ECONOMICS: THE FREE ENTERPRISE SYSTEM

ECONOMICS

THE FREE ENTERPRISE SYSTEM

H. Craig Petersen, Ph.D.
Professor,
Department of Economics
Utah State University
Logan, Utah

W. Cris Lewis, Ph.D.
Professor and Head,
Department of Economics
Utah State University
Logan, Utah

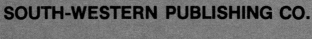

Published by

H38 **SOUTH-WESTERN PUBLISHING CO.**

CINCINNATI   WEST CHICAGO, IL   DALLAS   LIVERMORE, CA

ISBN: 0-538-08381-6

Library of Congress Catalog Card Number: 86-62132

3 4 5 6 7 8 D 3 2 1 0 9 8

Printed in the United States of America

PREFACE

The goal of *Economics: The Free Enterprise System* is to introduce you to the basic principles of a free enterprise economic system. By understanding these principles, you will be better able to function as a consumer, worker, and citizen. By applying the basic principles discussed in this book, you will be able to make better choices when purchasing goods and services, investing your money, and borrowing money. In addition, you will gain a greater appreciation of the advantages of living in an economic system that emphasizes and protects individual freedoms.

We are professional economists who have a strong commitment to the principles of free enterprise. We strongly believe that the free enterprise system is vastly superior to any of the alternatives. However, we also recognize that the free enterprise system has some shortcomings. You will find that this textbook presents a balanced view of the strengths and weaknesses of an economic system based on free enterprise.

The famous physicist, Albert Einstein, once stated that things should be made as simple as possible, but not more so. In writing this book, we have followed his advice. To assist you in learning this material, important ideas are presented in a concept/example format. First the concept is explained; then one or more examples are provided to demonstrate how the concept works and how it can be applied in the real world. In some cases, graphs and other diagrams have been used to explain certain concepts. Care has been taken to ensure that these illustrations are easy to understand.

Economics: The Free Enterprise System has many features to help you understand and remember the material. Each chapter begins with three questions that highlight interesting ideas and a preview that gives an example of the issues covered by the chapter. Next, the chapter objectives are listed. These objectives will help you focus on important concepts as you read the material. Throughout the chapter are "instant replays" that restate key ideas. The summary at the end of each chapter will help you to review the material that you have covered. Also, at the end of each chapter are a set of learning activities. These exercises are designed to help you evaluate your understanding, recall the important materials covered in the chapter, and develop specific skills. Finally, at the back of the book is a glossary that defines all of the terms that appear in the chapters.

It would be impossible to acknowledge all those who assisted in the development and writing of this book. Ruby Vazquez deserves special mention for her usual fine job of typing drafts of many of the chapters. We would also like to thank our families and our colleagues at Utah State University for their support and understanding during the period in which this manuscript was written.

Craig Petersen
Cris Lewis

CONTENTS

UNIT 1: AN INTRODUCTION TO FREE ENTERPRISE

Chapter 1 Freedom and the Free Enterprise System   2
The Economic System of a Society   3
Characteristics and Benefits of Free Enterprise
   Systems   6
Command Systems   9
Mixed Systems   10
Summary   12

Chapter 2 Choices in a World of Scarcity   15
Goods and Services Satisfy Human Needs and
   Wants   16
Resources Produce Goods and Services   19
Unlimited Wants and Limited Resources Cause
   Scarcity   23
Choices Have an Opportunity Cost   26
Three Basic Economic Questions   28
Equity vs Efficiency   30
Summary   31

Chapter 3 Markets and Money   34
Markets and Voluntary Exchange   35
Markets and the Circular Flow of Economic
   Activity   37
Markets and the Questions, *What, How,* and *for
   Whom to Produce?*   39
Barter and the Need for Money   44
The Three Functions of Money   46
Money in the United States   49
Summary   53

UNIT 2: THE FREE ENTERPRISE SYSTEM IN ACTION

Chapter 4 Supply, Demand, and Prices   58
Opportunity Costs and Prices   59
Prices as Signals   60
Prices and Resource Allocation   62
Demand   64
Supply   68
Determining the Equilibrium Price   70
Summary   74

Chapter 5   Profits and Competition   **77**
Profits as an Economic Incentive   78
Competition   85
Market Power in a Free Enterprise System   90
Summary   95

**Chapter 6   Economic Growth, Unemployment,
                Business Cycles, and Inflation**   **99**
Economic Growth   100
Unemployment   105
Business Cycles   109
Inflation and Deflation   111
Summary   116

UNIT 3: THE ROLE OF BUSINESS AND LABOR IN THE FREE ENTERPRISE SYSTEM

Chapter 7   Business Ownership and Organization   **120**
Forms of Business Ownership   121
Sole Proprietorships   124
Partnerships   126
Corporations   128
Types of Industries   133
Summary   137

Chapter 8   Basic Business Activities   **140**
Producing   141
Marketing   146
Advertising   150
Financing   153
Summary   159

Chapter 9   Organized Labor   **163**
A Short History of Organized Labor   164
Laws Affecting Organized Labor   165
Union Organization in the United States   168
Goals of Unions   170
Unions in Action   174
Summary   177

UNIT 4: GOVERNMENT AND THE FREE ENTERPRISE SYSTEM

Chapter 10   Government, Business, and the Individual 182
Government as a Referee   183
Government and Competition   186
Government and Consumer Protection   189
Government and Worker Protection   192
Government and Environmental Protection   194
Benefits and Costs of Government Regulation   195
Summary   196

Chapter 11   Banking and the Federal Reserve System   200
Banks as Financial Intermediaries   201
Fractional Reserve Banking   204
Commercial Banks and Other Financial
    Intermediaries   205
Federal Deposit Insurance Corporation   206
The Federal Reserve System   207
Summary   216

Chapter 12   Taxes   220
Purposes of Taxation   221
Progressive and Regressive Taxes   223
Personal Income Tax   225
Other Types of Taxes   229
Summary   232

Chapter 13   Government and the Economy   236
Government and Inflation/Unemployment   237
Government as a Producer of Goods and
    Services   241
Government Budgets   245
The National Debt   249
Summary   252

UNIT 5: THE WORLD ECONOMY

Chapter 14   International Trade   **258**
Benefits of International Trade   259
Importance of International Trade   263
International Finance   268
Restrictions on International Trade   271
Summary   274

Chapter 15   Economic Systems of Other Nations   **278**
Free Enterprise vs Command Systems   279
Capitalism and Socialism   282
Socialist Economic Systems: The U.S.S.R.   286
Worker-Managed Businesses: Yugoslavia   290
A Capitalist Success Story: Japan   291
Summary   294

UNIT 6: THE INDIVIDUAL AND THE FREE ENTERPRISE SYSTEM

Chapter 16   Earning a Living   **300**
The Opportunity Cost of Earning a Living   301
Sources of Income   302
Income Distribution   303
Why Some Jobs Pay More Than Others   305
Education and Job Opportunities   310
Finding a Job   312
Summary   317

Chapter 17   Borrowing, Saving, and Investing   **320**
Credit and Borrowing   321
Saving Money   324
The Role of Credit and Savings in the Economy   327
Investing in Stock   329
Summary   336

Chapter 18   Consumer Rights and Responsibilities   **340**
Consumer Rights   341
Consumer Responsibilities   347
Consumer Decisions and Principles of
    Economics   352
Summary   356

Chapter 19 **Consumer Economics** **360**
Budgeting Scarce Resources 361
Important Consumer Decisions 363
Consumer Fraud 373
Summary 376

Glossary **379**

Index **387**

UNIT 1

★ **Freedom and the Free Enterprise System**

★ **Choices in a World of Scarcity**

★ **Markets and Money**

H. Armstrong Roberts, Inc.

Consumer needs and wants are unlimited, but economic resources are scarce. Thus, individuals must continually make choices. In this unit, you will learn how consumers and producers make choices in the American free enterprise system. You will also learn how markets and money involve these choices in a circular flow of economic activity.

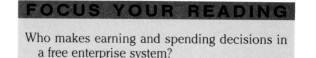

FOCUS YOUR READING

Who makes earning and spending decisions in a free enterprise system?

What freedoms do people have in a free enterprise system?

How is economic freedom related to political freedom?

CHAPTER 1

FREEDOM AND THE FREE ENTERPRISE SYSTEM

PREVIEW

Today is Sharon Lopez's twenty-first birthday. Unfortunately it's Monday and she must be at work by 8:00 a.m. Sharon is a riveter on a construction crew. She spends eight hours each working day building skyscrapers in Dallas.

Sharon's current project is a 60-story office building. A bank and a department store will occupy the main floor. The second floor will house the headquarters of a large company that makes furniture. On the upper floors will be real estate agents, lawyers, accountants, and dentists. Three to four thousand people will work in the building.

After work, Sharon meets her husband for a birthday dinner and a movie. When they return home, she reads the newspaper. One article tells about how people's last names may be based on the kind of work done by an ancestor. Her friend, John Smith, might have had a great-great-grandfather who was a blacksmith. A neighbor, Mary Tanner, probably had an ancestor who prepared leather. The origins of the names of Sharon's co-workers—Michael Farmer, Carma Hunter, Dwight Cook, and Pam Glover are easy to guess.

Sharon and her husband end their evening by watching the late-night news on television. The first story is about the President's new program for creating jobs. Another story discusses problems faced by young families trying to buy their first home. Sharon's husband comments that he would enjoy the news more if there were fewer commercials. In one half-hour they are asked to buy a new car, drink more milk, move into a high-rise condominium, and join a tennis club.

Think about Sharon Lopez's day. Much of her time involved activities dealing with either earning or spending money. Sharon's life is much like everyone else's. Everybody must decide how to earn and use money. Like Sharon, you have been faced with many such choices. As you continue through life, there will be many more decisions that must be made about earning a living and spending money wisely.

In this chapter you will learn about the ways earning and spending decisions are made. When you have completed the reading material and learning activities, you should be able to:

★ Explain what is meant by an economic system.

★ List the basic characteristics of a free enterprise system.

★ Discuss the differences between free enterprise, command, and mixed economic systems.

★ Explain the connection between political freedom and economic freedom.

THE ECONOMIC SYSTEM OF A SOCIETY

The story of Robinson Crusoe is known throughout the world. For years he lived alone on a desert island. During that time his life was difficult and tedious. He created many projects to amuse himself, because there was no one to talk to and no place to go. Perhaps worst of all, if any work was to be done, he had to do it.

The appearance of the man he called Friday made things a bit easier. There was still little companionship, but at least Crusoe had someone to help with the work. No longer was he responsible for each task necessary for day-to-day living.

Together, Robinson Crusoe and Friday formed a society on their island. A **society** is a group of individuals who have similar goals or interests. In their case, the goal was simple—to stay alive.

A person may belong to several societies. Your family is a small society. Each member of the family helps to meet the requirements of the family as a whole. The people who live in your town or city make up a society. They have a common interest in the activities of the community. On a larger scale, all the people living in the United States are part of the same society.

Societies exist because they make life better. Most people prefer living with others to living alone. They want friends they can call on in times of need. Most people want their work load to be shared.

Before Friday came along, Robinson Crusoe had to do all the fishing, cooking, sewing, and housekeeping. After Friday's arrival, each man could concentrate on the jobs that he did best. The same is true of the societies to which you belong. Although you have to work hard to earn the money that you need, you don't have to make everything that you use. Food can be purchased from the grocery store. Cars and buses are available for travel. Clothes are made in factories and sold by local

Each of us is a member of many societies.

The Rouse Company

businesses. The government protects you from criminals and threatening nations.

Clearly there are advantages to being part of a society. But there are also disadvantages. As people rely on others, life becomes more complicated. While Robinson Crusoe was living alone, he had few decisions to make. But with Friday's arrival, there were new choices to be made. Who would fish and who would cook? How should the food be divided?

In a modern society the choices are similar but much more complicated. Someone must determine what to produce and how to produce it. Someone must decide who are to be engineers and who are to be radio announcers. Decisions must be made about who will have expensive automobiles and who will have only bicycles. These decisions can be made in different ways. One alternative is for each person to make his or her own choice. Another possibility is for one person or a small group of people to make these decisions for everybody.

The way a society makes these choices is through its **economic system.** The economic system includes all the organizations, laws, traditions, beliefs, and habits that affect decision making in the society.

People often talk about the economy. For example, you might read, "The United States economy is the strongest in the world." Or a television newscaster might announce, "The outlook for the economy is

Societies make economic decisions about what to produce, how to produce, and for whom to produce.

Barnes Group Inc.

good." The term **economy** refers to all the places in society where spending and earning decisions are made. Two important parts of the economy are households and firms. A **household** is a small group of people who make their earning and spending decisions together. In most cases a household is the same as a family. A **firm** is another name for a business. For example, the Ford Motor Company is a firm. All the firms that make a particular product are referred to as an **industry.** The Ford Motor Company, General Motors Corporation, and the other car manufacturers make up the automobile industry.

INSTANT REPLAY

A society consists of people with similar goals or interests.

Living in a society allows a person to receive help from others.

The way spending and earning decisions are made in a society is referred to as the economic system of that society.

CHARACTERISTICS AND BENEFITS OF FREE ENTERPRISE SYSTEMS

The economic system of a society is determined by many factors, such as location, history, and tradition. Economic systems can be grouped into three broad categories:

★ Free enterprise

★ Command

★ Mixed

A **free enterprise system** is one in which households and the managers of firms are free to make their own choices about earning and spending activities. Such a system is based on **decentralized decision making.** That is, decisions are made by each individual rather than by one person or a small group of people. Because all countries have at least a few laws that apply to business activities, there are no pure free enterprise systems in the world today. But in free enterprise based systems, people are free to make their own choices, within the limits of these laws.

Decisions of individuals and business managers in a free enterprise system are not always wise. A person may purchase a bicycle that breaks down in a few months. Recording companies sometimes make tapes and albums that people are unwilling to buy. Living in a free enterprise system does not guarantee that people will make good decisions. It guarantees only that they will be free to make their *own* decisions.

There are at least four important freedoms that exist in a free enterprise system:

★ Freedom to own property

★ Freedom to buy

★ Freedom to produce and sell

★ Freedom to work

Freedom to Own Property

Sometimes the free enterprise system is referred to as a **private enterprise system.** The reason is that people make decisions as private individuals rather than as part of a public or government group.

Private property is a requirement of a free or private enterprise system. To have private property means to have things that belong to you. You have the right to decide what to do with this property. Unless you violate the law, private property cannot be taken from you. Of course, other people have the same rights to their private property.

For example, suppose you buy a car with money you have earned. Instead of being limited to baby-sitting or yard work in your neighborhood, you could now drive to a regular full-time job. This job will give you more money to spend and save. The car is your private property. As long as you don't break the law, you can use it any way you wish. You can drive it wherever you want. You don't have to share the car with any other person. You can paint it the color of your choice and decorate the interior to suit your tastes.

Freedom to Buy

In a free enterprise system, spending decisions are made by individuals. No one can force you to buy things that you don't want. Unless you break the law, you have complete freedom of choice in using your money. If you have enough money, you can buy a new suit or dress. If you want to go to a concert, all that is required is that you be willing and able to buy a ticket. Similarly, you have the right to buy all the meat and fruit you can afford.

Freedom to Produce and Sell

Firms are free to produce and sell whatever products they believe people will buy. An individual can open a new gas station on the corner even though the other three corners of the intersection already have gas stations. A supermarket is free to expand and sell cameras. Or a firm may decide not to sell anything anymore. For example, the managers of a movie theater can close down the business whenever they choose.

In a free enterprise system, firms can use whatever materials and methods the managers select for production. The firm can also charge whatever it wants for its product. The only restriction on price comes from buyers. If the price is set too high, then the firm will not be able to sell its product. Buyers will purchase from other firms instead.

Freedom to Work

Suppose you decide to baby-sit or do yard work. When you take a job, you are selling your skills. The person who pays you is buying your skills. This arrangement is an example of free enterprise. You are free to accept or refuse the work. The person who hires you is free to accept or reject your offer to do the work. An agreement is made between the worker and the employer. It exists because both parties believe that they will be better off as a result of their choices.

In the free enterprise system no one can force you into a career as a ballet dancer or a teacher. Similarly, no one can prevent you from trying to succeed in some other occupation. People make their own choices. Some of these choices may prove to be wise, and some may not. But the important point is that people are free to make their own choices.

INSTANT REPLAY

In a free enterprise system, earning and spending decisions are decentralized; that is, they are made by individuals.

Basic to the free enterprise system are the rights to own property, to buy, to produce and sell, and to work.

In the free enterprise system, people are free to make their own career choices.

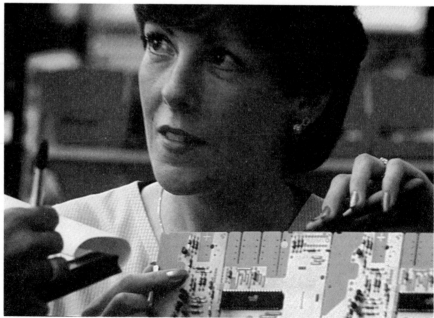

COMMAND SYSTEMS

In a **command system** the individual usually has little to say about economic decisions. In such systems the government is usually controlled by a small group of people. Members of this small group make most of the important economic decisions. They decide what and how much to produce in the economy. They select how products will be made and the prices at which they will be sold. The government decides where people will work and how much they will earn. It may be difficult to change jobs without government permission. Government control often extends even to finding a place to live. People are told where and in what kind of house or apartment they will live.

Under command systems individuals *are* allowed to have certain types of private property. For example, people own their clothes and the food they buy. Some people own bicycles and a few own cars. But all the businesses that make and sell these goods are owned by the government. Land, houses, and factories all belong to the government. The government also owns all the oil, coal, iron, and other natural resources.

A major difference between command and free enterprise systems concerns freedom. In a command system, a great deal of power is given to a small group of people. Almost always, the result is that the individual citizens have little freedom. People are told what to make, where to work, what they can own, and how much they will pay for the things they buy. That is, decisions are **centralized.** In contrast, you have already learned that choices are decentralized in a free enterprise system. There, individuals are free to make the decisions that they believe are best.

With the power to make economic decisions, government also gains the power to control its citizens in other ways. To understand how economic power can be used for control, consider jobs and housing. Under a command system the government tells people where they can work and live. People who want good jobs and a comfortable house or apartment do not criticize the government. Those who speak out are simply not allowed to have the best jobs. They are often given poor housing. If their criticism is loud enough, these people can be sent to prison.

Economic freedom and political freedom are closely connected. **Economic freedom** refers to the individual's right to make earning and spending decisions. **Political freedom** means being able to voice opinions, even though they may be unpopular. When economic freedom is taken away, political freedom is also reduced. In countries where the government has the power to refuse good jobs and housing to those who speak out, free speech can be risky.

No country in the world today has a complete command system. However, many of the nations of Eastern Europe are close to being command economies. The U.S.S.R. and East Germany are examples. Citizens of these two countries have only limited opportunities to make their own earning and spending decisions.

MIXED SYSTEMS

Life in a free enterprise system provides economic and political freedom. However, there can still be problems with such a system. Remember, choices and decisions are made by individuals. The people who make the decisions are free to consider their own best interests. Sometimes these people do not consider the needs and wants of the whole society. For example, a company that makes paper or chemicals may decide to use the cheapest way to dispose of its wastes. It may just dump them into a nearby river.

Putting the wastes in the river may be a good solution for the company, but not for society. The river will become polluted and the water unsafe. Fish in the river will be killed. The river can no longer be used for swimming. The source of drinking water for entire cities could be ruined. In a pure free enterprise system, there would be no way to stop this activity.

Clearly some controls are necessary. Individuals cannot be allowed to take actions or to exercise freedoms that hurt others. Therefore, laws are passed to control those activities of individuals and firms that harm others. For example, there are laws that prevent firms from polluting lakes and rivers. Other laws prevent the sale of unsafe drugs and foods. The courts and the police protect people against violence.

Passing and enforcing these laws cost money. It is unlikely that people would voluntarily provide enough money to government to pay the costs of these activities. As a result, tax laws require individuals and firms to give some of their earnings to the government. These laws restrict some economic freedoms, but are necessary to protect other freedoms. For example, paying taxes limits your spending opportunities, but the use of that money to pay for a fire department could save your house. Every country has such laws. As a result, no nation in the world today has a pure free enterprise system. However, the economic systems of the United States, West Germany, and Japan have many of the features of free enterprise. They are referred to as having mixed systems.

In a **mixed system** most decisions are left to individuals, but some decisions are made by government. For example, in the United States automobile makers and the government each have something to say about the cars that are sold. Automobile manufacturers can decide on style and price; the government sets standards for safety and air pollution. Of course, households finally decide whether or not to buy the cars. Thus, decisions about cars are made by individuals, business, and government.

INSTANT REPLAY

In a command system, earning and spending decisions are made by those who control the government.

Countries such as the U.S.S.R. and East Germany have command-type economic systems.

Because command systems limit economic freedom, they also can limit political freedom.

In a mixed system most decisions are left to individuals, but some are made by government.

Do you agree that some controls on personal freedom are necessary in a society?

RESERVED

SUMMARY

A society is a group of people with similar goals or interests. An advantage of living in a society is that people can concentrate on the tasks that they do best. The way spending and earning decisions are made in a society is referred to as the economic system of that society.

A free enterprise system is one in which earning and spending decisions are made by individuals. Free enterprise is also referred to as private enterprise. In such systems people have the freedom to own private property. They have the right to spend their money as they choose. They can make their own decisions about what to produce and how much to charge. They are free to decide which jobs to take.

In a command system one person or a small group decides what will be provided and how much it will cost. Where people will work and live is also controlled. Because economic freedom is limited in command systems, political freedom may also be limited. Many countries in Eastern Europe have command-type economic systems.

A mixed system leaves most decisions to individuals. However, some decisions are made by government to protect society. Examples of countries with mixed economic systems are the United States, West Germany, and Japan.

☆ LEARNING ACTIVITIES ☆

Building Your Vocabulary

On a separate piece of paper, write the numbers 1 through 14. Next to each number, write the term that correctly completes the sentence.

economic freedom
household
private property
industry
society
free enterprise
economic system
private enterprise
command
firm
economy
mixed
decentralized
political freedom

1. In a _Command_ system, decisions are centralized.

2. A _firm_ is another name for a business.

3. The ways by which earning and spending decisions are made is the _econ. system_ of a society.

4. People with similar goals and interests form a _society_.

5. Another name for free enterprise is _private enterprise_.

6. A system where decisions are made by individuals is called a _____ system.

7. The _economy_ is the place where spending and earning decisions are made.

8. A _household_ is a small group of people who make their spending and earning decisions together.

9. The right to make your own earning and spending decisions is referred to as _economic freedom_

10. _Decentralized_ decision making is a characteristic of a free enterprise system.

11. Freedom of speech is one characteristic of _free enterprise_.

12. In a _mixed_ system, decisions are made by individuals and government.

13. In a free enterprise system, people own _private prop._

14. An _industry_ consists of all the firms that make a particular product.

Reviewing the Facts

1. What are the advantages of living in a society?
2. What is the difference between a firm and an industry? Give an example of each.
3. List the four freedoms in a free enterprise system.
4. How are career choices made in a command system?
5. What is the connection between economic and political freedoms?
6. Name one country that has a pure free enterprise system. Explain.

Expressing Your Opinion

1. Would a command system work better in a small or large society? Why?
2. Suppose there were no laws that limited economic freedom. What are some of the problems a person might face living in such a society?
3. Are there any advantages to a command system? Explain your answer.
4. In a free enterprise system, what factors might limit your career choice?

Developing Your Attitudes, Values, and Skills

1. You read in this chapter that a society is any group of people that cooperates, from a small club to an entire nation. All societies establish goals that will help them satisfy the needs of their members. You belong to several societies; for example, your family, school, community, and state. How does each group decide what its goals are? How does each go about achieving its goals? Identify areas in which the goals of the different groups might conflict.
2. Choose one of America's major industries; for example, automobiles, textiles, oil, plastics, or agriculture. List five firms within that industry. Use library resources, such as encyclopedias, almanacs, and periodicals, to answer the following questions about the industry you chose: What products does it produce? What resources does it need? Where do its resources come from?

Where is it located? Why is it located there? What problems does it face? Be prepared to present your findings to the class.

3. The American free enterprise system is actually a mixed system, because the government makes some economic decisions while consumers and producers make others. The role of government in our economic system is often controversial. For example, the government can place limits on certain imports. It can introduce environmental protection laws that cause manufacturing costs to rise. What are the advantages and disadvantages of having such decisions made by the government? What might happen if *all* economic decisions were made by producers and consumers?

FOCUS YOUR READING

How does society deal with scarcity?

What do economists mean when they say that there are no free lunches in the economic system?

What is your opportunity cost of reading this chapter?

CHAPTER 2

CHOICES IN A WORLD OF SCARCITY

PREVIEW

"Should I have cereal or eggs for breakfast?" "Is *B* the right answer?" "Should I ask Tom or Mark to the dance?" "How can I pay for the dented fender on my parents' car?"

Each day you are faced with hundreds of choices. Some involve the use of your time. There are only 24 hours each day. So you must decide how many hours to sleep, how much time to devote to studying, how many television programs you are going to watch, and so forth.

Other choices deal with spending your money. Suppose that you were given $5,000 by a rich uncle. What would you do with those dollars? What part of your good fortune would be used to buy new clothes? How much would find its way to the local movie theater? Would some of the money go into a savings account? How about giving your parents $3,000 to help pay bills?

Sometimes the rules of society force people to choose between alternatives. For example, when you take a true-false test, you can select only one answer. Similarly, you can cast your vote for only one candidate for each position on the ballot in an election. Choices are a constant, if sometimes troublesome, part of everyday life. Everyone finds it difficult to make decisions at some time.

In this chapter you will learn about choices in the economic system. When you have completed the reading material and learning activities, you should be able to:

★ Explain the differences between needs and wants.

★ Define goods and services.

★ Explain what resources are and why they are limited.

15

★ Define scarcity and explain some of its causes.

★ Describe what is meant by the opportunity cost of making a choice.

★ Identify the three basic choices that must be made in every economic system.

GOODS AND SERVICES SATISFY HUMAN NEEDS AND WANTS

Have you ever been with a small child in a toy store? Do you remember the constant begging for dolls, trains, puzzles, games, baseball gloves, and other playthings? Did it seem that the child wanted almost every toy in the store?

Teenagers and adults are only slightly different from small children. As people get older, they don't stop wanting things. People just change the things they want. You may have heard the short rhyme: "The difference between men and boys is the price of their toys." A 4-year-old may want a car to push around the floor. At 12, the car must be radio controlled. Only the real thing will do at age 16.

Needs and Wants

In making decisions, you may find it is useful to distinguish between needs and wants. **Needs** are things that you must have to continue

Needs vs wants: Which is more valuable?

living. **Wants** are things you desire but could live without. They make life more pleasant.

An example of a need is a warm place to live during a cold winter. Another need is a coat for protection and warmth in a blizzard. The food necessary to provide energy for the body is also an important need for every person.

Many items belong in the category of wants. New speakers for a stereo system, a fashionable pair of jeans, and a sailboat are all examples of wants.

Sometimes, it is difficult to decide whether something is a need or a want. Everyone needs a place to live. But a house with a sauna and a swimming pool contains more than the basic needs for living. Similarly, everyone has to eat. But lobster and cheesecake are not absolutely necessary for survival and good health. In a country like the United States most (but not all) people are able to provide for their basic needs. As a result, people give much attention to satisfying the wants they believe will make their lives better.

The wants of one person may be quite different from those of another. A high school student's greatest desire may be for a car. A retired person may wish to travel to far-off places. Even for individuals at the same age level, wants can be different. One student may save money to buy a high-performance sports car; another may buy an economy car that has high gas mileage. One elderly couple sees Hawaii as the vacation spot of their dreams; another is happier with the excitement of the casinos in Las Vegas. The millions of products available in the economic system are an indication of the wide variety of individual wants.

Goods and Services

You don't have to spend money to satisfy all your wants. But there are many things you cannot get unless you are willing to buy them. When people make purchases, they are referred to as **consumers.** That is, they buy things that they will then use or consume. The use of these things is called **consumption.**

Consumer purchases can be divided into two categories: goods and services. **Goods** are objects that can be measured or weighed. Apples, books, dresses, and washing machines are all examples of goods. **Services** refer to help that is received from other people. When you have your hair styled, the barber or beautician provides you with a service. If you go to a rock concert, you enjoy the services of the performers. Taking karate lessons involves buying a service from your instructor.

Is this an example of a good or a service?

Bob Hahn/Taurus Photos Inc.

Unlimited Wants

In our society, consumption leads to more consumption. For example, a person with a new car may think about trading it in when next year's models come out. The couple who has just traveled to Spain may immediately start planning a vacation to China. The child who just got a Barbie® doll may begin asking for Barbie® clothes and Barbie® furniture. Most people develop new wants as old wants are satisfied. For this reason, consumer wants are said to be *unlimited*.

INSTANT REPLAY

Needs are things people must have to survive. Wants are things that make life more pleasant.

Goods are products that can be weighed or measured. Services are help received from other people.

Consumer wants are unlimited.

RESOURCES PRODUCE GOODS AND SERVICES

A **resource** is something that is available for use. **Economic resources** are used to produce the goods and services that people consume. Filling a cavity involves the time of a dentist. Producing electricity requires coal, oil, natural gas, or nuclear reactors. Manufacturing a new automobile enlists heavy machinery that stamps out the automobile body parts.

The economic resources used to produce goods and services are usually divided into three categories:

★ Human resources

★ Natural resources

★ Capital resources

Human Resources

Human resources are the efforts and skills that individuals can contribute to producing goods and services. The amount of human resources available is only partly measured by the total number of people available to produce the goods and services. Many other factors influence the amount of human resources available. Some of these factors are listed here.

Education. As individuals increase their education, they also increase their skills. An engineering student learns how to design roads and bridges. A medical student learns how to care for the sick. Once people have these special skills, they are able to contribute more human resources to society than before.

Age. The work that people can do changes with age. A 20-year-old may be able to do more physical labor than a 65-year-old. In some countries, there are few younger workers. For example, wars may reduce the number of young men available for work. In some countries it may be difficult to find enough young people to do jobs that require great physical strength.

Health. The amount of work that people can contribute is also determined by their health. In some countries many people have poor

When people acquire special skills, they are able to contribute more human resources to society than before.

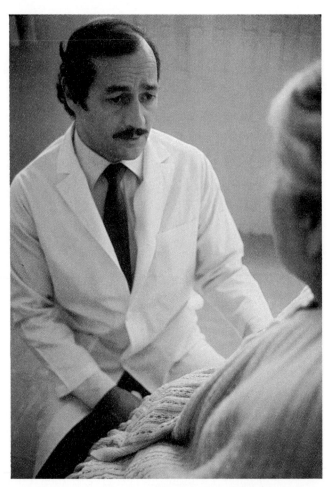

Photo courtesy of Abbott Laboratories

health because there is too little food or a shortage of doctors or drugs. Unclean living conditions also can lead to disease or poor health.

Although the total number of people in a country may be large, its human resources can be limited by one or more of the factors just described. A small country with healthy and well-educated people could actually have more human resources available for producing goods and services than a large country whose people have poor diets and inadequate education.

Natural Resources

All materials that come from the air, water, and earth are **natural resources.** Obvious examples are fuels such as oil and coal. Wood

One of our greatest economic problems is the conservation and wise use of natural resources.

COURTESY MICHIGAN TRAVEL BUREAU

from the forests, energy from the sun, and oxygen from the air are also in this category. Land is one of the most important natural resources. For example, suppose a developer wants to build a new shopping mall. A conveniently located piece of land is an important resource for a successful mall.

Capital Resources

The tools, buildings, and machinery used to produce goods or services are known as **capital resources** or **capital goods.** Capital goods are produced using human and natural resources. They do not directly satisfy human needs and wants. Instead, they assist in the production of goods or services that satisfy needs and wants.

A garden hoe is a simple example of a capital good. Few people buy hoes because they like to have them around. By itself, a hoe does not satisfy any human want. The value of a hoe is that it can be used to satisfy other wants. The owner of the hoe can rid the garden of weeds. With the weeds gone, the garden will grow more carrots and potatoes. The hoe is valuable because it helps gardeners satisfy their need for food.

Capital goods are important in the economic system. The electric razor that a barber uses to cut hair is an example of a capital good. The truck carrying lumber and the microphone held by an entertainer are capital goods. So is the typewriter on which an author writes a new novel.

An economic system with many capital goods can satisfy more needs and wants than a system that relies primarily on human and natural resources. Imagine what a new car would cost if it had to be made without machines. Today, companies like General Motors Corporation use capital goods (machines) to form sheets of steel into the body shapes. The body parts for a new car can be stamped out in just a matter of minutes. Auto manufacturers use robots to weld pieces of metal together. This is done more quickly, accurately, and cheaply by robots than by human labor.

Agriculture provides another example of the importance of capital goods. Using modern equipment, a farmer can work hundreds of acres of land. Without such capital goods, farmers would be able to produce only enough to satisfy their own food needs. Because of scientific advances in growing crops and an increase in the use of capital goods, farmers today produce much more food per acre than farmers did in the past. In the United States each year, the average farm worker produces enough food to feed 50 people. Capital resources used in agriculture, manufacturing, and other industries are largely responsible for the high standard of living enjoyed by many people in the United States.

Limited Resources

You have learned that economic resources are necessary to produce goods and services. It follows that the amount of economic resources available determines the amount of goods and services that can be produced. But only limited amounts of these resources—human, natural, and capital—are available in any economic system at any given time.

Why are human resources limited? As mentioned, an aging population, lack of education, and poor health can reduce the supply of human resources. Even if the total supply of human resources is large, there can still be problems. For example, there may be a shortage of people with particular skills. A scientist as talented as Albert Einstein is born only about every hundred years. Top-flight business managers are in short supply. In the sports world, the small number of superstars is another illustration of limited special talents. Few athletes are good enough to make the National Basketball Association (NBA). Even fewer become superstars.

Natural resources also can be scarce. Hidden in the earth are oil, coal, iron ore, gold, and other resources. Some of these resources are easily found and used, but obtaining additional amounts can be difficult and costly. For example, millions of barrels of oil have been pumped from under the plains of Texas. But finding more oil can involve difficult and costly pumping from the ocean floors.

Land for buildings and agricultural uses also is limited. There are thousands of unused acres in the deserts of Arizona and New Mexico; a large plot of land in a remote spot may cost only a few thousand dollars. Yet, additional land suitable for special purposes often is hard to find. A small piece of land on Manhattan Island in New York City could easily be worth a million dollars. The high price of land in Manhattan is the result of so little land being available there.

Capital resources are limited because a sacrifice is required to obtain them. Many countries of the world have few capital goods. As a result, the people in these countries have few goods and services. If such countries had more capital goods, their economic systems would be able to satisfy more human needs and wants. A basic problem faced by such countries is that they are not able to buy or produce capital goods. They cannot make the sacrifice because most of their resources are used just to satisfy the basic needs of the people.

Such countries need more capital goods to improve the standard of living of the people. Tractors and other farm machinery would increase the amount of food produced. Modern factories could increase the quantity and reduce the cost of manufactured goods. But with much of the population poorly clothed, living in unsatisfactory housing, and barely surviving on a poor diet, resources cannot be spared to buy or produce capital goods. Thus, the people in such countries are caught in an economic trap from which it is difficult to escape.

INSTANT REPLAY

Economic resources are used to produce goods and services.

These resources can be categorized as human, natural, and capital resources.

Economic resources are limited.

UNLIMITED WANTS AND LIMITED RESOURCES CAUSE SCARCITY

Resources are used to produce goods and services that satisfy human wants, but resources are limited. Thus, goods and services are

Some poor countries have few capital goods.

World Bank Photo by Ray Witlin

also limited. In contrast, people's wants are unlimited. The result is that an economic system can never satisfy all the wants of consumers.

When more goods or services are desired than are available, these items are said to be **scarce.** Scarcity is a problem faced by every economic system; no system can avoid it. Free enterprise, command, and mixed economic systems all must deal with the conflict between unlimited wants and scarce resources.

Economics is a science that attempts to explain how societies deal with the problem of scarcity. It is often defined as the study of how to allocate scarce resources. To **allocate** resources means to divide or direct them to specific uses. The task of economics is to find the best ways to use scarce resources, ways that will satisfy human needs and wants.

The difficulty of living in a world of scarcity is illustrated by a story told by Abraham Lincoln. Lincoln talked of walking down a dirt road in Illinois and finding two young boys fighting. Knowing that the two boys were usually close friends, he wondered what had caused them to fight. As he came closer, he could see a single large apple hanging from an old tree. When he was finally able to stop the fight, Lincoln learned its cause. The boys had both seen the apple at the same time, and each had decided that it was his. Unable to decide who was the rightful owner of the fruit, they attempted to settle the question by force.

Later, in talking to members of Congress, Lincoln observed that society faces the same problem as the boys: Who gets the apple? As long as wants exceed society's ability to fulfill them, scarcity will be a problem. Therefore, people need to study methods of allocating resources to the best uses.

Consider some ways of dealing with scarcity. The two boys in Lincoln's story chose *force* as a method. Clearly that is not a good approach. Unfortunately some of the bloodiest wars in history have been fought to solve the scarcity problem. For example, Japan's entry into World War II was partially due to the need to increase the scarce natural resources of that island nation.

Some societies approach the problem of scarcity by limiting the use of certain goods or services. This approach, called *rationing,* is used under the command systems in many of the countries of Eastern Europe. For goods such as meat, sugar, and heating oil, the government sets a maximum amount that each family can purchase. During hard times, these amounts may not meet the basic needs of the family.

Another approach is *substitution.* Suppose a good or resource is in short supply. It may be possible to deal with the scarcity problem by switching to other goods or resources. For example, as oil becomes more scarce, substitute energy sources may be used. These substitutes may include wind or solar power. During World War II, when the United States was unable to get supplies of natural rubber, scientists developed methods for making artificial rubber.

Finally, *prices* provide a solution to the scarcity problem. If goods or resources are scarce, one approach is to sell them to those who want them the most. The price people will pay for an item is a measure of how much they value it. In the free enterprise system, the price system is the method used to deal with scarcity. Chapter 4 covers the vital role that prices play in a free enterprise system.

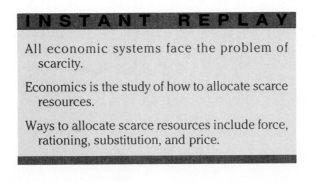

INSTANT REPLAY

All economic systems face the problem of scarcity.

Economics is the study of how to allocate scarce resources.

Ways to allocate scarce resources include force, rationing, substitution, and price.

CHOICES HAVE AN OPPORTUNITY COST

Suppose you choose to use your allowance or wages to buy a new suit or dress. Using the money in this way may mean you have to wait before you have enough to buy something else. For example, you may have to cancel or postpone plans for an exercise bench or a new pair of skis. Each time you make a choice, there are alternatives that you can no longer select.

The choices facing society also involve giving up alternatives. In the early 1960s, President Kennedy and Congress committed the resources of the United States to putting a man on the moon. On July 20, 1969, that dream was realized. Millions of Americans watched with pride as Neil Armstrong became the first person to set foot on the moon. But the total cost was over $30 billion.

The huge sum of money that was spent on the space program could have been spent on other worthwhile activities. For example, that same $30 billion could have paid for *all* of the following:

★ Granting 200 small colleges $10 million each

★ Awarding 50,000 graduating high school seniors seven-year scholarships of $4,000 per person, per year

★ Feeding 5 billion meals to hungry people around the world

★ Developing more than 1,500 miles of new highways

How do you think the money should have been used? Were the benefits of the space program greater than the value of the alternative uses of the money? Obviously, President Kennedy and Congress decided that the space program made the best use of the resources available.

Government officials at all levels must constantly make similar decisions. The national government is currently faced with such alternatives as space exploration, the development of new missile systems, and the construction of dams. There is a common problem to all these decisions: Whenever resources are used in one project, they are not available for other projects. More missiles may mean less medical care. The building of new dams may use dollars that could have been spent to reduce pollution.

An *acronym* is a word made up of the first letters of other words. Economists sometimes use the acronym TANSTAAFL to summarize the problem of making choices. The acronym means *There Ain't No Such*

What were the opportunity costs of this moon walk?

NASA

Thing As A Free Lunch. In a world of scarcity, nothing can be free. Each time that one course of action is chosen, it is necessary to give up something else. And even when some things appear to be free, they are not—someone is paying for these things.

The alternatives given up when a choice is made become the opportunity cost of the choice. Thus, the term **opportunity cost** is defined as the value of resources in their best alternative use. For the space program, the opportunity cost was the education, help for the poor, and highway programs that could not be provided. On a simpler level, if an individual buys a new pair of shoes, the opportunity cost is what could have been the best alternative use of the money, such as a tennis racket. Choices involving time also have an opportunity cost. An hour spent watching television is an hour that cannot be used to study for a test. Thus, the opportunity cost of watching television might be the time that is given up from studying.

Opportunity cost is an important idea. Government officials, managers, and individuals all should consider the opportunity costs of choices they make. Sometimes, choices are made without a clear understanding of opportunity costs. An example is the popularity of wood-burning stoves. In recent years, thousands of these stoves have been purchased by people who want to reduce their heating bills. In many cases people with stoves believe they can cut the wood for nothing in nearby forests. Even when the cost of gasoline and a chain saw is considered, the use of a wood-burning stove seems cheap.

However, the true opportunity cost of heating with wood involves more than just the money that must be spent. Other resource costs include the value of time spent doing the cutting, loading the stove, and cleaning the ashes. For example, suppose the same time could be spent at a paying job. In that case, the true cost of heating with wood may not be so low. The opportunity cost would include the dollars lost by not working. Even if the time would otherwise be used for recreation, there is still an opportunity cost. Unless the person enjoys the activities required to maintain the wood-burning stove, the satisfaction from recreational activities is lost in working on the stove. Sometimes individuals make poor choices because they fail to recognize the true opportunity costs of their actions.

INSTANT REPLAY

The opportunity cost of a choice is the value of the resources in their best alternative use.

The opportunity cost of time is often ignored in making choices.

THREE BASIC ECONOMIC QUESTIONS

Almost all the choices that must be made in an economic system can be divided into three categories:

★ What to produce

★ How to produce

★ For whom to produce

What to Produce

*?
of
equity
efficiency*

Scarcity limits the amounts and kinds of goods and services that can be produced. Think about the rare athlete who has the ability to be a professional in both basketball and football. Unfortunately there is an overlap between the two seasons. Both sports have games in the fall. So, even though the person has the skill to play both, that person is forced to make a choice between the two.

The question, *what to produce,* must be answered by every economic system. Some businesses make a variety of products. But most specialize in one area such as clothing, food, machines, or energy. Even within their areas, managers must decide which of thousands of possible products will be produced. For example, the manager of a large farm must choose whether to produce wheat, corn, or potatoes.

How to Produce

efficiency

Once the economic system decides what to produce, it must determine the best way of producing the needed goods and services. Often a good or service can be produced in many different ways. For example, consider frozen meat pies. As a shopper, you learn quickly that different companies have made different decisions concerning ingredients. Some pies have only a single crust; others have two. Some brands are stuffed with meat; others have only a trace of meat. One brand may have corn, peas, and potatoes. Another may be mostly gravy with a few peas floating in the middle.

The question, *how to produce,* also refers to the methods used to produce the good or service. Compare a neighborhood bakery with a large company that provides baked goods to a grocery store. The neighborhood bakery may make pies largely by hand; the large firm may use capital equipment that mixes the crust, rolls it, cuts it and adds filling automatically. The final products, the pies, may be quite similar, but the production methods are very different.

For Whom to Produce

equity

Remember Lincoln's story about the two boys? Even after the apple had been "produced," there was still a problem deciding who was to have it. The same difficulty exists in every part of the economic system. Who gets the goods and services once they are produced? Almost everyone would like to own a new Cadillac, a two-carat diamond ring, or a plantation on Maui in the Hawaiian Islands. Unfortunately, few people can have all their wants satisfied. Many people are forced to go without goods and services that they want. An important question that must be answered is, For whom are the goods and services produced?

EQUITY VS EFFICIENCY

Two important ideas in the study of economics are equity and efficiency. They can be easily understood by imagining all the goods and services that are produced as being part of a huge pie.

Equity means fairness and refers to how the pie should be divided. Who gets the big pieces and who gets the small pieces? In the real world, equity is concerned with the distribution of goods, services, and resources. **Efficiency** involves using scarce resources to make the pie as big as possible; that is, producing the maximum amount of goods and services from a given amount of resources.

The question, *how to produce,* clearly deals with efficiency. A society should use those production methods that result in the best use of scarce resources. *For whom to produce* is a question of equity. *What to produce* deals with both equity and efficiency. The goods and services produced should be selected to satisfy the maximum amount of wants possible. But since people have different wants, the choice also involves equity. If resources are used to produce the goods desired by one person, they will not be available to produce the goods desired by another person.

The study of economics is primarily concerned with efficiency, that is, making the economic pie of goods as large as possible. This is a desirable objective; if resources can be allocated to produce more goods and services, then everyone can be better off.

Equity questions are more difficult. No matter how a society distributes or divides the pie of goods and services, one person benefits only if another person does not. For example, if mountain areas are set aside for sheep grazing, then they will not be available for summer homes. Thus, sheep ranchers are better off, but vacationers are worse off. Whether or not this is a good policy depends on your views about the two groups. Such judgments are not part of the study of economics.

They should be made by politicians or others in government. However, economics may be able to help evaluate the outcomes of such judgments.

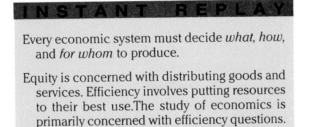

INSTANT REPLAY

Every economic system must decide *what, how,* and *for whom* to produce.

Equity is concerned with distributing goods and services. Efficiency involves putting resources to their best use. The study of economics is primarily concerned with efficiency questions.

SUMMARY

Needs are things people must have to survive. Food, clothing, and shelter are examples. Wants are things that make life more pleasant. Because people always want more, it is said that their wants are unlimited.

Economic resources are used to produce the things that satisfy needs and wants. Human resources are the efforts and skills of individuals. Natural resources are those substances available from the air, water, and earth. Capital goods (or capital resources) are tools such as machinery. These are used to produce other goods and services. The amounts of human, natural, and capital resources are limited.

The combination of limited resources and unlimited wants results in scarcity. Economics is the study of how to deal with the problems of scarcity. Because of scarcity, every choice should be measured by what must be given up. In making decisions, a person should recognize the true opportunity cost.

Every economic system must answer three basic questions. The question, *what to produce,* involves choices between the thousands of goods and services that might be produced. The question, *how to produce,* refers to the method of producing a product. Who gets the goods and services once they are produced is the focus of the question, *for whom to produce.*

Efficiency involves using resources to satisfy the greatest amount of needs and wants. Who gets the goods and services is an equity question.

☆ LEARNING ACTIVITIES ☆

Building Your Vocabulary

On a separate piece of paper, write the numbers 1 through 14. Next to each number, write the term that correctly completes the sentence.

- ✓goods
- ✓equity
- ✓resources
- ✓capital
- ✓needs
- ✓opportunity cost
- ✓consumption
- ✓natural
- ✓scarcity
- ✓wants
- ✓service
- human
- ✓consumers
- ✓efficiency

1. The _opportunity cost_ of going to a concert might be missing a football game on television.

2. Housing and food are examples of _needs_ .

3. Oil and gas are _natural_ resources.

4. When the barber cuts your hair, that is a _service_ .

5. Things that make life more pleasant are _wants_ .

6. Limited resources and unlimited wants cause _scarcity_

7. A machine is an example of a _capital_ good or resource.

8. The use of goods and services is called _consumption_

9. Who gets goods and services is a question of _equity_ .

10. Things available to produce goods and services are called _resources_

11. _goods_ are things that can be weighed or measured.

12. _Efficiency_ is concerned with using resources to produce the maximum amount of goods and services.

13. _Consumers_ are people who buy goods and services for their own use.

14. More education increases the _human_ resources of a society.

Reviewing the Facts

1. What is the difference between needs and wants?
2. Give an example of a good and a service.
3. What are the three types of economic resources?
4. Give an example of a capital good.
5. What is meant by the acronym TANSTAAFL?
6. What are the three questions faced by every economic system? Which question involves both equity and efficiency?

Expressing Your Opinion

1. Suppose that the people in a society have everything they need to live, such as food, water, air, and shelter. Will these people experience scarcity? Explain.
2. Consider the story Abraham Lincoln

told about the two boys who fought over ownership of an apple. What alternatives to fighting could the boys have found?

3. Suppose you were the manager of a radio station. What are some of the questions you would face concerning the question, *What to produce?*

4. Why does the study of economics deal with efficiency more than with equity?

5. What is the opportunity cost of doing an hour of homework in the evening?

Developing Your Attitudes, Values, and Skills

1. Choose one natural resource from this list: marshes, oil, rivers, trees, gold, farmland. Using books, magazines, and newspaper articles, research the status of this resource in the United States today. How is the resource used by industry? Is it widely available? If it is being used up, can it be replaced? If not, when will the resource run out? If there is a shortage, what caused it? How would things change if the resource suddenly became available in unlimited supply? Who would benefit? Who would be hurt? Write a summary of your conclusions.

2. How did the Americans at the time feel about the money and resources that President Kennedy and Congress spent to send an astronaut to the moon? Track public opinion through newspaper and magazine articles of the 1960s. If the class works in groups, you can divide the research by years. How did most people think the money and resources should have been used? At what times did opinions about its use change? What did people perceive as the opportunity costs? Did some people disagree about the way resources were portioned? Why? Prepare a time line or a graph to present your results to the class. A similar issue today is the development of the Strategic Defense Initiative System, called Star Wars. Do some background reading in newspapers and magazines. How are public opinions about Star Wars similar to the attitudes you found toward space exploration in the 1960s? How do they differ? Why?

3. People often debate issues that arise from the three basic economic questions, and newspapers often carry accounts of such debates. From reading the newspaper, choose an issue that illustrates one of the questions: what to produce, how to produce, and for whom to produce. For example, how much money should we spend on national defense, on vocational education, or on disposal of nuclear waste materials? Interview family members, friends, and teachers about your topic. Ask them how they think resources should be allocated in your example. Ask them about the opportunity costs. Try to get opposing points of view. Compare the responses to your questions, and prepare an oral report for the class.

FOCUS YOUR READING

What do salt, playing cards, and tobacco have in common?

What is the "invisible hand" that guides a free enterprise system?

Why is money called the "oil" of an economic system?

CHAPTER 3

MARKETS AND MONEY

PREVIEW

"The job *market* is awful."

"The gold *market* has been strong recently."

"The farmer's *market* has a good buy on oranges."

"To *market,* to *market,* to buy a fat pig— Home again, home again jiggity jig."

Jobs, gold, oranges, and pigs have something in common. These and thousands of other goods, services, and resources are bought and sold in markets. In the free enterprise system, markets play an important role in deciding *what, how,* and *for whom to produce.*

Exchanges that take place in markets usually involve the use of money. But what is money? That seems like a simple question. Money is what you get on payday. Money is what you use to buy goods and services.

Money is what people sometimes run short of in checking accounts.

Today, most people have a general understanding of the word *money.* But money has been different things at different times. Primitive tribes used the bones of certain animals as money. The ancient Romans used cattle and salt. American Indians relied on strings of colored shells, which they called wampum. In colonial times the use of tobacco as money was approved by the government of Virginia, and the South Carolina legislature granted citizens the right to pay their taxes with rice. During that same period, the military governor of Canada paid his troops with playing cards. On the back of the cards he wrote the amount and signed his name. These cards were used as money in Canada for over 70 years.

In this chapter you will learn about the operation of markets and the important role of money in the economic system. When you have completed the reading material and learning activities, you should be able to:

★ Discuss the differences between product and resource markets.

★ Explain the circular flow of economic activity.

★ Describe how a market economy answers the questions of what to produce, how to produce, and for whom to produce.

★ Explain why barter is inefficient in a market economy.

★ List the three functions of money.

★ Describe three types of money used in the United States.

★ Explain what is meant by the term *fiat money*.

MARKETS AND VOLUNTARY EXCHANGE

Trade is the exchange of goods, services, and resources between individuals and firms in the economic system. Voluntary trade occurs only when both of the trading parties believe that they will be better off after the exchange. Farmers sell apples because they value the money more than the fruit. At the same time, buyers trade their money for the apples because the fruit is valued more than the money spent.

Voluntary exchange does not always require money. Suppose, for instance, the manager of a nearby business asks you to wash the firm's windows. In return, the manager agrees to let you use the firm's tools to work on your car. In deciding whether to make the exchange, you must determine if the use of the tools (a capital resource) is more valuable than the time (a human resource) that would be necessary to wash the windows. This trade of your time for the firm's equipment will occur only if you both decide that you will benefit by the exchange.

Voluntary exchange is important in a free enterprise system. Such trade allocates goods, services, and resources to those who value them most. The fact that both parties agree to the exchange guarantees that the new allocation is an improvement over the allocation that existed before the trade was made. Otherwise, the trade would not have been made.

Markets exist to make voluntary exchange easier. A **market** is an arrangement that allows buyers and sellers to come together to trade goods, services, and resources.

We usually think of a market as a place where people buy something, but to economists, the meaning is much broader.

Chicago Mercantile Exchange

Markets at Work

Trading in a market is based on trial and error. Sellers set the prices at which they are willing to offer their wares. Buyers make known the prices that they are willing to pay. If sellers set their prices too high, they will be unable to sell their goods, services, or resources. This causes them to lower their prices. On the other hand, if buyers offer prices that are too low, no one will sell to them and they will not be able to get the things they want, so they increase their bids. Finally, by trial and error, buyers and sellers agree on prices, and exchanges are made.

The sale of a motorcycle is a simple example of markets at work. Suppose the owner of a used Honda needs cash to go to college. An advertisement is placed in the local newspaper offering the cycle for sale at $2,500. Three people see the ad and come to look at the cycle. Two lose interest because of the high price. The third offers to buy but is willing to pay only $2,000.

This lack of success tells the cycle owner that the price probably is too high. The unwillingness of the owner to sell tells the interested buyer that the offer was too low. As a result, the owner responds by reducing the price to $2,300 and the interested buyer offers $2,200. This trial-and-error process has brought them closer to an exchange. However, they must alter their prices even more if the trade is to be made. If the buyer and seller can agree on a price between $2,200 and $2,300, the motorcycle will have a new owner and both parties should be happier as a result of the exchange.

Product and Resource Markets

Markets can be classified as either product markets or resource markets. **Product markets** involve the exchange of goods and services. A grocery store is part of a product market for goods. Barbershops are part of a product market for services.

Resource markets exist to assist in exchanging human, natural, and capital resources. When an oil company buys oil from producers in Saudi Arabia, the firm is involved in a resource market. You participate in a resource market when you search for a job.

Product and resource markets serve the same purpose. They bring buyers into contact with sellers for voluntary exchanges. By making trade easier, markets assist in efficiently allocating goods, services, and resources in a free enterprise system.

> ### INSTANT REPLAY
>
> Voluntary exchange makes both parties better off as a result of the exchange.
>
> A market is an arrangement that brings buyers and sellers together to exchange goods, services, or resources.
>
> Goods and services are traded in product markets. Resources such as labor are exchanged in resource markets.

MARKETS AND THE CIRCULAR FLOW OF ECONOMIC ACTIVITY

You just learned that product markets involve the exchange of goods and services. They bring together sellers (businesses) and buyers (households). You also learned that resource markets exist for the trading of economic resources, such as labor and land. Usually individuals or households are the sellers of these resources and businesses are the buyers.

Notice that businesses and households trade roles in going from one market to another. Businesses are usually the sellers in product markets, but they are the buyers in resource markets. In contrast, households are sellers in resource markets, but buyers in product markets.

Product and resource markets work together in a free enterprise system. Figure 3-1 illustrates the connection between these two types of markets. It shows a circular flow of economic activity between product and resource markets.

The term **circular flow of economic activity** refers to the continuous movement of income between resource and product markets. **Income** is the total value of earnings that a household receives from the sales of its resources.

In the resource market, businesses offer dollars to the owners of resources. For example, a worker is paid for his or her labor, or a landowner receives money for oil discovered on her or his land. These resources are then used by businesses to produce goods and services.

The income received by households from the sale of resources (usually labor) is spent in product markets to purchase goods and services. This money then becomes income to businesses and is used by them to purchase more resources from households. In turn, households use this income from the sale of resources to buy more goods and services from businesses. This flow of economic activity between businesses and households in product and resource markets is a continuing process.

The circular flow of economic activity shown in Figure 3-1 indicates that households and businesses must work together in the economic

FIGURE 3-1
The connection between product and resource markets is shown in this circular flow of economic activity.

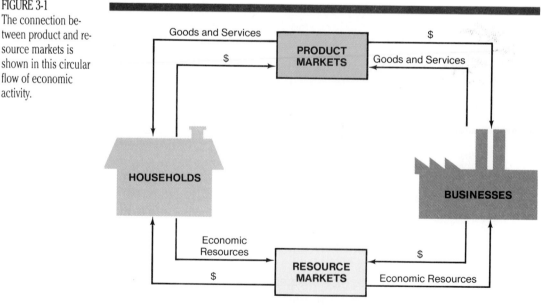

All economic systems depend on a flow of exchanges between producers and consumers.

system. If the exchange of goods, services, and resources breaks down at any point, the system will cease to work. If households do not sell the resources that they own, businesses will be unable to produce goods and services. At the same time, if businesses stop purchasing resources, then households will lose their source of income. Within the economic system, businesses depend on households and households depend on businesses.

INSTANT REPLAY

There is a circular flow of economic activity that connects products and resource markets.

Businesses and households must work together in the economic system.

MARKETS AND THE QUESTIONS, *WHAT, HOW,* AND *FOR WHOM TO PRODUCE?*

Chapter 2 explains that scarcity occurs because wants are unlimited and resources are limited. Scarcity results in the need to make decisions about *what, how,* and *for whom to produce.* These choices must be made in every economic system. In a free enterprise system they are made through the operation of markets. That is why a free enterprise system is often referred to as a **market economy.** In such a system the questions of *what, how,* and *for whom to produce* are determined by the operation of markets.

What to Produce?

Businesses must continually make choices about what to produce. These decisions involve questions such as, Should the local movie theater show more westerns or rely on science fiction films? Should scarce oil be used to make gasoline or heating oil? Should General Motors Corporation concentrate on manufacturing luxury automobiles or airplane engines?

In a market economy, the "dollar votes" of consumers guide businesses in their decisions about what to produce. Businesses produce what they wish in a free enterprise system. Consumers spend their incomes as they please. If businesses provide products not wanted by households, those products will go unsold. Thus, successful businesses must be responsive to the needs and wants of consumers. This idea is referred to as **consumer sovereignty.** It means that consumers are the real decision makers in determining what will be produced.

Consumers vote in favor of a good or service by buying it. If they purchase enough of the product, it will continue to be produced. However, if the good or service is not accepted by consumers, the firm must change the product, produce a different good or service, or go out of business.

In the late 1950s the Ford Motor Company introduced a new car named the Edsel. The Edsel was probably as good a car as most of the other models around, but car buyers did not like it. The reasons are unclear. Some people believe that the grill (which looked a lot like a horse collar) was a factor. Others suggest that the name *Edsel* was a poor choice. Whatever the explanation, consumers indicated their dislike by buying very few Edsels. The consumers' lack of dollar votes convinced Ford that a mistake had been made. The company soon took the car off the market. The introduction of the Edsel resulted in a loss of at least $50 million for the Ford Motor Company.

In a market economy, decisions about *what to produce* are made by trial and error. Although businesses try to provide the goods and services that will be accepted by consumers, they often fail.

Before a good or service comes to the market, there is no way of knowing for sure whether consumers will like it. For example, a movie studio may spend $25 million to make a new film. A very successful

Consumers vote in favor of a good or service by buying it.

movie could earn ten times that amount in tickets sold; an unpopular movie could leave the producers with millions of dollars in unpaid bills. Although a good advertising campaign could help sales, it is the consumer who finally determines whether the show is a success or a failure.

Markets and consumer sovereignty aid in the efficient allocation of resources. Resources that formerly had been used to produce unsuccessful products can be used to produce goods and services that consumers value more highly. Thus, the market allocates resources to produce those goods and services that will best satisfy human needs and wants.

How to Produce?

Chapter 2 explains that most goods and services can be produced in several ways. Suppose two individuals are each in the business of selling firewood. One cuts the wood slowly but surely with an axe. The other uses a chain saw, which cuts the wood quickly. Which person will be able to sell wood at a lower price?

Although the chain saw may have cost the second owner several hundred dollars, that person cuts more wood each day than the owner who cuts the wood with an axe. Thus, that person can sell the wood at a lower price. The owner cutting wood with the axe is now faced with the decision to buy a chain saw or lose business.

Changes in radios over the last 20 years also show the impact of markets in the decision *how to produce*. For many years radios were made using vacuum tubes. These tubes were expensive, bulky, and un-reliable. The invention of the transistor made the vacuum tube obsolete. Because the transistor had so many advantages, radio manufacturers no longer used tubes. Firms were forced to switch to the transistor or fail.

These examples are typical of the way in which *how to produce* decisions are made in a market economy. Companies using the most efficient methods of production stay in business. Inefficient firms are forced out of the market because they cannot meet the prices of other, more efficient businesses. Thus, the efficient use of scarce resources is encouraged by the operation of the market.

Changes in radios over the last 20 years show the impact of markets in the decision of how to produce.

For Whom to Produce?

Decisions must also be made to determine who will get the goods and services that are produced. Does a new stereo go to you or to your friend down the block? Does your family get a new house or does it go to the Jefferson family?

Answers to these and other questions concerning *for whom to produce* are determined mainly by how income is distributed in the economic system. You learned that income is received by households from the sale of resources. Because some households have more valuable resources to sell than others, they receive more income from the sale of those resources; that is, income is not distributed equally.

In a market economy, goods and services go to those who have the money and are willing to spend it. However much you might like to buy a new stereo, it will not be yours until you have the money. Even then, you must be willing to pay the price. Similarly, your parents may want a luxury home. However, the Jeffersons will be the new owners if they can pay the price and your parents cannot.

Adam Smith and the Invisible Hand

The year 1776 was important for Americans. That was the year in which the Declaration of Independence was signed. That document stressed the need for political freedom. The year 1776 was also an important date for the study of economics. In that year Adam Smith published *An Inquiry Into the Nature and Causes of the Wealth of Nations,* which deals with another important kind of freedom—economic freedom.

Smith argued that the economic system is best able to satisfy human needs and wants when people are allowed to act freely in a market economy. He said markets work as if they were guided by an *invisible hand.*

Adam Smith's "invisible hand" is not a difficult idea. People in society want to earn money to buy goods and services. But an individual's success in earning income depends on how well the needs of other groups are satisfied. The resource owner must provide resources that meet the needs of business. Otherwise, the resources cannot be sold. At the same time, the success of a business depends on satisfying the needs and wants of consumers.

Both resource owners and businesses are in the market to satisfy their own needs. But in meeting those needs, they also assist others. As Adam Smith looked at this result, it seemed to him that an invisible hand was guiding the system to achieve an outcome that was good for all.

I N S T A N T   R E P L A Y

In a free enterprise or market economy, the *what to produce* decision is determined by the dollar votes of consumers. This is called consumer sovereignty.

The most efficient methods of production guide the choice of *how to produce.*

For whom to produce is decided by the distribution of income. Goods and services go to those who have the money and are willing to pay the price.

A market economy works for the good of all as if guided by an invisible hand.

BARTER AND THE NEED FOR MONEY

The exchange of goods and services in a market does not require that money be used. Think about two children trading baseball cards. One has a card that the other wants. By trial and error they attempt to find a price that they can both agree on. But that price may not be in terms of money. The trade could involve the exchange of one card for another. Or it could be the baseball card for three video arcade tokens. When goods are traded directly without the use of money, the exchange is called **barter.**

Barter is a cumbersome method for trading goods and services. The problem with a barter system is that, for a trade to take place, each person must have something that the other wants. Often, this matching of wants does not occur. Suppose that you need a new pair of shoes. You have a tennis racket that you are willing to trade for the shoes. Someone else has a pair of shoes, but is looking for an electric drill. No trade will take place because the wants of both traders cannot be satisfied.

To get what you want in a barter system, you might have to make a series of trades. You might, for example, find someone with whom you could exchange your tennis racket for an electric drill. Then you could trade the drill for the shoes you need. There might be additional trades in between. Imagine how time-consuming and frustrating it would be if you had to trade in this way for all the things that you need and want.

The basic problem with barter is that it is inefficient, because it requires people to use a great deal of their time and effort in trading. This time and effort could be better spent in producing goods and services or in enjoying leisure activities. Bartering simply is not a satisfactory method of exchange in our modern world.

Money is anything that people are willing to accept as payment for things they sell or work they do. Although money is not necessary for trading goods and services, it certainly makes exchanges easier. Money can be exchanged for the goods and services you want. If you have money and go to the owner of the shoes, you should have little trouble making the trade. Agreeing on the price might be the only problem. In turn, the seller will be able to use the money to buy the electric drill directly. You no longer need to become involved in a long series of trades in order to match wants. Since money is accepted by everybody, all you need to do is to find someone who has what you want at the price you are willing to pay. Then the money you offer will be accepted.

Money is sometimes referred to as the "oil" that makes an economic system work more efficiently. Oil reduces friction and makes an engine run smoothly. Money functions in much the same way. The

Throughout history, people have been willing to accept many things as payment for the work they do.

advantage of money is that it reduces the transaction costs involved in an exchange. A **transaction cost** is an expense associated with a trade or transaction.

In a barter system, transaction costs are high. These costs are the time and effort used to find trading partners. Money greatly reduces transaction costs. Because money is accepted by everyone, trading for goods and services is much easier than in a barter system.

Money on Rossel Island

Tobacco, cattle, beads, and beaver skins have all been used as money at one time or another. The list could also include gold, silver, wheat, spices, and hundreds of other items. The money of Rossel Island, near New Guinea in the South Pacific, is an interesting example. Until recently, the population of about 1,000 natives used shells to pay for pigs, canoes, wives, and everything else that was traded. Different kinds of shells had different values. They were recognized by their colors and shapes. White shells were the least valuable and red the most prized. There were more than 1,000 of the low-valued shells, but only 8 or 10 of the precious red shells.

The natives of Rossel Island believed that the highest valued shells had a magical content. Some were considered so sacred that they were always kept in a box and never saw the light of day. When passed from person to person, they were handled with great reverence; the two people would kneel with heads bowed.

Other shells were used only for special purposes. For example, the natives used to have a custom that when a chief died, one of the inhabitants of a neighboring village would be killed. The victim's relatives were then paid these sacred shells.

THE THREE FUNCTIONS OF MONEY

In a market economy, money has three main uses or functions. The most important use of money is as a **medium of exchange.** Money is useful only as long as people are willing to accept it in exchange for goods and services. The beginning of the chapter pointed out that many things have been used as money. These things could be referred to as money only because people considered them money. As soon as tobacco, wampum, or salt was no longer generally accepted, it could not be considered money. The point is so important that it needs to be repeated: Something is money only if people accept it as money.

If people lose confidence in a society's money, they may not be willing to accept it as payment for goods or services. The money then loses its usefulness. For example, if prices increase too fast, people may believe their money will have little value in the future. As a result, they refuse to accept money and resort to bartering goods and services.

The second use of money is as a **unit of account.** Suppose you go into a store and see a dress or suit that you like. The price could be expressed in many ways. For example, the price could be in pounds of rice or in tickets to the Super Bowl. But these measures would not give you a clear idea of the opportunity cost of buying the clothing. In contrast, if the suit or dress carries a price tag of $100, you know exactly what the opportunity cost is—the other goods that could be purchased for $100.

Because money is so commonly used, everybody in the nation has a clear idea what is meant by a dollar. Instead of prices being expressed in terms of different items, all prices are counted in dollars. Thus, the dollar is said to be the unit of account in the United States. In all countries, the basic unit of money is the unit of account for measuring prices. For example, in Mexico prices are stated in pesos. In Japan the prices of rice and fish are measured in yen. Table 3-1 shows the unit of account in other nations.

TABLE 3-1

MONETARY UNITS OF ACCOUNT IN OTHER NATIONS

Country	Unit of Account
Argentina	Peso
Canada	Dollar
China	Yuan
France	Franc
Germany (East & West)	Mark
Great Britain	Pound
Greece	Drachma
India	Rupee
Israel	Shekel
Italy	Lira
Japan	Yen
Mexico	Peso
Poland	Zloty
Saudi Arabia	Riyal
Sweden	Krona
U.S.S.R.	Ruble

A third use of money is as a **store of value.** If you don't want to buy goods and services with your money today, you can save it to buy things in the future. Suppose you have a small farm and produce eggs. The eggs must be sold or they will spoil. By selling your eggs for money, you have traded a good (eggs) that will become worthless if kept. You have received a good (money) that you can store until you want to make a purchase in the future.

INSTANT REPLAY

Barter is the direct exchange of goods and services without the use of money.

Barter is inefficient, because the time and effort required to find trading partners result in high transaction costs.

Money is anything that people will accept in payment for things they sell or work they do. It oils the economic system by reducing transaction costs.

Money functions as a medium of exchange, a unit of account, and a store of value.

The money shown here is based on each country's unit of account.

MONEY IN THE UNITED STATES

To be useful, money must be scarce. If individuals had the right to print money, the economic system would soon be flooded with useless money. Hence, in modern societies the privilege of creating money is given to the national government. In the United States, the Constitution gives the federal government the right to produce money:

> No state shall...coin money...The Congress shall have power...To coin money, and regulate the value thereof...

Coins, Currency, and Demand Deposits

There are three important kinds of money used in the United States:

★ Coins

★ Currency

★ Demand Deposits

Coins. **Coins** are money made of metal, such as nickels, dimes and quarters. The oldest coins still in existence today were made in about 600 B.C. in what is now Turkey. They were bean-shaped lumps of gold and silver.

All the coins used in the United States today are made by the Department of the Treasury. The Treasury has mints in Denver, San Francisco, and Philadelphia. You can tell where a coin was made by looking at the date. Coins minted in Denver have a "D" after the date; those minted in San Francisco have an "S." There is no letter following the date on Philadelphia-made coins.

Currency. **Currency** is paper money, such as dollar bills. The Chinese were the first to use paper money. When Marco Polo returned from his travels to China he reported:

> All of his [the Chinese emperor's] subjects receive it [paper money] without hesitation because, wherever their business may call them, they can dispose of it again in the purchase of merchandise they may require.

All United States currency is printed by the Treasury under the direction of the Federal Reserve System. Look at the front of any denomination of paper money. At the top the words *FEDERAL RESERVE NOTE* appear. The Federal Reserve System has been given the right by Congress to print money and also to regulate banking throughout the United States. You will learn more about the Federal Reserve System in Chapter 11.

Demand Deposits. **Demand deposits** are money that people keep in their checking accounts. Suppose you take $100 to the bank and open a checking account. The bank will give you credit for demand deposits in the amount of $100. You then have the ability to write checks up to $100.

These checks can be used like coins and currency to pay for the things you buy. When a purchase is made using a check, the person or business who receives it can present the check to the proper bank for payment. The bank must make payment immediately. That is, it must pay "on demand."

Since so many people pay for goods, services, and resources by check, demand deposits are the most important type of money in the United States. Total demand deposits are much greater than coins and currency combined.

Who's Who on United States Currency

Traditionally, the faces of government leaders or other famous people have been placed on coins and currency. The Caesars appear on the coins of ancient Rome. The kings and queens of England adorn British coins. This custom has been continued in the United States. Coins and currency usually carry the pictures of former presidents or great patriots. Below is a list of the individuals whose likenesses currently appear on United States coins and currency.

COINS

Penny	Abraham Lincoln
Nickel	Thomas Jefferson
Dime	Franklin D. Roosevelt
Quarter	George Washington
Half-Dollar	John F. Kennedy
Dollar	Susan B. Anthony

CURRENCY

One-Dollar Bill	George Washington
Five-Dollar Bill	Abraham Lincoln
Ten-Dollar Bill	Alexander Hamilton
Twenty-Dollar Bill	Andrew Jackson
Fifty-Dollar Bill	Ulysses S. Grant
Hundred-Dollar Bill	Benjamin Franklin

Until 1969, currency in denominations of $500, $1,000, $5,000, and $10,000 was issued by the Federal Reserve System. However, these bills were rarely used by the public. Since 1969, the $100 bill has been the largest unit of United States currency printed.

Demand deposits, or checkbook money, are popular because of their advantages over coins and currency. Purchases of expensive items, such as a television or a car, can be made by writing a single check. If a large sum of cash is lost, it is usually much more serious than if you lose your checkbook. When cancelled checks are returned to you by the bank, they may be used as receipts. Also, checks provide an easy method for keeping track of how much money you spend and what you purchase.

Fiat vs Commodity Money

Until the 1930s, the United States Treasury minted coins made of gold. The amount of gold in these coins was equal to the value of the coin as money. For example, a $20 gold coin contained twenty dollars' worth of gold. Money that is made of valuable metals such as gold is called **commodity money.** Until 1971, the Treasury minted silver half-dollars. These coins are another example of commodity money. They each contained fifty cents' worth of silver.

The coins used in the United States today are not commodity money. The value of the metal from which they are made is usually much less than the value of the coin. For example, a Kennedy half-dollar is a sandwich of metals. The outer edges are made of nickel and copper; the middle is pure copper. The total value of these metals is considerably less than the fifty cents that the coin is worth.

Paper money clearly is not commodity money, but in the past it was possible to convert currency to gold or silver. The holder of a dollar bill could require the government to give a dollar's worth of gold or silver in exchange for the bill. The conversion of currency to gold ended in 1933. The printing of currency that could be exchanged for silver ended in 1965.

Today, all the money printed in the United States is fiat money. The word *fiat* means "by decree or order." **Fiat money** is not made of valuable metals. It is money because the government has decreed or ordered that it be money. On the face of each piece of currency printed in the United States are the words "THIS NOTE IS LEGAL TENDER FOR ALL DEBTS, PUBLIC AND PRIVATE." The phrase **legal tender** means that paper money must be accepted as payment for goods, services, and resources. Suppose you owe someone $100 and offer to pay that person with a $100 bill. That person is legally required to accept the currency as payment for the debt. The person cannot make you pay in gold, silver, or anything else.

How much is the metal in these coins worth?

Fiat money has some advantages over commodity money. One advantage is that valuable metals are saved for other uses. A second advantage is that the amount of money in circulation can be increased when necessary to meet the needs of a growing economy. If all money was made of gold, then the total amount of money in the economy would be determined by the amount of gold that was mined. If gold was not mined fast enough to meet the needs of the economic system, there would not be enough money available.

There are also some dangers in the use of fiat money. The value of such money depends on the confidence people have that they can continue to use it as a medium of exchange. Unlike commodity money, the only use of fiat money is as money. The materials used to make the coins or currency are worth very little.

During the Civil War, the United States government printed over $400 million of fiat money. Because of their color, these bills were called "greenbacks." Like our money today, this currency was designated as legal tender but could not be converted into gold or silver. The usefulness of greenbacks depended on people's confidence in them as a medium of exchange. Their value rose and fell with the fortunes of the government in the war. During one bleak period, a $1 greenback was worth only 35 cents in gold.

The Confederate government also printed fiat money during the Civil War. As the South suffered defeats, the value of this money declined. At the end of the war, Confederate fiat money was essentially worthless.

Fiat money is widely used throughout the world. However, three requirements must be met for fiat money to be valuable. First, the government of the country must decree that the money is legal tender. Second, the government must keep its money relatively scarce. Finally, and most important, the people in the country must be willing to accept the fiat money as a medium of exchange.

I N S T A N T   R E P L A Y

Coins are minted by the Treasury. Currency is printed under the direction of the Federal Reserve System.

Demand deposits are the most important form of money used in the United States.

Commodity money is made of valuable metals. Fiat money is money by government decree or order.

All the money used in the United States today is fiat money.

S U M M A R Y

Voluntary exchange occurs when buyers and sellers are both made better off by a trade. Markets exist to make exchange easier. Prices in a market are determined by trial and error. Goods and services are traded in product markets. Human, natural, and capital resources are traded in resource markets.

There is a circular flow of economic activity between product and resource markets. Businesses provide income to households in exchange for resources. Households use that income to buy goods and services from businesses. Businesses then use the money to buy additional resources.

In a market economy, decisions about *what to produce* are based on consumer sovereignty. In spending their dollars, consumers vote for the goods and services that they want. The *how to produce* question is determined by firms in their search for the most efficient methods of production. *For whom to produce* is determined by who has the income and how they decide to spend it. The operation of markets results in an efficient allocation of resources. To Adam Smith it seemed as if markets were guided by an invisible hand.

The direct exchange of goods and services is called barter. Bartering is inefficient, because trades can take place only if each party has exactly what the other wants. Money reduces transaction costs associated with trading. Since everyone wants money, much less time and effort are required to make exchanges.

Money has three functions in a market economy. It serves as a medium of exchange, a unit of account, and a store of value.

The three most important forms of money used in the United States are coins, currency, and demand deposits. Because of their advantages, checks are the most frequently used medium of exchange in payment for goods, services, and resources.

Commodity money contains valuable metals. Fiat money is valuable by order of decree of the government, not because of its content. Most economic systems use fiat money. Three requirements of fiat money are that the government designate it as legal tender, that it be kept scarce, and that people accept it as a medium of exchange.

☆ LEARNING ACTIVITIES ☆

Building Your Vocabulary

On a separate sheet of paper, write the numbers 1 through 14. Next to each number, write the term that correctly completes the sentence.

consumer sovereignty
unit of account
barter
resource markets
coins
store of value
legal tender
fiat
trade
circular flow of economic activity
medium of exchange
currency
commodity
money

1. _____ oils the economic system by reducing transaction costs.

2. _Coins_ are money made of metal.

3. Gold and silver coins are examples of _Commodity_ money.

4. When money is used to add to a person's wealth, it is acting as a _store_ of _value_

5. Paper money is called _currency_.

6. The continual movement of income between product and resource markets is the _circular flow of_.

7. _Resource ma_ assist in the exchange of economic resources.

8. The *what to produce* decision is determined in a market economy by _Consumer so_

9. _Trade_ is the exchange of goods, services, and resources between individuals and firms in the economic system.

10. A _legal tender_ is something that is widely accepted in payment for goods, services, and resources.

11. As a method of expressing prices, money functions as a _____.

12. Money by government order or decree is called _fiat_ money.

13. Direct exchange of goods and services is _barter_.

14. Something that *must* be accepted in payment for goods, services, and resources is said to be _legal tender_.

Reviewing the Facts

1. Give an example of a good or service that is sold in a product market. Give an example of something sold in a resource market.
2. How do the resources owned by a household affect the amount of income that a household can earn?
3. Why are inefficient companies likely to fail in a market economy?
4. Why is barter an inefficient method for making exchanges?
5. Why must money be scarce?
6. Why is checkbook money called demand deposits?
7. Give an example of commodity money currently in use in the United States.

Expressing Your Opinion

1. What are some of the markets that you have participated in during the last week? Describe these markets.
2. Which are most important—product markets or resource markets? Why?
3. What determines the resources that a household has to sell?
4. How does advertising affect the principle of consumer sovereignty?
5. Could the modern economic system function without money? Explain.
6. Why don't people use large denominations ($500 or more) of currency?

Developing Your Attitudes, Values, and Skills

1. For money to have value, it must be accepted in exchange for goods and services. Some people feel safer if money is guaranteed by a precious metal that always has value, such as gold. The United States stopped backing its money with gold in 1933. Read some background material on the gold standard. Examine the arguments on both sides of the question, Should all money be backed by gold reserves? Draw your own conclusions about the importance of gold in our society.
2. In our society, most exchanges of goods and services involve money. But there are times when people barter, or exchange goods and services directly. Ask family members and friends to recount their bartering experiences. What kinds of goods and services have they exchanged? With whom? How frequently? Do they enjoy bartering, or do they prefer using money? Do they expect to barter in the future? Compare the answers you receive, and form conclusions about the role of barter in our economy.
3. When a government prints too much

money, the money loses value. This happened in Germany in the 1920s, in China and Hungary after World War II, in Chile in the 1970s, and in Israel in the 1980s. Read an account of one of these situations, and describe what happened to the society as a result. Explain why money lost its value.

4. When you see the word **market,** you probably think of a farmer's market or a flea market. But the word has a much broader meaning. Read again the definition of market in this chapter. Then explain why each of the situations listed below could be described as a market transaction. Who is the seller? Who is the buyer? What good, service, or resource is being traded? What is it exchanged for?

a. Hiring a babysitter.

b. Buying food.

c. Ordering mail-order seeds.

d. Selling a house.

e. Renting a car.

What are some other examples of markets?

UNIT 2

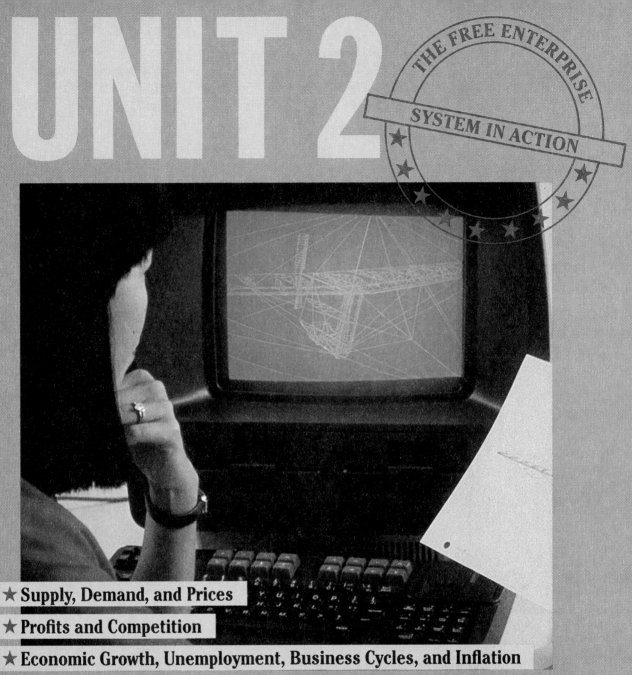

★ **Supply, Demand, and Prices**

★ **Profits and Competition**

★ **Economic Growth, Unemployment, Business Cycles, and Inflation**

Photo courtesy of Hewlett-Packard Company

The focus of this unit is the operation of the free enterprise system. You will learn about supply and demand and how prices are determined. You will read about the roles of profit and competition in the American market system. In addition, you will learn to relate business cycles, deflation, and inflation with economic conditions.

FOCUS YOUR READING

How do business managers know what and how much to produce for consumers?

Why do people buy more of a product when it is on sale?

What happens when there is an excess supply of a product?

CHAPTER 4

SUPPLY, DEMAND, AND PRICES

PREVIEW

In Chapter 2, you learned that an economic system must answer questions concerning *what to produce*, *how to produce*, and *for whom to produce*. In the United States, thousands of firms are producing goods and services for more than 200 million consumers. How do these firms know what consumers want to buy? How do these firms know which natural resources, capital goods, and labor to use in producing their product? How much will these firms send to stores in Seattle, Washington, and how much will they send to stores in Atlanta, Georgia?

In some countries, the government decides the answers to these questions, but such economic systems usually do not work well. Some goods and services that consumers want are not available, while unwanted goods remain unsold. Such a system wastes a country's resources and fails to satisfy its consumer's wants and needs.

The free enterprise system is a more efficient alternative. This approach is based on the markets you learned about in Chapter 3. Recall the principle of consumer sovereignty. Consumers decide what is produced by voting with their dollars in the market. This market approach is based on the idea that when people act to make themselves better off, they also make others better off. This idea is what Adam Smith meant when he said the economic system works as if it were being guided by an invisible hand.

But how does such a system work? Does someone have to organize all this activity? The answer is no. The system will organize itself. It is organized through prices that continually provide signals to producers and consumers. Just as the quarterback of a football team calls the play in the huddle so that the other players know what to do, the price system "calls the plays" for all the producers and consumers in the economy. In fact, each of us helps to call the plays in the free enterprise system whenever we buy or sell something.

58

In this chapter you will learn about the role played by prices in the free enterprise system and how prices are determined in a market. When you have completed the reading material and learning activities, you should be able to:

★ Explain how prices reflect opportunity costs.

★ Show how prices serve as signals for producers and consumers.

★ Explain how prices influence the decisions about what, how, and for whom to produce.

★ Explain what is meant by the law of supply and the law of demand.

★ Describe how supply and demand work together to determine the equilibrium price.

OPPORTUNITY COSTS AND PRICES

In the United States, prices of goods, services, and resources are usually expressed in terms of dollars. These prices help us to identify and measure the opportunity costs of our choices.

Table 4-1 lists prices for several goods and services. Suppose you are thinking about buying a new pair of shoes. The shoes cost $25 a pair. What is the opportunity cost of buying the shoes? That is, what must you give up to have them? For $25, you could buy a steak and a new cassette. Another alternative would be a ski pass and a movie ticket. Because there are so many possibilities, sometimes it is difficult to make a decision. You might want to have all those things and more, but your choices are limited to those that can be purchased for $25.

How do you decide what to buy? Clearly, you choose the goods and services that will bring you the most satisfaction. But you also base your purchases on the price of each product; that is, on how much of your money you are required to exchange for each item. This method of putting a monetary value on products is known as a **price system,** and it is the foundation of free enterprise. Prices help you calculate the opportunity cost of each purchase quickly and easily. Imagine, for example, that you decide to buy a jacket for $20 instead of one for $15, because you feel that the style and the color of the more expensive jacket are worth the extra $5 to you. Now imagine that the two jackets do not have price tags and you have no idea how much they cost. You might find it impossible to decide which one to buy, or whether to buy a jacket at all.

Prices not only help make choices about which goods and services to purchase, they also act as a bridge between goods and services and

TABLE 4-1

PRICES OF GOODS AND SERVICES	
Item	Price
Sweater	$20
Shoes	25
Movie Ticket	5
Socks	2
Record	8
Cassette	10
Calculator	15
Steak Dinner	15
Ski Pass (one day)	20
Tennis Balls (3)	3
Gasoline (gallon)	1
Electric Razor	30
Haircut	15

economic resources. Suppose you have a job that pays $5 an hour. That is the price of your labor services. Thus, you know the price of your labor and the prices of the goods and services that you want. With this information, you can determine how much work is required to buy an item.

Table 4-1 shows that sweaters cost $20 each. If you receive $5 an hour after paying taxes, you must work four hours to earn enough money for one sweater. Thus, the opportunity cost of a sweater is four hours of work. What is the opportunity cost of an electric razor in hours of work? You find the answer by dividing the price of the razor, $30, by $5 per hour. The answer is six hours. Four hours of work will buy a ski pass; less than one hour will buy a can of tennis balls.

In making a decision to buy any of these goods or services, you compare effort with satisfaction. The effort is the amount of time you must spend working to earn enough to buy an item. Satisfaction is how much you will enjoy having the item. If the value of satisfaction is greater than the necessary effort, you will make the purchase. This decision is made much easier because all prices are given in terms of money.

PRICES AS SIGNALS

The price system sends signals to producers, telling them what goods and services consumers want. Suppose a company is trying to decide whether to manufacture microwave ovens. One of the first things the company does is to determine the prices of microwave ovens. Then

Prices help the consumer make choices about which goods and services to purchase.

the company has to determine whether it can produce a product comparable to those on the market for the same price or less.

In this case, assume that the company's planners determine that the average consumer spends about $200 for a microwave oven, but they also determine that it is impossible for their company to manufacture a similar oven for less than $300 each. Obviously, if consumers can buy a product of the same quality for $200, they are not going to buy it for $300. Therefore, the company can expect to fail in the microwave oven manufacturing business.

However, if the planners determine that the company can produce a comparable oven profitably for $150 each, they can expect their company to be successful at making microwaves. In fact, the company can expect to sell many more ovens than its competitors because it can offer a product of the same quality at a lower price.

Of course, businesses cannot always determine the best price for their products beforehand, so a company will often set a price on a new product and then wait to see if the item sells. If the item does not sell well, that is a signal to the company that it has set the price of the product too high. It will reduce the price until it finds the price that most consumers are willing to pay. This system is an example of consumer sovereignty. By buying or not buying, consumers dictate the price to the producers.

Prices also send important signals to consumers. Telephone service is a good example of this. Telephone users decide whether or not to make a call in the same way that they make other buying decisions. If the value of a call is greater than the opportunity cost, the call will be made, but if the opportunity cost is greater than the value of the call, it will not be made.

Some areas of the United States use a flat-rate pricing system for local telephone service. The user pays a certain amount, a flat rate, for telephone service every month. Local calls are free once the flat monthly service charge has been paid. Long-distance calls are extra.

When a telephone user in a flat-rate system makes a local call, the only opportunity cost is the time and effort required to make the call. The call itself is free. Because the opportunity cost is low, many unimportant phone calls are made.

In other areas of the country, the telephone company uses measured-service pricing. With measured service, the basic monthly charge for phone service is smaller, but phone users are charged for each local call they make. Therefore, the opportunity cost of local calls is greater than under the flat-rate system because each call costs money as well as time and effort.

Not surprisingly, when flat-rate and measured-service systems are compared, measured-service users make fewer local calls. This example illustrates how prices act as signals in the economic system. Under flat-rate pricing, users get the signal that the opportunity cost of local calls is small, and they therefore make many calls. However, with measured-rate pricing, users get the signal that the opportunity cost is more expensive, and as a result, they limit the number of calls they make.

Electricity is almost always sold using measured-service pricing. The monthly bill depends on the amount of electricity used. Have you ever been told to turn off the light in your room? The reason is that electricty is expensive, and the person in your household who pays the electric bill is responding to market signals. The signal comes each month with the bill.

Suppose a household's electric bill was the same each month regardless of the amount of electricity used. Then there would be no price signal telling people to conserve electricity. Would anyone still be as concerned about your leaving the light on in your room?

PRICES AND RESOURCE ALLOCATION

Prices also help businesses decide what to produce, that is, whether or not to allocate a company's resources to making a product. Suppose you are the manager of a copper mining company. Often silver is found

High energy prices signal consumers to conserve on energy use.

in small amounts where copper is mined. When silver prices are low, you may decide not to use your company's equipment and workers to separate the silver from the copper, because the cost is too great. But suppose the price of silver increases substantially. The higher price signals to you that it would now pay to use the company's resources to recover the silver. This example illustrates how prices guide firms in deciding what to produce. In this case, when the price of silver went up, its value increased, and the opportunity cost of not recovering it increased.

Prices also affect a firm's choice of how to produce a product. Suppose you manage an electric company. Your first big decision is how to produce electricity for your customers. Your generating equipment can burn either coal or oil to make electricity, so how do you choose which fuel to use? Price can be the deciding factor. If the price of coal is higher than the price of oil, you buy oil; if the price of oil is higher than

Prices provide signals to guide producers in deciding what goods to make.

Courtesy of Burlington Industries, Inc.

the price of coal, you use coal. Clearly, prices help decide which resources will be used to produce goods and services.

Finally, prices are important to help determine who gets the goods and services. Since prices measure opportunity costs, they help you decide whether to sell a product or service and to whom. For example, suppose you decide to sell expensive, inground swimming pools. If only a few people in your area can afford these pools, you will not sell many pools and you will not make much money. Therefore, you may decide to sell cheaper, aboveground pools. If you are successful and sell a large number of aboveground pools, your success is a signal that you are selling the right items to the right people at the right price.

INSTANT REPLAY

Prices measure the opportunity cost of purchasing goods and services.

Prices provide signals that guide consumers in deciding what to buy and guide producers in determining what to make and sell

DEMAND

Demand refers to the relationship between the price of a good and the quantity of that good that consumers want to purchase. An example will help to explain this relationship. How many hamburgers do you buy each week? If the price of a hamburger were $10, how many would you buy? If the price were 15 cents, how many would you buy? If you are like most people, you would buy fewer at the higher price and more at the lower price. This relationship is true for almost all goods and services. It is known as the **law of demand** and means simply that people tend to buy more of something at lower prices than they do at higher prices.

There are three reasons that this law holds. First, when prices rise, you cannot afford to buy so many units of the product as you did before. If you had $15 to spend each month and every hamburger cost $1.50, you could buy ten hamburgers. But if the price increased to $3, you could buy only five hamburgers.

The second reason is that the opportunity cost of buying something increases when its price increases. Suppose the price of a movie ticket is $3. When the price of hamburgers was $1.50, the opportunity cost was one-half of a movie ticket. When the price of hamburgers increased to $3, the opportunity cost increased to one movie ticket. Because the opportunity cost is higher, people probably will buy fewer hamburgers than before.

The third explanation for the law of demand is that often the more you consume of something, the less enjoyment or satisfaction you receive from consuming another unit of that product. An example will help to explain this point. A hamburger at lunchtime can be truly enjoyable. A second one may also be good, but it probably does not hit the spot the way the first one did. That is, the second one gives less satisfaction than the first. The satisfaction received from a third hamburger will be even less, and so on.

Because the first hamburger delivered more satisfaction than the others, you would be willing to pay more for it. You might buy two at lunch if the price were a little lower. It is doubtful that you would buy a third hamburger unless it was very inexpensive.

The Demand Schedule

The **demand schedule** shows the amount demanded by consumers at different prices. Consider the market demand schedule for gasoline shown in Table 4-2. Note that the law of demand is in operation here. As the price goes up, the amount of gasoline purchased goes down. The formal way of discussing these numbers is to say that the *quantity of gasoline demanded* at a price of 50 cents per gallon is 60 million gallons per day. At a price of $1.50 per gallon, the quantity demanded is 20 million gallons per day. As the price increases, the quantity of gasoline demanded decreases. On the other hand, as the price decreases, the quantity demanded increases. Thus, consumers want more gasoline at lower prices than they do at higher prices.

Less gasoline is demanded at higher prices than at lower prices.

Kerr-McGee Corporation

TABLE 4-2

DEMAND SCHEDULE FOR GASOLINE	
Price of Gasoline per Gallon	Millions of Gallons Purchased per Day
$ .50	60
.75	50
1.00	40
1.25	30
1.50	20
1.75	10

It is important to understand that a demand schedule refers to a particular period of time. For example, the schedule in Table 4-2 shows the demand for gas for a period of one day. There would be a different schedule for a month or a year. Clearly, the longer the period, the greater the quantity demanded at each price.

The Demand Curve

Sometimes information is easier to comprehend when it is presented in a graph. A graph is a drawing that depicts a relationship between two or more sets of numbers. For example, a graph might show how a nation's population has increased or decreased over several decades, or how much of a person's tax dollar was spent on defense in each of the last ten years. Graphs are important tools in economics. They can present many types of numerical information in a way that is quickly and easily understood.

Figure 4-1 is a graph of the numbers from the demand schedule in Table 4-2. The amount of gasoline is measured along the bottom of the graph, the horizontal axis. The price of gasoline is measured up the side of the graph, the vertical axis. The line marked with a *D* at each end is called a **demand curve.** In this example, the curve is actually a straight line. The demand curve is drawn with information from the demand schedule. For example, the demand schedule shows that a price of 50 cents per gallon, 60 million gallons of gasoline will be sold each day. To

FIGURE 4-1
This graph shows the demand curve for gasoline. It corresponds to Table 4-2.

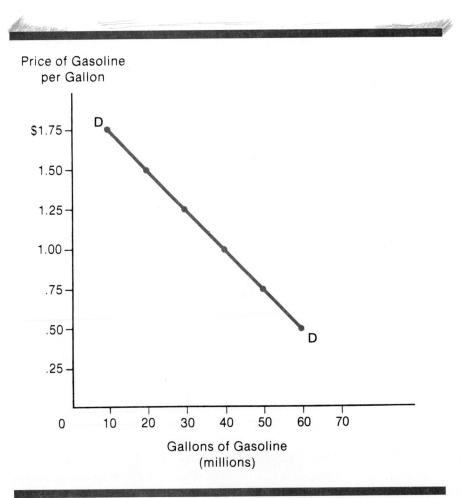

enter this information on the graph, go up the side until you come to a price of 50 cents. Then go out along the bottom line to 60 million gallons. That point on the graph gives the same information as the first row in the demand schedule.

The same method is used to place the other points on the graph. Note that there are six points on the graph. Each corresponds to one of the six rows in the demand schedule. Also, note that the curve slopes downward from left to right. This slope shows that there is an inverse relationship between quantity demanded and price. That is, when the one goes up, the other goes down. Thus, the graph illustrates the law of demand.

Once the points are plotted on the graph, the demand curve is drawn with a line connecting the six points. Take a moment to compare the information in Table 4-2 and Figure 4-1. The graph is a picture representing the same information as the numbers in the demand schedule.

I N S T A N T   R E P L A Y

The law of demand states that more of a good or service is demanded at lower prices than at higher prices.

The demand schedule or demand curve shows the relationship between the price of a product and the amount that consumers want to buy at that price.

SUPPLY

Supply refers to the amount or quantity of a good or service that firms will provide at given prices. Table 4-3 shows the **supply schedule** for gasoline. The schedule shows how many gallons of gas oil companies will offer for sale at each possible price. For example, if the price is $1 per gallon, firms will supply 25 million gallons per day. If the price increases to $1.50 per gallon, oil companies will increase the amount supplied to 35 million gallons each day. Thus, the quantity of gasoline offered for sale will increase as the price increases.

Like the demand schedule, the supply schedule can be shown as a graph, as in Figure 4-2. Each of the six combinations of price and quantity is plotted as a point on the graph. Then these points are connected to form a **supply curve.** The supply curve rises as it moves from left to right. This rise shows a direct relationship between quantity supplied and price. Look at each of the points on that supply curve. Notice that they show that producers will supply more gasoline at higher prices. A price of $.50 results in a supply of 15 million gallons of gas. At a price of $1.75, the quantity supplied increases to 40 million gallons.

TABLE 4-3

SUPPLY SCHEDULE FOR GASOLINE

Price of Gasoline per Gallon	Millions of Gallons Supplied per Day
$ .50	15
.75	20
1.00	25
1.25	30
1.50	35
1.75	40

FIGURE 4-2
The quantity of gasoline supplied each day will increase as the price increases. This curve corresponds to Table 4-3.

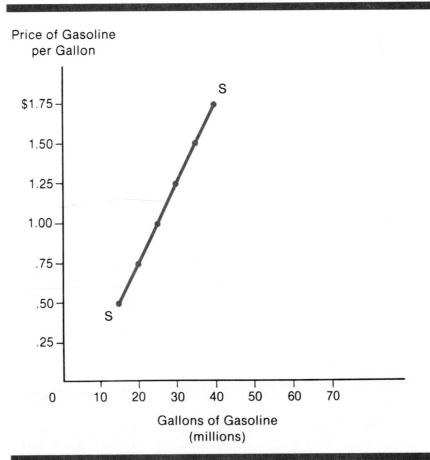

The supply curve illustrates an important concept in economics: the **law of supply.** This law states that firms will produce more of a good at higher prices than they will at lower prices.

In the case of gasoline production, the company's costs include buying crude oil, converting it to gasoline, and delivering it to service stations. Each additional gallon of gas the company produces represents an extra cost to the company. This cost—the cost of producing one more unit of output—is called the **marginal cost.**

Think about what an oil company has to do to provide more gas. The first need would be to get more oil. Suppose that all of a company's oil comes from wells drilled in the United States. To get more oil, the company will have to drill more wells. This might mean drilling wells into the ocean floor, working in temperatures of 80° below zero in Alaska, or exploring remote areas of Wyoming. Any oil that comes from these areas will cost much more than oil already pumped in the Southwest. That is, the marginal cost of this new oil will be higher than the cost of oil currently being produced. Thus, the company will not pay these additional costs unless the gasoline can be sold at higher prices. The increasing marginal cost of getting additional oil is the reason that the supply curve for gas slopes upward.

The supply curves for other goods and services slope upward for the same reason. As companies produce more of a good or service, the marginal cost increases. Firms will always use the least expensive way of producing first and then will go to more expensive ways of producing.

INSTANT REPLAY

Supply refers to the quantity of a product that will be offered for sale at different prices.

The law of supply states that more will be offered for sale at higher prices than at lower prices. That is, the supply curve is upward sloping.

The supply curve is upward sloping because, for most products, the marginal cost of producing increases as output increases.

DETERMINING THE EQUILIBRIUM PRICE

You often hear people refer to "the law of supply and demand." They think of these two concepts as one law. In effect, they are one law because they work together to determine the prices of goods and services in a free enterprise system. They are like the two arms of a scale always seeking to balance the wants and needs of consumers and producers. This tendency toward balance is how the free enterprise system organizes itself without the need for the government to make all the nation's economic decisions. Here is how supply and demand work together.

Table 4-4 shows the gasoline supply and demand schedules together. These schedules come from Tables 4-2 and 4-3. Suppose the price of gasoline was $1 per gallon. At that price, the quantity supplied would be 25 million gallons and the quantity demanded would be 40 million gallons. Because more gas is demanded than is supplied (15 million gallons more to be exact), there is said to be **excess demand.**

What happens when there is excess demand for a good or service? Because more gas is demanded than is available, some people are unable to get as much as they want to purchase at that price. To get more gasoline, some consumers will pay a higher price. Suppose the price goes up to $1.25. At this higher price, some consumers decide to use less gasoline. Table 4-4 shows that at this higher price, the quantity demanded falls to 30 million gallons per day.

TABLE 4-4

SUPPLY AND DEMAND SCHEDULE FOR GASOLINE		
Price of Gasoline per Gallon	Millions of Gallons Supplied per Day	Millions of Gallons Demanded per Day
$ .50	15	60
.75	20	50
1.00	25	40
1.25	30	30
1.50	35	20
1.75	40	10

But consumers are not the only ones who change their behavior when prices rise. Producers of gasoline also respond to this higher price by supplying more gas to the market. By looking at the supply schedule in Table 4-4, you see that the quantity supplied at a price of $1.25 per gallon is 30 million gallons. Thus, the quantity demanded (30 million gallons) is the same as the quantity supplied (30 million). There is no excess demand. Consumers are able to purchase all they want at this price, and producers are able to sell all that they produce at this price. Neither buyers nor sellers have any reason to change the price. This price, determined by a trial and error process in the market, is sometimes called the **equilibrium price.**

Equilibrium is a condition where opposing forces are exactly balanced. For example, if you put equal weight on both sides of a balance scale, the scale will be in equilibrium. The force pulling on one side exactly offsets the force pulling on the other side. Think of the market as a balance scale with supply on one side and demand on the other. In equilibrium, the forces of demand are equal to the forces of supply. This market scale is in balance, or in equilibrium.

What happens if the price is above the equilibrium price? Suppose that the price is $1.75 per gallon. Producers will supply 40 million gallons, but consumers will want to purchase only 10 million gallons. Because supply is greater than demand, there is said to be **excess supply** at that price. The amount of the excess supply is the difference between the quantity supplied and the quantity demanded. In this case that difference is 30 million gallons.

Producers who are unable to sell the amounts they have on hand will be disappointed at the lack of customers and will lower their prices. Lower prices will increase the amount that consumers will want to purchase and will decrease the amount that producers will supply. The result of these two forces working together will be to eliminate the excess supply.

The price will fall until it reaches $1.25 per gallon. As you have already seen, that is the equilibrium price. At that price the quantity demanded by consumers is equal to the quantity supplied by producers. Neither group has any reason to change the price. The market is now in equilibrium.

How is the equilibrium price determined? If the price is above the equilibrium price, there is excess supply. As a result, the price is brought down until supply and demand are equal. If the price is below the equilibrium price, there is excess demand. The price is driven up until supply and demand are again in balance. Once the amount supplied is equal to the amount demanded, there is no reason for the price to change. Unless consumers change their demand decisions or producers change their supply decisions, the price will stay the same.

You have seen how the supply and demand schedules in Table 4-4 are used to show how the price is set in the market. This equilibrium price also can be determined using the supply and demand graphs. Figure 4-3 shows both the supply and the demand curves drawn on the same graph. Notice where the two curves cross. This point is the equilibrium point. The equilibrium quantity is 30 million gallons, and the equilibrium price is $1.25 per gallon. This price brings demand and supply into balance.

You can see from the figure that any price above the equilibrium price will result in excess supply; the quantity supplied will be greater than the quantity demanded. Similarly, any price below the market price causes excess demand. Demand and supply are in balance only where the curves cross.

INSTANT REPLAY

Excess demand means the quantity demanded exceeds the quantity supplied. As a result, the price will rise.

Excess supply means that the quantity supplied exceeds the quantity demanded. As a result, the price will fall.

The equilibrium price is determined where supply equals demand.

FIGURE 4-3

The equilibrium price is determined at the point where the demand and supply curves cross.

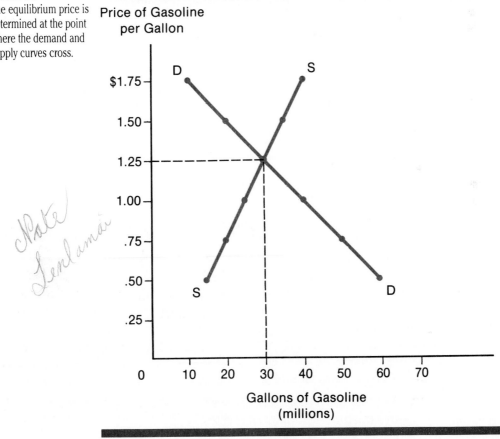

S U M M A R Y

The free enterprise system is based on markets where goods and services are bought and sold. The prices of these goods and services are expressed in dollars, and they send signals to both producers and consumers. Prices give producers signals about what consumers want to buy, and they give consumers signals about the opportunity costs of their choices.

Which goods and services you buy depends on the amount of money you have to spend and the prices of these goods and services. The signals from prices guide producers in deciding what goods to manufacture and how to make those goods, and they guide consumers in deciding what products to buy.

Demand is the relationship between the price of a good or service and the quantity of that good or service that consumers want to purchase. The law of demand states that more is demanded at lower prices than at higher prices. The demand schedule shows the quantity demanded at each price. The demand curve is a graph of the demand schedule.

Supply is the relationship between the price of a good or service and the quantity that firms will offer for sale. The supply schedule shows the quantity offered for sale at each price. The supply curve is a graph of the supply schedule. The law of supply states that more will be supplied as the price increases. The additional cost of producing one more unit of output is known as marginal cost.

When the quantity demanded exceeds the quantity supplied, there is excess demand. The result is an increase in price. If the quantity supplied exceeds the quantity demanded, there is excess supply. As a result, the price declines. The market is in equilibrium when the quantity demanded is equal to the quantity supplied. On a graph, equilibrium is where the supply and demand curves cross.

☆ LEARNING ACTIVITIES ☆

Building Your Vocabulary

On a separate piece of paper, write the numbers 1 through 10. Next to each number, write the term that correctly completes the sentence.

law of demand
excess supply
excess demand
equilibrium price
demand schedule
supply

1. A graph that shows the relationship between price and the quantity of a good that consumers want to buy is known as a _demand_ _curve_.

2. The _____ is found where the demand and supply curves cross.

3. A _____ is a table that shows the amount of a product demanded by consumers at different prices.

supply schedule
marginal cost
demand curve
law of supply

4. The _law of demand_ states that consumers will buy more of a good or service at lower prices and less at higher prices.

5. _Supply_ is the relationship between price and the quantity of a good that will be offered for sale.

6. The _law of supply_ states that firms will produce more of a good at higher prices than at lower prices.

7. The expense of producing an additional unit of output is called _marginal cost_.

8. If producers are offering more for sale at some price than consumers want to buy, _excess supply_ is said to exist.

9. If consumers want to buy more of a good than is offered for sale, this condition is called _excess demand_.

10. A _supply schedule_ is a table that shows how much of a product manufacturers will offer for sale at different prices.

Reviewing the Facts

1. If you have a job that pays you $5 an hour, what would be your opportunity cost, in hours of work, for a new ten-speed bicycle selling for $195?
2. Would you be more concerned about repairing a leaky faucet if your water company charges you for water use by the gallon or at a flat rate each month, regardless of the amount used?
3. How do prices send signals to producers and consumers? What do these signals guide?
4. What are three reasons for the law of demand?
5. What is the relationship between a demand curve and a demand schedule?
6. What is the law of supply, and why does this law hold?
7. If the equilibrium price of a product is $4 and the market price is $5, would there be excess supply or excess demand for this product?
8. If there is excess demand in a market, will the price rise or fall to eliminate that excess demand?

Expressing Your Opinion

1. Do you think the government should organize all the production and consumption decisions for our economy? Why or why not?
2. What signals are provided by the price tag of a $100,000 diamond bracelet? What do the signals tell you about the producers and consumers of such an item?
3. Think about the goods and services that you buy regularly. If the prices of all food items doubled while the prices of all other things were cut in half, how would your consumption habits change?

Would you be better or worse off?

4. If it were determined that a particular food product caused cancer, how would the demand for the product change? Do you think there should be governmental regulations prohibiting the sale of cancer-causing products? Why or why not?

5. If the equilibrium price of gasoline were $1.50 but a government rule required that gas be sold for no more than $1 a gallon, what problems could occur?

Developing Your Attitudes, Values, and Skills

1. Interview two or three local business people, such as the owner of a gas station or the manager of a fast-food chain. Ask them these questions: How do they decide what products to offer in their store? How do they set prices on their products? Do they compare their goods and prices with those of competitors? How do they decide to raise or lower prices? What factors are involved in deciding to put certain items on sale? What do they do with goods that they cannot sell? Do they ever have more demand for some items than they are able to supply? Compare your answers with those of your classmates.

2. Many companies now offer long-distance telephone service at different rates. Prices vary according to distance, time of day, length of the call, and so on. These factors can make it difficult for consumers to shop for long-distance telephone service. Suppose that you are shopping for long-distance phone service. Choose two long-distance telephone calls from your city to another American city. Make one a weekend call and one a weekday call. For example, you might choose a 15-minute call to San Francisco on Sunday afternoon and a half-hour call to Chicago on Wednesday morning. Call several long-distance telephone companies, and ask for their rates for your calls. How did the rates vary? Which service was the most expensive? The cheapest? Can the company with the highest rates tell you why its service is more expensive than its competitors? Are there monthly charges for service? Which company would you select? Why?

3. Ask a guest to speak to your class. Choose someone who has lived or traveled in a country in which the government makes most or all of the production and consumption decisions. How does the country compare with the United States in the availability and prices of consumer goods, such as automobiles, televisions, video-cassette recorders, microwave ovens, and computers? Does the country suffer from shortages of manufactured goods? How many hours does a person have to work to pay for a television, a suit of clothes, or a pair of shoes? How do these numbers compare with those in the United States? Can you find out who makes the economic decisions or how they are made? Are the country's consumers consulted? How are prices set? Are there any benefits to a government-controlled economy? What are they?

FOCUS YOUR READING

Which company used a waffle iron to design shoes?

On the average, what percentage of the selling price of a product goes to profit?

How many colors were available to the buyers of early Fords?

CHAPTER 5

PROFITS AND COMPETITION

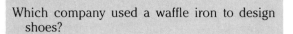

PREVIEW

In the early 1970s, companies started making hand-held calculators that would not only add, subtract, multiply, and divide, but also do other mathematical problems such as compute square roots and find logarithms. Unfortunately, the average student could not afford these products because they cost several hundred dollars each.

Today, many firms manufacture small calculators that can perform just about any mathematical operation. Prices have fallen so dramatically that a calculator costing $300 a few years ago now costs less than $30. A basic four-function calculator sells for less than $10.

What caused the prices of calculators to drop so much? The answer is competition between the firms that make these products. Each company wanted to increase its share of the calculator market. But to win sales from other firms, these businesses had to improve their product and reduce their prices. The heart of the free enterprise system is the competition between businesses as they seek to increase their profits.

In this chapter, you will learn about the role of profits and competition in a free enterprise system. When you have completed the reading materials and learning activities, you should be able to:

★ Describe what is meant by the profit motive.

★ Explain the important role that entrepreneurs play in the free enterprise system.

★ Discuss how profits provide signals in the free enterprise system.

★ Identify the most important uses of profits.

★ List four ways that businesses compete for customers.

★ Explain how society benefits from competition.

★ Describe the problems that occur when firms have market power.

PROFITS AS AN ECONOMIC INCENTIVE

Profits are the money left over after a business has paid all its expenses. Profits reward persons who have used their money to start or improve a business.

American consumers sometimes become upset because they believe that business profits are too great. Some businesses do earn large profits. However, many people overestimate the amount of profit earned by the average business. A recent survey asked people to estimate business profits after payment of taxes as a percentage of dollars received from sales. The average estimate was 32 percent.

The same group was then asked to indicate what they thought would be a reasonable profit as a percentage of sales. The average estimate was 26 percent; that is, 26 cents out of each sales dollar. Yet in recent years, the average profit as a percentage of sales for manufacturing industries has been less than 5 percent. That is, only 5 cents of every sales dollar represents profits received by business owners. Note that this is only one-fifth of what the survey group considered to be a reasonable profit.

The Entrepreneur

Business successes occur because someone sees a need and can meet that need. Sometimes a person can take a good idea and a little money and make millions of dollars. Some people who have done just that are discussed on page 80. People who are willing to take risks in order to earn profits are referred to as **entrepreneurs.**

In Chapter 2 you learned that human, natural, and capital resources are used to produce goods and services. When resources are put to use, they are called **factors of production.** To get goods and services, these factors must be used in the right way. For example, manufacturing a television requires more than just having the workers, parts, and machines available in the economic system. Someone with talent has to organize and direct the use of these factors of production. Organization and direction are the entrepreneur's contribution to society; profits are the reward for using this talent.

Not everyone is cut out to be an entrepreneur. Most people feel more comfortable with a job that provides a guaranteed salary. They know that they may never become wealthy, but they are also unlikely to go broke.

Entrepreneurs are different. They are not content with an average standard of living. Instead, most entrepreneurs are willing to risk their money and use their talents for a chance to become wealthy. Although entrepreneurs often are in charge of a company, they are different from managers. Usually a manager works for a salary. In contrast, the entrepreneur's payment comes from profits.

Entrepreneurs take risks in the hope of making large profits.

Berg & Associates/Photo by Michael Plack

Some Successful Entrepreneurs

Phil Knight

Twenty years ago, no serious distance runner would have considered using American-made running shoes. They were too heavy and clumsy. In the 1960s Phil Knight started Nike, Inc., to compete with foreign-made shoes. In 1975 his partner, Bill Bowerman, experimented with a piece of rubber in his wife's waffle iron. The waffle iron was ruined, but Nike's famous waffle sole was born. Today, Nike, Inc., sells over $600 million worth of shoes each year. World-class runners and weekend joggers alike use Nike shoes.

Chester Carlson and Joseph Wilson

In 1938 Chester Carlson, a law student, was frustrated by the problem of getting copies of documents and drawings. At that time about the only alternative was to take a photograph. Working on his own, he developed the basic ideas now used for photocopying. Carlson took his invention to more than 20 companies, but none were willing to risk the money necessary to develop the product. After six years of disappointment, he found a small firm that would take on the project. The Xerox Corporation, headed by Joseph Wilson, worked on photocopying machines for the next 14 years. It was not until 1960 that the first copier reached the market.

Today, photocopying has completely changed office practice. Carlson's invention is considered one of the most important of the twentieth century. Although Carlson had the original idea, Wilson's contribution was just as important. He organized the factors of production necessary to transform a good idea into a successful product. Both Carlson and Wilson became wealthy as a reward for their efforts.

Mary Kay Ash

For many years Mary Kay Ash sold products to people in their homes. As a salesperson, she gained valuable insights about what consumers desire and how to meet their needs. Desiring to test her skill as an entrepreneur, she took $5,000 from her savings and started a business that sold skin cream. Initially the firm had only nine employees and operated out of a small rented office.

Today, Mary Kay Cosmetics, Inc., is a giant business with sales of over $200 million each year. In addition to the skin cream, the firm sells products such as cosmetics, toiletries, and jewelry. More than 200,000 people work part- or full-time for her company.

The Profit Motive

When an entrepreneur launches a new business, the risks are often great; but if the business succeeds, so are the rewards. One common risk is that the new business will fail to earn a profit and will go out of business. If a business fails, the entrepreneur may have nothing to show for an investment of considerable effort and money. On the other hand, if the business is a success, the entrepreneur's reward will come in the form of high profits. Profits are the entrepreneur's prize for taking risks. People will not take the chance of losing everything unless there is also a possibility of becoming a big winner. The desire to earn profits is called the **profit motive.** It is the profit motive that makes the free enterprise system work.

Suppose there was no chance of earning huge profits when participating in a business venture. Without the possibility of profits as a reward, there would be far fewer entrepreneurs. What would the free enterprise system be like without these risk-takers? For one thing there would be much less change in the economic system.

Entrepreneurs play an important role in the development of new products. Home computers, copying machines, telephones, and electric lights were all introduced by entrepreneurs. Life would be much harder without these products.

In addition to developing new products, entrepreneurs play an important role in helping society use its factors of production efficiently. Remember, the amount of profits earned by the entrepreneur depends on how much is left after all the expenses of the business have been paid. One way for the entrepreneur to make more profits is to reduce expenses. By finding ways to cut the cost of producing products, entrepreneurs increase their rewards. Cost-cutting benefits society as well as the entrepreneur. If ways can be found to use scarce resources more efficiently in making a product, then the resources saved can be used to satisfy other human wants.

An example of how an entrepreneur can help society conserve resources is Henry Ford's assembly line for producing automobiles. In the early 1900s, Ford realized that he could build cars for less money than other firms if the vehicles were placed on a moving belt and moved from worker to worker. The assembly-line idea made the Ford Motor Company the most successful automobile manufacturer for many years. Henry Ford's reward was millions of dollars in profits. Society's reward was less expensive cars, which were produced with fewer scarce resources.

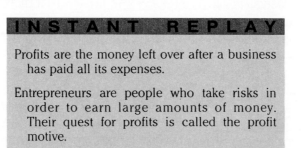

INSTANT REPLAY

Profits are the money left over after a business has paid all its expenses.

Entrepreneurs are people who take risks in order to earn large amounts of money. Their quest for profits is called the profit motive.

By organizing the factors of production, entrepreneurs produce goods and services more efficiently and create new products.

Henry Ford's invention of the assembly line still works today to conserve resources.

Courtesy United Technologies Corporation

Profits as Signals

In Chapter 4 you learned that in a market economy, prices act as signals to consumers. High prices discourage consumers from purchasing goods and services; low prices encourage them to buy more. Prices also provide signals to producers that help them decide what to make and how to allocate their factors of production.

Profits also serve as signals. Specifically, they guide entrepreneurs in deciding how and where to use their time, money, and effort. Suppose that you are an entrepreneur who has started a clothing store that is not making a profit. The reason seems to be that there are too many clothing stores in your community. Your lack of profit indicates that you are failing to obtain the rewards you expected for your risk-taking. This signals you to spend your time and dollars elsewhere.

You become aware that large amounts of profit are being earned by companies selling home computers. The above-average profits being earned by these companies attract your interest. Convinced that the clothing store will continue to be a losing proposition, you sell the business and use the money to start a computer business. If you can develop a product that consumers want and if you are a good manager, you may be able to share in the success of the industry.

In a free enterprise system, profits cause entrepreneurs to respond to the wishes of consumers. High profits signal that consumers desire the good or service provided by a business. They indicate that more of society's scarce resources should be used to produce that good or service. Entrepreneurs react to this signal by using their money and skills to increase the supply of the product.

The home computer industry is a good example of how profits can attract entrepreneurs. At first, only a few small firms were in the business. The success of these companies attracted other entrepreneurs, who started their own firms. Finally, large businesses such as IBM and Tandy Corporation entered the field. New companies will continue to enter the computer field as long as entrepreneurs believe that above-average profits can be earned in the industry.

However, losses or minimal profits may signal that consumers do not desire the product being provided by a business. They indicate that scarce resources could be better used in other ways. They tell entrepreneurs that their time and effort should be shifted to other goods and services.

CB radios are a good example. Having a Citizen's Band radio in a car was very popular a few years ago. Dozens of firms entered the field in the attempt to capture some of the profits. Unfortunately the fad faded quickly and most of these companies found themselves losing money. A lack of profits caused many firms to leave the field and concentrate on other products.

Truck drivers use CB radios, but for many consumers the product was a fad. Most companies producing CBs lost money.

Ford Truck Operations

In Chapter 2 you learned that resources are scarce. The signals provided by profits guide entrepreneurs in their use of these resources. Low profits cause resources to be shifted out of an industry. High profits cause more resources to be devoted to an industry. Thus, in a free enterprise system the scarce resources of a society are efficiently used.

research
new products
taxes
workers
new businesses
firm grow

INSTANT REPLAY

Profits act as signals in a free enterprise system. They help assure that scarce resources are efficiently used.

Entrepreneurs shift resources from uses where profits are low to uses where profits are higher.

Uses of Profits

Not all the profits earned by a business find their way into the entrepreneur's pocket. A large share of the profits is generally put back into the company, especially if it is a new business.

Remember that high rates of profit are a signal that society wants more of a company's goods or services. Some of the profits may be used to buy additional capital goods to produce more of the product. For example, Apple Computer, Inc., started production in a small garage. The company soon found that it could not fill the orders for its product in this small building. Therefore, some of the early profits were used to obtain more space and to purchase capital equipment that would allow the firm to produce more efficiently.

In some businesses, profits may be used for research to improve the company's product or to develop new ideas. Mary Kay Cosmetics employs people to develop new lipsticks and powders. Xerox spends millions of dollars to study ways of making faster and better copying machines. Nike is constantly trying to find new materials that will make its running shoes lighter and more durable.

Sometimes profits are used to buy other businesses. A large computer company might buy a smaller maker of computers that has just developed a promising new product. A chain of grocery stores might buy a trucking company to deliver merchandise to each store. A television station might buy a baseball team or vice versa. In each case, the buying firm sacrifices present profits in the hope of earning even more profits in the future.

Part of a company's profits are taken as taxes to pay for government activities such as road building and police protection. An example is the corporate income tax, which is based on the amount of profits earned by a firm. You will learn more about taxes in Chapter 12.

Some businesses donate profits to support charitable causes. A firm may give money to build a park in a local community or to buy equipment for a university. For example, the Hershey Chocolate Company has given millions of dollars to make Hershey, Pennsylvania, a more pleasant place to live.

Finally, profits can be used to aid the workers in a firm. Sometimes employees are allowed to share in the profits of a business. Apple Computer, Inc., boasts that dozens of its employees have become millionaires through sharing the firm's profits. Even if employees are not allowed to share profits directly, they still can benefit from high levels of profit. If the firm responds to the signal of high profits by expanding, more jobs will become available. As the firm grows, there will be more opportunities for advancement. Workers may also be able to share profits through wage increases and profit-sharing plans.

INSTANT REPLAY

Not all of a firm's profits are taken by the entrepreneur for personal use.

Profits may be used to (1) help the firm grow, (2) create new products and improve existing products, (3) acquire new businesses, (4) support government through taxes, (5) support charitable activities, and (6) benefit workers.

6) Expand
charity
benefit workers
support gov.
create new products
buy new business.

COMPETITION

How would you go about buying a new car? First, you must decide what make of car you want. Suppose a new Ford seems right for you and there are four Ford dealers nearby. From which dealer will you purchase your car? It is likely that you will do some price shopping before making your decision. You will haggle with each dealer to find out who will give you the best buy. The successful dealer will probably be the one who offers the lowest price.

Car dealers are aware that you are looking for the best deal. They know that they must beat the prices of the other dealers. Setting a high price is of no value to them if they do not sell any cars. As a result, they cut their prices to persuade you to buy their car. If they fail to get your business, they are signaled that their prices are too high. Thus, the next customer who comes into their showroom may be offered a slightly lower price.

Car dealers compete in product markets to sell cars. **Competition** in product markets refers to the attempts by businesses to attract customers. Consumer dollars available for buying cars are scarce. Sellers are in a contest to see who can win the largest share of these dollars.

In this market, consumers are free to use their dollars wherever they can get the best deal. They can choose to either buy or not buy from a particular business. On the other side of the market, sellers are free to use any legal means to persuade the consumer to buy from them. As long as they do not lie, steal, or use force, they have the legal right to compete aggressively for sales.

Because consumer dollars are scarce, not every business will end up a winner all the time. However, companies that win often are signaled by profits that they should remain in the market, while firms that do not win very often are signaled to use their resources in another part of the economic system. Thus, by directing factors of production to the best uses, competition assists the efficient allocation of society's scarce resources.

Methods of Competing

In a football game the objective is to score more points than the other team. There are several ways that points can be scored. The kicker can boot a field goal. The quarterback can toss a long bomb for a touchdown. The star running back can break loose for an 80-yard scoring run. A defensive back can return a pass interception for a touchdown.

In the contest between businesses, the objective is to earn profits. As with football, there are a number of ways that firms can compete in the quest for profits. Some of the most important forms of competition are discussed here.

Price Competition. A company can compete by cutting its prices below those of competitors. Look in your local newspaper. You will see supermarket advertisements for a "great buy" on chicken thighs, bread, TV dinners, or soft drinks. A trip downtown or to a shopping center will reveal discount stores claiming the "lowest prices ever" on cameras, camping gear, and gardening tools. Almost daily the mail brings news of specials on books, magazines, and other reading matter.

Cutting prices is a common way that sellers compete for consumer dollars.

Lenore Weber/Taurus Photos Inc.

Cutting prices involves a trade-off. Lower prices are likely to increase sales. But lower prices also reduce the profit that the firm makes on each sale. The manager of each competing firm must decide what price will result in the greatest total profit for the company. Competition usually drives prices down until managers believe that it is better to lose some sales than to reduce prices further.

Advertising Competition. Advertising is an important way that firms compete. Almost every large firm budgets a significant sum of money for advertising. For instance, the Procter and Gamble Company spends nearly $2 billion each year to tell consumers about its soap, toothpaste, and other household products.

Companies advertise for two reasons. The first is to convince consumers that they should buy more of the industry's product. For example, advertisements paid for by members of the dairy industry try to increase the demand for milk by promoting its virtues. Prune growers and beef ranchers have a similar objective in spending dollars to advertise their products.

The second reason for advertising is to take sales away from competitors. The Coca-Cola Company takes the approach that only a Coke® will satisfy your taste. At the same time, Pepsico, Inc., advertises that people prefer the taste of Pepsi®. Airline commercials compare service and comfort, such as legroom. Automobile advertisements compare cars for the smoothest ride and the best gas mileage.

Quality Competition. Some businesses compete by trying to offer a product that is superior to that of their competitors. Fine restaurants fit into this category. If you go to one of these restaurants, you know that the bill is likely to be high, but you also know that the food should be good. It may be worth an extra $5 for a steak if you can be sure that it will be tender and cooked just the right amount. A pleasant atmosphere and a good location may also draw you to the nicer restaurant.

Quality competition is important in many industries. Cars such as those made by Mercedes-Benz have a reputation for fine workmanship and long life and therefore can be sold at a higher price. Makers of fine watches can survive in the marketplace even though their products may have prices that are ten times higher than those of some other brands. A particularly good movie will draw a full house even though ticket prices are higher than at those theaters where less popular movies are being shown.

Variety Competition. Henry Ford was the leading producer of automobiles during the 1920s. In those years, he told consumers that they could have a Ford in any color they wanted—as long as they wanted black! Although Fords could be purchased for a low price, there was no variety. The buyer was stuck with the one basic model that the company produced. Indeed, one of the reasons that the price was so low was that only one kind of car was produced. There was no need to train workers to do many different jobs. Machines could be designed for very specific purposes. Large quantities of paint and other materials could be purchased at discount prices. All of the firm's resources were geared to the production of the basic Ford automobile.

Although the early Fords were unusually good cars, not everyone's favorite color was black. Some consumers were willing to pay a higher price for a car that was more to their liking. As a result, other manufacturers were able to capture a share of the market by offering consumers a choice. Their cars were not necessarily better or cheaper than Ford's, but they were different.

Companies can often compete successfully in a market by offering consumers a wide range of choice. A clothing store may be successful because it stocks clothing not sold by other stores in the community. For example, some clothing stores specialize in fitting tall, short, or heavy people. Some stores offer the latest fashions for teenagers. Others feature comfortable clothes for pregnant women. Such stores may offer no advantage in price or quality and may not spend much on advertising. Still, they can survive in the marketplace because they increase the variety of goods and services available. Their success is based on their ability to meet the special wants of some consumers.

Benefits of Competition

Consumers are the winners in the game of competition. The consumer is free to buy a good or service from the seller who offers the best deal. Thus, businesses must try to meet the needs and wants of consumers. Similarly, if the wants and needs of consumers change, competition forces businesses to respond to these changes.

Each form of competition benefits consumers in a different way. Price competition between sellers results in lower prices as businesses struggle to win customers. Advertising competition, although sometimes confusing, gives consumers information about products and prices. Quality competition encourages firms to improve their products. Companies that offer goods or services of poor quality will be forced out of business unless they make improvements. Variety competition gives the consumer a much wider range of choice. Because people have different wants and needs, it is impossible to satisfy everyone with a single product. Competition causes companies to seek out and meet the wants

One of the benefits of competition is that it gives consumers a wide range of choices.

of small groups of consumers. These groups are better off than if they were forced to select from a narrow range of products.

Competition is important for society because it causes scarce resources to be used efficiently. Businesses that use factors of production wastefully will have higher costs than their more efficient competitors. Unless they become more efficient, they will fail because they are unable to match the prices of other firms. Furthermore, companies offering products that are not acceptable to consumers will also be forced out of business. The factors of production used by these firms are then available to produce other products that are valued more highly in the marketplace.

INSTANT REPLAY

Firms compete to attract customers in product markets.

Methods of competing include cutting prices, advertising, improving quality, and offering a greater variety of goods and services.

Competition results in lower prices, more information, higher quality, and greater variety for consumers. It also assists in efficiently allocating society's scarce resources.

MARKET POWER IN A FREE ENTERPRISE SYSTEM

If consumers can take their business somewhere else, firms are forced to compete for sales. However, a company may be the only seller of a good or service, or there may be only a few other sellers. If so, there is little pressure to compete. Businesses that have only a limited need to compete are said to have **market power.**

For example, suppose you decide to build a new house. If there is only one cement company within a hundred miles of where you live, that company has market power. The cost of hauling cement makes it unlikely that you will select a distant cement supplier. The importance of cement in home construction also makes it unlikely that you can find another material. Thus, the local company has power over the market for cement. It does not have to cut prices, advertise, worry about quality, or offer a variety of cement types. Because buyers of cement have no real alternative, the company does not have to compete for business.

Causes of Market Power

Why do some firms face intense competition in selling their product, while others have little need to compete? There are a number of reasons that some firms gain market power.

Superior Management Skill. Not all businesses are equally efficient. Some have the advantage of superior managers, who use their skills to enhance their companies in many ways. Under the leadership of a superior manager, a company may produce better products or devise more effective advertising campaigns. The manager may make the company more efficient than other companies, so that it can produce and sell goods at lower prices than those charged by its competitors. The manager may also decide to abandon the manufacture of low-profit products and to concentrate the company's resources on high-profit items. As a result of this leadership, the superior manager's company will do well while competing companies will earn lower profits or be forced out of business.

Control over Resources. Some products require special resources for their manufacture. A good example is aluminum. One of the basic ingredients in aluminum is bauxite. Bauxite is mined from the earth and is found in only a few locations. Until World War II, the Alcoa company owned all the bauxite mines in the United States. As a result, Alcoa was the only seller of aluminum. Alcoa's total control of this market was finally ended by the federal government because of the urgent need for aluminum during the war.

Sometimes a firm's location determines market power. A fast-food restaurant located next to a high school may have an advantage because students find it easy to go there for lunch, while a similar fast-food restaurant located four blocks away might do much less business because its location is not so good.

Economies of Scale. Some products can be produced more efficiently by large firms. This advantage of a large-scale business is known as **economies of scale.** A local garage, for example, could never make automobiles as cheaply as General Motors or Toyota can. When thousands of cars are produced each day, it is possible to use capital equipment that small car-makers could not afford. These machines make it possible to produce large numbers of items more cheaply than if only a few were made. By reducing the cost of production, economies of scale allow large firms to sell their products at a lower price than small companies. As the small firms are forced from the market, the large firms gain market power.

Advertising. A company can develop market power by advertising. If consumers can be convinced that a firm's product is superior to that of other companies, then that firm will have market power. You have already learned that advertising is a form of competition. Yet, when a firm is successful in advertising its product, then it reduces the need to compete in other ways, such as lowering prices.

Government Assistance. Often, help from the government enables a company to obtain market power. Electric companies illustrate this idea. How many different electric companies sell power in your community? In all but a few cities, there is only one supplier of electricity. One reason is that there are economies of scale in selling electricity.

Perhaps more important is the fact that only one company has been given a franchise to sell electricity. A **franchise** is the legal right to sell a good or service in a specific area. The market power of the electric company results from the government franchise that protects it from competition. Natural gas and cable television companies are other businesses that are sometimes granted freedom from competition.

Problems Created by Market Power

Competition works to the benefit of consumers. Market power, on the other hand, usually does not benefit consumers. When companies have less need to compete for sales, they also have less reason to respond to the wants and needs of consumers.

Competition keeps prices down. But when a company has market power, it is under less pressure to keep prices low. Next time you go to a movie, compare the price of drinks inside the theater with those at a nearby fast-food restaurant or some other eating place. Once you are inside the building, the manager of the theater has market power. You are no longer able to go somewhere else to buy a drink. Many theaters also prohibit bringing drinks into the building. Because they are the only sellers, they are likely to charge more for a soft drink than other places where sellers face competition.

Competition forces companies to improve the quality of their products. In contrast, a business with market power may worry less about quality. Because the consumer's ability to buy elsewhere is limited, complaints may be ignored. If there is only one television repair shop in town, the owner of a broken television is forced to use that service. The quality of repairs may be poor, but the lack of choice creates

Turn to 12

market power. However, if a new shop opens, then the older repair center will have to improve or lose business.

Competition results in the offering of a large variety of goods and services to consumers. Companies with market power may provide only a narrow range of products. It was competition that finally forced Henry Ford to start offering different models and colors of automobiles. It was competition that caused telephone manufacturers to offer answering machines and cordless telephones.

The basic problem with market power is that it can cause inefficient use of scarce resources. A firm faced with competition must use factors of production efficiently or go out of business. But the firm with market power may be able to survive even though it is relatively inefficient. Competition directs resources to uses that can best satisfy consumer wants and needs. In contrast, the firm with market power may be much less responsive to such needs and wants.

Monopoly and Oligopoly

When there is only one company that supplies a good or service, that firm is called a **monopoly.** The term comes from the Greek language and means "single seller." Monopolists have a great deal of market power. As the only seller, the monopolist does not have to worry about competitors. The firm can set its price at the level that provides the maximum profit. Consumers must either pay the price set by the monopolist or go without the good or service.

For a firm to be a monopoly, two conditions must be met. First, it must be the only convenient seller of a good or service. The cement company mentioned earlier was a monopoly because, although there were other cement companies, they were so far away that they could not effectively compete.

The second condition is that there be no good substitutes for the product sold by the monopoly. If the house in the example could be built using stone or steel, then the local cement company would not be totally free from competition. If the company's price of cement was too high, builders could use the other materials to build the house. Hence, the availability of these substitutes would limit the market power of the cement company.

In some markets there are only a few sellers. A market with few important sellers is called an **oligopoly.** Oligopolies are much more common in the United States than are monopolies. Many important products in the United States are produced in markets with a small number of sellers. The automobile industry is an oligopoly. About 98

Local telephone companies are monopolies.

Reproduced with permission of AT&T Co.

percent of all the cars sold in the United States are made by eight firms—General Motors, Chrysler, Ford, American Motors, Toyota, Volkswagen, Nissan, and Honda. Copper mining and the manufacture of rubber are also oligopolies. In each case, over 80 percent of all sales are made by the eight largest firms.

Firms in an oligopoly must compete with one another. However, they often develop their own style of competition. Sometimes they avoid competing on price but spend large sums on advertising. On other occasions they may avoid any form of active competition by agreeing on prices and other matters. When oligopolists stop competing, consumers are the losers. Chapter 10 discusses efforts by government to increase competition between the firms in an oligopoly.

INSTANT REPLAY

Businesses that have little competition are said to have market power.

A business may have market power because of superior skills of its management, control over important resources, economies of scale, advertising, or assistance received from government.

Firms with market power may charge higher prices, be less concerned with the quality of their products, and offer less variety than firms that are forced to compete. Market power may also result in a less efficient allocation of scarce resources.

A single seller of a good or service is called a monopoly. An industry with only a few sellers is referred to as an oligopoly.

S U M M A R Y

Profits are the dollars left over after a company has paid all of its expenses. Entrepreneurs are persons willing to take risks in order to earn profits. This desire to earn profits is called the profit motive. Entrepreneurs perform the important function of organizing the factors of production in the economic system. They take the lead in developing new products. Their search for profits also helps society to use scarce factors of production efficiently. High profits signal entrepreneurs that more resources should be used in a particular industry. Losses or low profits indicate that society would be better off if fewer resources were devoted to a particular activity.

The profits earned by business are not all used by the entrepreneur. Profits are also used to help the firm grow, to pay for research on new or better products, to purchase other businesses, to pay taxes, to support charitable activities, and to benefit workers.

Competition involves efforts by businesses to win consumer dollars. Competition may include cutting prices, advertising, offering better quality products or improved service, and providing consumers with a variety of choices. Competition benefits society because scarce factors of production are used more efficiently.

When companies are partly freed from the need to compete, they are said to have market power. Market power occurs because some businesses have superior managers or they control scarce resources. Economies of scale, advertising, and help from the government can also lead to market power. Higher prices, lower quality, less consumer choice, and inefficient use of resources usually result from market power.

A single seller of a good or service is called a monopoly. An industry with only a few important sellers is referred to as an oligopoly. Firms in an oligopoly often try to avoid competing with one another.

☆ LEARNING ACTIVITIES ☆

Building Your Vocabulary

On a separate piece of paper, write the numbers 1 through 10. Next to each number, write the term that correctly completes the sentence.

profit
entrepreneurs
factors of production
profit motive
competition
market power
economies of scale
franchise
monopoly
oligopoly

1. The risk-takers in an economic system are called _entrepreneurs_.

2. An industry with only a few major sellers is an _oligopoly_

3. The money left over after a company has paid its expenses is _profit_.

4. When businesses try to attract buyers to their products, this is called _competition_

5. The desire to earn profits is the _profit motive_.

6. A company's employees, buildings, equipment, and resources are its _factors of production_.

7. When products are produced more efficiently by large firms, this is due to _economies of scale_

8. Businesses that have little need to compete are said to have _market power_

9. A _franchise_ is the legal right to provide a good or service in a specific area.

10. When only one company provides a good or service, it is said to be a _monopoly_

Reviewing the Facts

1. How do entrepreneurs contribute to the efficient use of scarce resources?
2. How do profits act as signals to entrepreneurs?
3. What are five uses for profits?
4. How can advertising be used as a substitute for price competition?
5. Why does competition between firms

usually result in a greater variety of goods and services for consumers?

6. How can a franchise give a company market power?

7. Why do economies of scale provide an advantage for large firms?

8. What are the two conditions for being a monopoly?

Expressing Your Opinion

1. Should the government limit the amount of profits that can be earned by a business? Why or why not?
2. How would the amount of risk involved in a business be related to the amount of profit required by entrepreneurs? Explain.
3. Is advertising really helpful to the consumer? Do you know more about products after seeing commercials or reading advertisements about them?
4. Aside from the possibility of becoming rich, are there any other reasons that people would want to be entrepreneurs?
5. Would society be better off if large automobile or oil companies were divided into many smaller firms? Why or why not?

Developing Your Attitudes, Values, and Skills

1. Research a large corporation such as IBM, Federal Express, Ford Motor Co., Apple Computers, Inc., General Motors, or AT&T, and try to answer the following questions: How did the company get started? Who were the entrepreneurs who started it, and what risks did they take in going into business? How does the company compete with other businesses? Does it have market power? How did it gain market power? Is it a monopoly or a member of an oligopoly? What have the company's profits been for each of the last ten years, and what percentage of the selling price of its products goes to profits? (You may find books about some corporations, such as the Ford Motor Co. and AT&T, and you should be able to find magazine articles about other corporations in periodicals such as *Business Week, Forbes,* and *Fortune.* You can locate these articles by using the Periodicals Guide in your school or public library.)

2. Get permission to conduct a survey in another class to determine whether people tend to overestimate or underestimate a company's profits. Find a business magazine article about a corporation that reports its annual sales and profits (sometimes referred to as net income), and calculate what percentage of the company's sales go to profits. (*Fortune* magazine prints a list of annual sales and net income of major corporations each spring.) Ask 10 people to estimate the company's percentage of profit. How many of the 10 guessed too high, and how many guessed too low? How do your results compare with those of your classmates?

3. At a department store, an appliance store, or an electronics store, examine a group of similar items such as cameras, tape recorders, televisions, or computers. Analyze how the manufacturers

compete with one another. Are they competing on the basis of price, advertising, quality, or variety? Are they using a combination of techniques? If you were going to buy an item, which brand would you buy? Did you choose the cheapest product? If not, what factors persuaded you to choose a more expensive one? If other classmates analyzed the same group of products, what brands would they have bought? Did their choices agree with yours? How did they arrive at their selections?

FOCUS YOUR READING

Why is it important for an economic system to produce more goods and services each year?

What steps can be taken to reduce the number of people who do not have jobs?

How can some people benefit from inflation?

CHAPTER 6

ECONOMIC GROWTH, UNEMPLOYMENT, BUSINESS CYCLES, AND INFLATION

P R E V I E W

An important part of life is measuring performance. In a recent basketball game, Debbie O'Brien of Central High School scored 29 points, pulled down 12 rebounds, and had 6 assists. Later that evening, Pat Schwartz, a member of the gymnastics team, scored a 9.7 on the balance beam and a 9.1 on her floor exercise. By any standard, these were outstanding performances.

Measuring the performance of the economic system is also important. Three measures of economic performance are:

1. The growth in the amount of goods and services produced each year

2. The number of workers who are unable to find a job

3. The rate of inflation

Generally, if the production of goods and services increases, people will be able to consume more, and additional jobs will be created. If such growth does not occur, many people may be unable to find employment. Most economic systems are able to achieve increased production, although the gains are not always steady. A more typical pattern is a period of growth followed by a shorter period of decline in production.

Stable prices are also an important economic goal. When prices increase, problems may occur. For example, in 1922 the prices of goods and services in Germany increased at a monthly rate of 322 percent. The average price of a good or service was increasing more than four times each month. At that rate, an ice cream sundae costing $1.50 today would sell for $475 in just four months! In 1946 prices increased in Hungary even more rapidly. For almost a year, prices rose at a monthly rate of 19,800 percent. At that rate, the $1.50 sundae would cost $297 one month later, $58,806 two months later, and almost $12 million at the end of three months. Although these figures may not seem possible, prices actually did increase that fast in Germany and Hungary during those times.

In this chapter you will learn about the performance of the free enterprise system in terms of producing goods and services, providing jobs, and maintaining stable prices. When you have completed the reading material and the learning activities, you should be able to:

★ Explain what is meant by gross national product.

★ Describe how economic growth occurs and why it is important.

★ Explain what is meant by the unemployment rate and why it is an important measure of economic performance.

★ Describe the business cycle.

★ Explain what inflation means.

★ Describe the two main causes of inflation.

★ Identify some positive and negative effects of inflation.

ECONOMIC GROWTH

One measure of how an economy is performing is gross national product (GNP). **GNP** is the value of all *final* goods and services produced in the economy in a calendar year. The word *final* is important because certain goods and services have to be excluded or they would be counted twice. For example, steel and rubber are materials that go

Only final goods and services are counted in the GNP.

into the production of automobiles. Assume there is $1,000 of steel and $100 of rubber in a $12,000 car. If you add the value of the steel and rubber ($1,100) to GNP, as well as the value of the car ($12,000), the steel and rubber would be counted twice. Those materials have already been included in the value ($12,000) of the car. Goods that are used to produce other goods are called **intermediate goods** and are excluded when computing GNP.

One important goal of virtually all economic systems is to promote a steady, moderate rate of economic growth, as measured by increases in GNP. Some countries experience more rapid rates of economic growth than others. For example, during the 1980s, GNP increased at a rate of about 2 percent per year in the United States compared with a rate of about 4 percent per year in Japan. Growth that occurs too rapidly or too slowly can lead to periods of inflation and unemployment. A steady, moderate rate of growth results in a stable and prosperous economic system.

The Importance of Economic Growth

Why is economic growth such an important goal? Why do most countries strive for increases in GNP? There are several reasons. The population in most countries of the world is increasing. Thus, each year more people are looking for jobs. A growing economy creates additional jobs each year. When demand increases, firms need more labor to produce additional output. Therefore, an expanding GNP results in the hiring of more people. Without growth, the number of jobs does not increase. The result may be an increase in the number of unemployed people.

You have learned that all people have wants and needs. Those living in very poor countries have difficulty meeting the basic needs of food, clothing, and housing. Economic growth will allow these people to meet their basic needs and to have something left over to spend on goods and services that meet some of their wants.

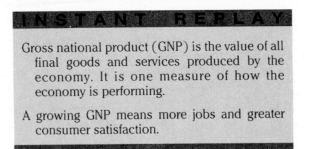

INSTANT REPLAY

Gross national product (GNP) is the value of all final goods and services produced by the economy. It is one measure of how the economy is performing.

A growing GNP means more jobs and greater consumer satisfaction.

Achieving Economic Growth

Increased GNP is achieved in the following ways:

★ Increasing productivity

★ Improving resource allocation

★ Increasing labor, capital resources, or both

Increasing Productivity. Improvements in the quality of capital equipment, worker training, and management techniques can result in more output from the same amounts of capital and labor. This increase in goods and services from the same amounts of capital and labor is called **productivity increase.**

An example will help to explain this concept. Suppose that a pencil factory has 1,000 employees and 500 machines. Every year the manager conducts training programs that improve the productivity of the workers so that they can do their jobs faster and with fewer mistakes. As a result, output from this factory increases each year. Productivity is measured in terms of the number of pencils produced per worker. As shown in Table 6-1, the number of pencils produced per worker has increased 10 percent each year. In other words, productivity has increased 10 percent per year.

TABLE 6-1

| | | | PRODUCTIVITY INCREASE | |
Year	Number of Workers	Pencils Produced (millions)	Pencils Produced per Worker (millions)
1983	1000	1,000	1.00
1984	1000	1,100	1.10
1985	1000	1,210	1.21
1986	1000	1,321	1.32
1987	1000	1,453	1.45

United States agriculture offers another excellent example of productivity increase. American farmers are the most productive in the world. In 1950 the average farmer in the United States produced enough food for about 16 people. By 1986 the average United States farmer was producing enough food to feed more than 70 people. In contrast, the average Russian farmer feeds only about 7 people.

Improving Resource Allocation. A second way to achieve economic growth is through better resource allocation. Sometimes resources are not put to their best use. For example, to employ a skilled brain surgeon as a worker in the pencil factory would be a poor allocation of resources. If the factory sells pencils for 2 cents each, the value of each worker's output in 1987 would be $29,000; that is, 2 cents multiplied by the 1.45 million pencils that the worker helps to produce. As a brain surgeon, this person might perform 200 operations per year, each valued at $1,000 for a total of $200,000. Shifting this person from the pencil factory to the operating room would result in a GNP increase of $171,000. That is, pencil output would decrease by $29,000, but medical output would increase by $200,000.

There are always many people who are changing jobs. Usually they are moving to a better job—one that pays more and perhaps offers more interesting and challenging work. Capital resources also move from one industry to another. Suppose a building once used for a small grocery store was converted into a video game arcade because a nearby modern supermarket had taken much of the business away from the small corner grocery store. Converting that grocery store building into a video game arcade should increase gross national product.

Increasing Labor and Capital Resources. Labor and capital are brought together to produce goods and services. For example, the pencil factory uses workers and machinery to produce pencils. It can increase the production of pencils by adding more workers and machinery. The same is true for the economy. An important source of economic growth is an increase in the number of workers and the amount of capital they have to work with.

The capital resources of an economy increase when people shift part of the GNP from consumer goods to capital goods. To do this, they must hold back part of their income from consumption. This part of income becomes **savings.** If everyone spent all of their income on consumer goods and services, there would be nothing left for spending on machinery, trucks, and other capital goods. Dollars used to purchase capital goods are referred to as an **investment.** Savings make money available for investment.

People in the United States typically save about 6 to 8 percent of their income. Most of this money is available for investment in capital goods. In some other countries, a much higher percentage of income is saved. For example, about 15 percent of income is saved in Japan. This high saving rate has resulted in more capital goods being available and has allowed Japan to achieve a higher rate of economic growth than the

Savings and investments are important sources of economic growth.

United States. Over the past 20 years, the rate of GNP growth in Japan has been more than twice that of the United States.

Production of goods and services also increases if the amount of labor is increased. The number of people available for work increases when population grows or when a larger proportion of a given population decide they want to work. Of course, merely having people available for work is not enough. If people are to produce goods and services, there must be jobs available for them. And people must be trained for the jobs that are available.

INSTANT REPLAY

Economic growth is achieved by increasing productivity, improving resource allocation, or increasing labor and capital.

An increase in productivity can be achieved by improvement in the quality of worker training and equipment or by better management of resources.

Capital resources are increased when people hold back part of their income in the form of savings and invest their savings in capital goods.

UNEMPLOYMENT

Having a job is an important part of life for most people. In high school you may hold a part-time job to provide money for consumption or to save for college. As an adult, you will use the income from your job to provide food, clothing, and shelter for yourself and your family. Your income will also go toward purchasing consumer goods that will make your life more comfortable and enjoyable. In addition, as you spend the income from your job, you help provide employment to workers who are needed to produce the goods you purchase. Of course, not everyone wants or needs a job, but two-thirds of all Americans over 16 years old are either employed or seeking a job. These 120 million workers form the nation's **labor force.**

The Bureau of Labor Statistics is part of the United States Department of Labor. One task of this agency is to measure the labor force and the number of unemployed people each month. To be included in the labor force, a person must be at least 16 years old, available for full-time work, and either employed or actively seeking employment. Those members of the labor force who do not have a job are considered **unemployed.**

Some people want to have a job but have given up looking for one. These people are called **discouraged workers** and are not counted as part of the labor force or as being unemployed because they do not meet the criteria outlined above. If they were included, the unemployment rate would be even higher than that reported.

Measuring Unemployment

You probably have heard about the unemployment rate on television or have read about it in a newspaper. The **unemployment rate** is the percentage of the labor force that does not have a job. This rate is computed in the following way:

$$\left(\begin{array}{c} \text{Number of} \\ \text{Unemployed} \end{array} \div \begin{array}{c} \text{Number in} \\ \text{Labor Force} \end{array} \right) \times 100 = \begin{array}{c} \text{Unemployment} \\ \text{Rate.} \end{array}$$

For example, suppose the labor force was 120 million and there were 7 million unemployed. The unemployment rate would then be

$$(7 \text{ million} \div 120 \text{ million}) \times 100 = 5.8\%.$$

This figure would mean that almost 6 out of every 100 members of the labor force do not have a job.

It would be impossible to reach every person to compute the unemployment rate. In practice, the Bureau of Labor Statistics surveys about 50,000 people each month. Those surveyed are selected from all races, occupations, and regions of the United States. If 6 percent of the people surveyed are classified as unemployed, then it is assumed that the unemployment rate for the entire labor force also is about 6 percent.

Table 6-2 shows the unemployment rates for selected years from 1960 through 1986. Clearly, the economy has performed better in some years than in others. For example, in 1970 the unemployment rate was 4.9 percent. In 1982 the unemployment rate was almost 10 percent, or twice the 1970 level. By 1986 the unemployment rate had declined to 7.2 percent.

TABLE 6-2

UNEMPLOYMENT RATES: SELECTED YEARS (1960–1986)			
Year	Total	Married Household Heads	Teenagers (16-19 years)
1960	5.6%	3.1%	14.7%
1970	4.9	2.6	15.3
1980	7.1	4.2	17.7
1982	9.8	7.1	28.7
1983	9.6	5.6	21.1
1986	7.2	4.2	15.7

Source: U.S. Department of Labor, Bureau of Labor Statistics, *Employment and Earnings* (Washington: U.S. Government Printing Office).

Table 6-2 also shows the unemployment rate for married adults and for young people 16 through 19 years of age. Notice that the unemployment rate for teenagers is consistently higher than that for adults. In 1986 about 16 out of every 100 teenagers who wanted a job were unable to find one.

Why do young people have more difficulty than adults in finding employment? There are two reasons. First, some teenagers have not completed high school and lack important work skills. If they dropped out of high school, employers may think they have poor work habits. Their writing and speaking skills may also be poor. Second, teenagers have the least work experience. They may be the last to be hired during a period of economic growth and the first to be laid off when a business reduces the number of employees to cut expenses.

The group of unemployed people is constantly changing. As some lose their jobs and join the pool of unemployed, others find jobs. There are an unfortunate few who may be without jobs for many months or years, but this is not typical. The average period of unemployment is about five weeks when the economy is performing well.

Types of Unemployment

The economy is said to be at **full employment** when the unemployment rate is about 5 percent. Why not define full employment as zero percent unemployment? The reason is that at any one time there are always people who have left one job and are waiting a few weeks for a new job to begin. Unemployment that results when workers change jobs is called **frictional unemployment.** About 5 percent of the labor force fits into this category. Thus, a 5 percent unemployment rate generally is considered to be full employment.

frictional - workers change jobs

There are three other types of unemployment. **Cyclical unemployment** happens when there is too little demand for goods and services in the economy. As a result, there is a low demand for labor. When the free enterprise system does not produce enough jobs to keep all the labor force employed, more people are unemployed than when the economy is strong. With **structural unemployment,** there are many job openings and many people seeking employment. However, the skills of the job seekers do not match the requirements of the jobs. Some unemployment is **seasonal.** Jobs that offer employment for only part of the year often cause seasonal unemployment. For example, ski instructors may work every day in the winter and early spring and then not work at all during the summer months. The reverse is true for lifeguards.

Cyclical - little demand for goods /services

structural - skills of workers don't match job they're seeking

Seasonal - different seasons affect

Solving the Unemployment Problem

A number of things can be done to reduce the unemployment rate. Clearly, one strategy is job retraining. Unskilled workers and those with skills that are no longer in demand can be retrained for vacant jobs. Government and private businesses offer numerous training programs. Another strategy is to provide better information about job openings and people available for work. Again, private and governmental employment agencies provide services of this type. These organizations maintain files of job applicants and lists of employment opportunities.

Seasonal workers are employed at jobs like this only a few months of the year.

Berg & Associates/Photo by Kirk Schlea

The task of these agencies is to match qualified applicants with the appropriate job openings.

Probably the single most important condition for full employment is a strong economy where gross national product is growing steadily. Steady growth in GNP not only provides employment for current members of the labor force but also generates new jobs for people entering the labor force as they finish school, technical training, or military service. In Chapter 16 you will learn more about employment opportunities and earning a living.

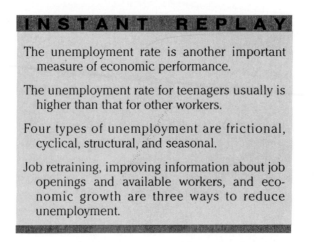

INSTANT REPLAY

The unemployment rate is another important measure of economic performance.

The unemployment rate for teenagers usually is higher than that for other workers.

Four types of unemployment are frictional, cyclical, structural, and seasonal.

Job retraining, improving information about job openings and available workers, and economic growth are three ways to reduce unemployment.

BUSINESS CYCLES

Ideally, economic systems should grow at a smooth, even pace, but in reality, they progress in erratic waves of ups and downs. Each alternating wave of growth and decline in GNP is called a **business cycle.** When an economic system is in the growth part of the cycle, it is said to be in a period of **expansion;** when it is in the downward part of the cycle, it is in **recession.**

Figure 6-1 depicts a business cycle graphically. When an economic system is in the expansion phase, GNP, income, and the number of available jobs increase while the unemployment rate decreases. When the expansion phase ends, the economy is at its **peak** and the recession phase begins. Then GNP, income, and the number of available jobs all decrease while unemployment rises. When the recession ends, the economy is at a **trough** and expansion begins again.

FIGURE 6-1
The business cycle is characterized by alternating periods of expansion and recession.

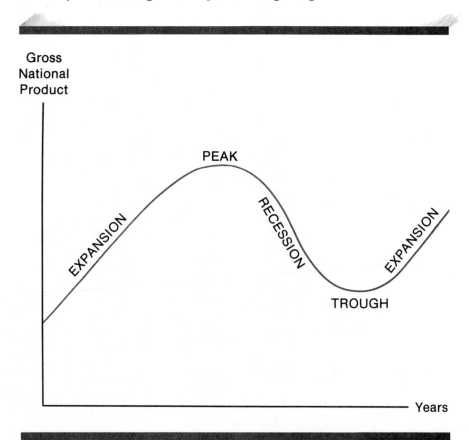

No two business cycles are the same, but in the U.S. economy the average period of expansion has been about four years and the average period of recession has been one year. Because expansions are longer than recessions, GNP in the United States has generally been increasing. You can understand this increase better if you think of our economy as a flight of stairs. If you climbed the staircase two steps at a time but fell back one step each time, you would still eventually make it to the top. In the same way, the nation's economy has grown despite periods of recession.

A period when real GNP is falling rapidly and the number of people without jobs is very high is called a **depression.** The United States and many other countries experienced a major depression that began in 1929. GNP declined for four years, and then the expansion phase was very slow to begin. For more than ten years, the unemployment rate was very high. It was a period of severe hardship for many people who lost their homes, farms, and businesses. This period is usually referred to as the Great Depression, or simply the Depression.

The Great Depression was a period of enormous hardship caused by high unemployment and a falling GNP.

The Bettmann Archive Inc.

I N S T A N T   R E P L A Y

The business cycle is characterized by alternating periods of expansion and recession.

A recession that is long and unusually severe is referred to as a depression.

INFLATION AND DEFLATION

Have you ever purchased something for $10 only to discover later that the price of this product had increased to $12? This change in price may or may not have been the result of inflation. **Inflation** is defined as an increase in the overall price of a market basket of goods and services. A **market basket** is a set of goods and services that a typical family purchases. When economists compare the costs of the same items at some time in the past, they can see whether the prices have increased, decreased, or stayed the same over time. An increase in the price of one item does not constitute inflation; it is only when the prices of many goods and services increase that inflation occurs.

Inflation is measured by means of a price index developed by the United States government. Actually, the government has several price indexes. Of these, the **consumer price index (CPI)** is the most important. This index measures the change in the overall cost of a market basket purchased by the average family.

The period of the 1970s was one of rapid inflation in the United States. On the average, the consumer price index increased at a rate of 8 percent per year. At that rate, a typical product that sold for $10 in 1970 would have cost $10.80 in 1971, and $11.70 in 1972. By 1980, the price of this product would have increased to $21.60. That is, the price would have more than doubled in ten years. Of course, this increase is just the average. The price of some products increased at a faster rate, while the price of others increased at a slower rate. The price of a few products, including cameras and electronic calculators, actually decreased during the 1970s.

Deflation is defined as a decrease in the overall price of a market basket of goods and services. Although the economy in the United States has generally experienced inflation rather than deflation, there have been some periods when prices have declined. Perhaps the most notable case occurred during the Great Depression. Between 1929 and 1933, prices declined about 25 percent.

Causes of Inflation

Economists disagree about the causes of inflation. However, two types of inflation are generally identified—demand-pull inflation and cost-push inflation.

Demand-Pull Inflation. Chapter 4 describes how the equilibrium price is determined by supply and demand. Figure 6-2 shows a supply curve (S) and a demand curve (D) for television sets. The curves cross where the price is $500, the equilibrium price of television sets.

FIGURE 6-2
This graph shows the supply and demand curves for television sets. Increased demand, indicated by the D* curve, causes the equilibrium price to increase, creating demand-pull inflation.

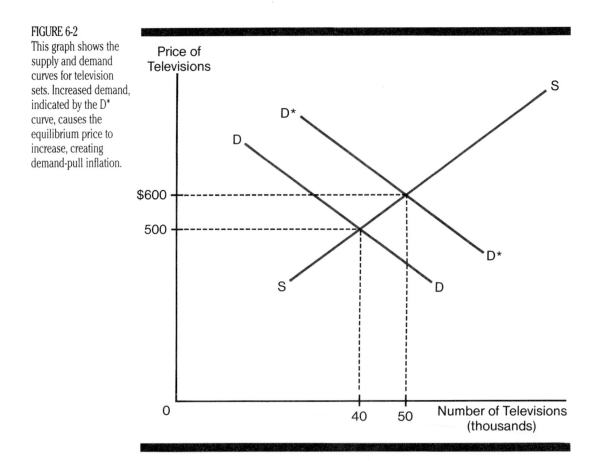

Suppose more people want to buy television sets than before. Perhaps the networks are showing more football games or have scheduled better movies for the coming year. The increased demand for television sets is shown by the new demand curve D*. It indicates that, at each price, more people want to buy television sets than before.

The new demand curve and the original supply curve cross at a price of $600. The new equilibrium price is higher than before. The increase in demand has caused an increase in price, but this increase in price does not mean that the economy has experienced inflation. An increase in the price of one product, or a few products, is not referred to as inflation.

However, suppose the overall demand for many goods and services increased. This could happen if there were more people in the economic system, or if individuals had more money to spend. Just as in the television set example, the increase in demand would cause the prices of many goods and services to rise. This general increase in prices would qualify as inflation. **Demand-pull inflation** often is described as too much money chasing too few goods. In other words, the production or availability of goods has not kept up with demand.

Cost-Push Inflation. The prices of goods and services are affected by the costs of producing them. Usually when costs go up, prices also go up. In the 1970s the price of crude oil went from about $3 a barrel to more than $30 a barrel. As a result, the price of gasoline, heating oil, and other oil products increased rapidly. People in the economic system soon realized that their incomes were not keeping up with the price changes. Many workers demanded and received higher wages. In turn, these higher wages increased the costs of producing other goods and services. Thus, businesses had to increase prices even further. When prices are pushed higher by increasing costs, this is called **cost-push inflation.**

INSTANT REPLAY

Inflation is defined as an increase in the overall price of a market basket of goods and services.

Demand-pull inflation is caused by too much money chasing too few goods.

Increases in the cost of producing goods and services may result in cost-push inflation.

Coping with Inflation

Most people think inflation is harmful. As consumers, they have to pay higher prices for the things they buy; therefore, as wage earners, they have to earn more money to maintain the same standard of living.

But many people also benefit from inflation; as producers and sellers, they receive higher prices for the goods and services they sell. Part of that higher price usually goes toward increasing the salaries of employees so that they can keep up with inflation.

For the individual, then, the effects of inflation may be beneficial or harmful. For the economy, inflation is usually harmful because it can reduce the rate of economic growth. Some of the consequences of inflation are summarized below.

Making Fixed Payments. Many contracts require that a regular payment be made each month or year for some time period. Sometimes, this period is specified as a certain number of years. For example, a car loan usually requires that a payment be made monthly for three or four years. In other cases, the period is not specified. For example, a retirement program may specify that a person is to receive a payment of $800 per month for as long as that person is alive. Many of these arrangements do not allow for a change in the amount of the payment as an adjustment for inflation. In general, inflation hurts the one receiving the fixed payment and benefits the one making the fixed payment. Each fixed payment received purchases fewer goods and services as prices rise.

Some elderly people receive a fixed retirement payment that does not increase with changes in the prices of goods and services. The period from 1974 to 1982 was one of rapid inflation. During these eight years, prices doubled in the United States. Thus, people with a fixed payment as their only source of income could purchase only half as much in 1982 as they could in 1974. If the fixed income is low to begin with, as is often the case with pensions, rapid inflation can impoverish people with fixed incomes and cause them to suffer great hardships. However, most older persons receive Social Security benefits, and in recent years these payments have been adjusted annually to keep up with inflation.

Borrowing and Lending. Many businesses and government agencies borrow money regularly. A firm may borrow money on the following terms. A lender (a bank or individual) gives the firm $1,000 today, and the firm promises to pay the lender $50 each year for ten years and to repay the $1,000 at the end of that period. If prices rise, the purchasing power of those $50 payments and the $1,000 final payment is reduced. In terms of the real value of the payments, the borrower benefits and the lender loses. Usually borrowers benefit in times of inflation.

Inflation hurts people on fixed incomes, such as pensioners, unless their payments are adjusted to compensate for rising costs.

Planning. Inflation makes it difficult to predict future prices and to plan for them. Workers may agree to work for the next year at a given wage only to discover a few months later that higher prices have caused a reduction in the purchasing power of their wages.

Also, if people expect prices to increase, they may rush out to buy things they will not need for some time. Others may try to buy large amounts of an item in the hope of reselling these items later at a much higher price.

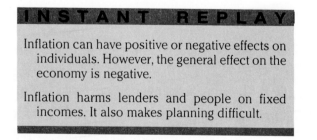

INSTANT REPLAY

Inflation can have positive or negative effects on individuals. However, the general effect on the economy is negative.

Inflation harms lenders and people on fixed incomes. It also makes planning difficult.

S U M M A R Y

Economic growth refers to a steady increase in the production of goods and services in an economic system. Economic growth is important because it provides jobs and enables people to better meet their needs and wants. Growth in GNP is a goal of virtually all countries. It is achieved by increases in productivity, better allocation of resources, and increases in labor and capital.

Providing jobs for members of the labor force is an important economic goal. The unemployment rate measures the performance of the economy in providing jobs. Four types of unemployment are frictional, cyclical, structural, and seasonal. Solutions to the unemployment problem include job retraining, providing better information about jobs and applicants, and improving the performance of the economy so that more jobs are created.

A period of economic expansion followed by a recession is a business cycle. A depression is a recession that is long and accompanied by an unusually high unemployment rate.

Inflation is defined as an increase in the overall price of a market basket of goods and services. Deflation occurs when the price of that market basket declines. Demand-pull inflation occurs when increased demand pulls up the prices of many goods and services. Often, it is described as too many dollars chasing too few goods and services. Cost-push inflation occurs when the cost of producing goods and services increases. Prices then have to be raised to cover the higher costs.

Inflation can have positive and negative effects. For example, lenders and people living on a fixed income suffer a decline in purchasing power when inflation occurs. However, sellers may benefit when inflation increases the price of the goods and services they sell.

☆ LEARNING ACTIVITIES ☆

Building Your Vocabulary

On a separate piece of paper, write the numbers 1 through 12. Next to each number, write the term that correctly completes the sentence.

depression
demand-pull inflation
full employment
seasonal
  unemployment
market basket
inflation

1. People who are more than 16 years old, available for work, and employed or seeking employment are members of the __labor force__.

2. A __productivity__ means that more goods and services can be produced using the same amounts of capital and labor.

3. A member of the labor force who does not have a job is __unemployed__.

4. A __market basket__ is a list of goods and services purchased by consumers.

gross national
    product
labor force
productivity increase
unemployment rate
unemployed
recession

5. When the unemployment rate is about 5 percent, the economy is at _full employment_.

6. The total value of all final goods and services in an economy is its _GNP_.

7. An increase in the overall price of a market basket of goods and services is _inflation_ while an overall decrease in prices is _deflation_.

8. When the number of unemployed is divided by the number in the labor force, the _unemployment rate_ is determined.

9. Too much money chasing too few goods is called _demand-pull inflation_.

10. A _recession_ is said to occur if the gross national product declines.

11. If GNP declines over a long period of time and the unemployment rate becomes very high, the economy is said to be in a _depression_.

12. Workers at beaches and ski resorts may experience _seasonal unemployment_.

Reviewing the Facts

1. Why are only final goods and services included when GNP is calculated?

2. If the population is growing at a rate of 4 percent per year and GNP is increasing at 2 percent per year, is the average person likely to be better off or worse off? Why?

3. Describe three sources of economic growth.

4. List and define four types of unemployment.

5. Describe three strategies for reducing unemployment.

6. Describe two types of inflation, and explain how they occur.

7. Why does inflation hurt people living on fixed incomes?

8. If the price of automobiles increased by 20 percent each year for the last three years, does this mean that inflation occurred? Why or why not?

9. In a period of rapid inflation, would you rather be a borrower or a lender?

10. Describe the phases of a business cycle, and explain what occurs in each phase.

Expressing Your Opinion

1. Some people argue that environmental problems like air and water pollution could be resolved by reducing the amount of goods and services produced. What do you think of this idea? Do you see any problems with it?

2. Why does the unemployment rate probably understate the actual rate of unemployment? Think about the criteria for being included in the unemployed category.

3. Having two people share the same job and reducing the standard workweek from 40 hours to 30 hours have been suggested as ways to reduce the unemployment rate. Do you think these

ideas would work? Why or why not?

4. Many unemployed people receive money each week from the government in the form of unemployment compensation. Some argue that unemployment compensation causes some unemployed people to stop looking for a job and this may be one reason that the unemployment rate has remained high. Do you agree or disagree?

Developing Your Attitudes, Values, and Skills

1. Make your own market basket list of 10 to 15 common items. These can include bread, milk, cars, televisions, steaks, hair dryers, shoes and records. Now, using old newspapers on file at your local library, look through the newspaper's advertisements to find out what the prices were for the items on your list a year ago, ten years ago, and twenty years ago. How does your list of prices for each of these past years compare with today's prices? Did the prices of one or two items change more substantially than the total dollar figure for the overall list? Put the information you have gathered into a table showing the items and prices for each year.

2. Interview friends or family members who remember the Great Depression. Ask them how their lives were affected. Did they lose their jobs? Did they benefit from the Great Depression? If so, how? Were their savings affected? Did they have trouble finding work? Did they have to rely on family members or friends to help them survive? Did they understand what was happening to the economy, or were they puzzled by it?

Did they lose faith in the American system, or did this experience somehow make them feel more patriotic? Did they become politically active, or did they feel there was nothing they could do to affect the system? Compare and summarize these personal testimonies, and describe to your class what life was like during the Depression for people who lived through it.

3. Using the *World Almanac,* the *Hammond Almanac,* or a similar reference book, compare our present GNP with those of nine other countries. Rank the GNPs from highest to lowest. Where do we stand? Now list the population of each of these countries. Divide the GNP of each country by its population. This gives the per capita GNP for each country. Rank the per capita GNPs. Where do we stand? Does the country with the highest GNP also have the highest per capita GNP? What does this tell you about productivity in each country? Summarize your findings about GNP for the countries you have studied, and report your results to the class.

UNIT 3

★ **Business Ownership and Organization**

★ **Basic Business Activities**

★ **Organized Labor**

This unit is concerned with the role of business and labor in the American free enterprise system. You will learn about the major types of business ownership, the production of goods and services, the marketing of those goods and services to consumers, and the financing of business activities. You will also learn about the role of organized labor.

How does a corporation differ from a partnership?

In terms of sales, what is the largest corporation in the United States?

What is the difference between trade and service industries?

CHAPTER 7

BUSINESS OWNERSHIP AND ORGANIZATION

PREVIEW

"The business of America is business."
Calvin Coolidge

There are about 15 million businesses in the United States. This total includes more than 200,000 grocery stores, almost that many service stations, and about 50,000 drugstores. Some of these businesses are very small. For example, a corner newsstand in New York City might consist of little more than a wooden shelter, a magazine rack, newspapers, and a few dozen magazines.

In contrast, some businesses have grown to gigantic size. A few years ago, the American Telephone & Telegraph Co. (AT&T) provided jobs for about one million people. At that time, there were more AT&T employees than there were people living in Idaho, North Dakota, or Vermont.

Later, AT&T was divided into several separate businesses. The new firms created by dividing AT&T are still large, but the General Motors Corporation is now the largest employer in the United States. More than 700,000 people get their paychecks from General Motors.

There are many differences between General Motors and the corner newsstand. Size is the most obvious, but another important difference involves the legal rights and responsibilities of the owners. These rights and responsibilities are determined by the form of ownership used in the business.

In this chapter you will learn about various types of business ownership and types of industries. When you have completed the reading material and learning activities, you should be able to:

★ Define the terms *sole proprietorship, partnership,* and *corporation.*

★ List the advantages and disadvantages of a sole proprietorship, partnership, and corporation.

★ Describe different types of industries and the kinds of goods and services they produce.

FORMS OF BUSINESS OWNERSHIP

Have you ever thought about starting your own business? What would you sell? How would you get the money necessary to begin? Whom would you ask for help?

Suppose your favorite aunt leaves you her secret recipe for fudge. You decide you could earn a lot of money by making this fudge and selling it to local candy stores.

What will you need to get started? First, you must have a place equipped for making candy. Perhaps your parents would be willing to let you use their kitchen. Next, you would need money to buy sugar, chocolate, nuts, and the other ingredients necessary for making fudge. The dollars you have saved for a summer vacation may be enough to pay for the first batch of supplies.

In the beginning, you may be able to take care of everything by yourself. You should have plenty of time to make the fudge and to deliver it to the stores. Later, if you have many requests for the candy, you may have to hire some friends to help fill orders. Also, your parents may decide that they want their kitchen back. As a result, you will have to find another location for your business. You will also need a stove, mixer, refrigerator, and other items. Unless you are wealthy, you may have to borrow from friends, parents, or the bank.

At this point, your candy business is called a **sole proprietorship.** That is, you are the only owner of the business. Any other people who work for you are your employees. An **employee** is a worker whose income in wages or salary is set by agreement with the owner. An employee's income is usually not affected by how much profit is earned by the business. Rather, an employee is paid **wages** for time worked— usually according to the number of hours. Or an employee receives a **salary,** a regular income paid for a set time period such as a week or a month. A salary usually does not depend on the number of hours worked.

The owner of a sole proprietorship is entitled to all the profits of the business. These profits need not be shared with anyone. However, the owner is also responsible for any losses. If your candy business does not sell enough fudge to cover expenses, you, as the owner, must still pay the bills. If a large sum of money is involved, you could be forced to sell your car or some other personal possessions in order to make these payments.

Suppose the fudge business does well. As a result, you decide to expand and open your own candy store. One of your first needs will be more money—a lot more money—to lease the store, purchase equipment and fixtures, hire more employees, build up your stock of goods, and so on. Another need is for someone to share the risk. A bigger operation can produce more profits, but it also can mean more losses. A third need is for someone to do the bookkeeping. You are an excellent candymaker but may not be particularly good with numbers.

Because of these needs, you decide to look for a partner. After a short search, you find someone who has the money to invest in the candy business. Luckily, this person also has a college degree in accounting. When the two of you join together, the business becomes a partnership. Although there are only two partners in your business, a partnership may involve any number of people. The feature that makes a business a **partnership** is that two or more people share ownership. They also share the profits and the responsibility for any losses of the business.

You soon learn that your new partner has some great ideas. Not only does she understand accounting, she also knows how to sell fudge. As a result, the business becomes very successful. To keep growing, you now need a full-scale candy factory, delivery trucks, and some advertising. Your partner estimates that a million dollars should do the job.

At this point, you and your partner start to worry. The possibility of having to repay a million dollars is frightening. Looking for ideas, you go to your lawyer.

The lawyer suggests that you form a corporation. A **corporation** is a special form of business that is owned by several people, each of whom invests money in the business and owns a share of any profit, but has limited liability. **Limited liability** means that each owner cannot lose more than she or he has invested in the business. For example, if you had put $500 into the corporation, that is the most that you could lose. Even if the company lost the entire million dollars, your possible loss would be limited to $500. Because of limited liability, it is often easier to find investors for corporations than it is for partnerships.

Your fudge business started out as a sole proprietorship, became a partnership, and finally ended up as a corporation. Not all businesses go through all three forms of ownership. However, many large corporations began as sole proprietorships or partnerships. For example, J. C. Penney

Company, Inc., and F. W. Woolworth Co. both started out as sole proprietorships. So did the Marriott Corporation, which began as a small root beer stand in Washington, D.C. The stand grew to become a restaurant, and then the business was expanded to include many restaurants. Today, the Marriott Corporation owns over 1,600 restaurants and operates hotels with over 70,000 rooms.

Usually, a sole proprietorship or partnership is not the right form of ownership for a very large business. Similarly, most new businesses do not start out as corporations. Each form of ownership has its advantages and disadvantages. In the next sections you will learn more about sole proprietorships, partnerships, and corporations.

Although the Marriott Corporation started out as a root beer stand, sole proprietorships usually do not become large corporations.

Boston Marriott/Copley Place, courtesy of Marriott Corporation

INSTANT REPLAY

A sole proprietorship is a business owned by one person.

A partnership is a business that has two or more owners. In most partnerships each person has unlimited liability.

A corporation is a form of business ownership that allows its owners to have limited liability. That is, they cannot lose more than they have put into the business.

SOLE PROPRIETORSHIPS

The sole proprietorship is the simplest form of business organization. More than 500,000 such businesses are started in the United States each year.

Advantages

The three main advantages of the sole proprietorship are as follows:

★ Ease of start-up

★ No sharing of profits

★ Complete control

Ease of Start-Up. Starting a sole proprietorship often requires little more than deciding to go into business. A license may be required, but usually it is easy to obtain. A license application must be submitted to the local government where the business is to be located. A typical application requires the name, location, and type of business. Before granting the license, the fire department may check that there are no fire hazards. The police department may also check to determine whether the owner of the business has a police record. A history of problems with the law could cause a license application to be refused.

No Sharing of Profits. Any profits earned by the business belong to the owner. The owner decides how those profits are to be used. In some cases, they may be used to improve or expand the business. In other cases, the owner may take every dollar of profit for personal use.

Sole proprietorships are easy to start, and any profits belong to the owner.

Jose Carrillo

Complete Control. The owner is totally responsible for decisions about the business. He or she has the right to decide what goods and services will be produced and the methods used to produce them. Although advice may be received from other people, the owner is free to accept or reject this advice. The owner is the decision maker.

Disadvantages

The three main disadvantages of the sole proprietorship are as follows:

★ Difficulty of expansion

★ Unlimited liability

★ Limited management skills

Difficulty of Expansion. Owners of a sole proprietorship often have difficulty finding the money necessary to expand the business. Building a new plant or purchasing new capital goods can be very expensive. The average person rarely has enough money saved to meet the needs of a growing business.

Unlimited Liability. Although the owner does not have to share profits, she or he also has no one to help share losses. The owner's personal savings and other possessions, as well as any money invested in the firm, can be lost if the business does not have enough money to pay its debts.

Limited Management Skills. Few people have all the skills necessary to manage a business. Often, a person with good ideas may be poor at managing money. Or a good money manager may be a poor people manager. The lack of management skills may cause a promising proprietorship to fail.

PARTNERSHIPS

Partnerships are formed for a number of reasons. Friends or relatives become partners because they have trust and confidence in one another. In other businesses, the partnership results because each partner has special skills. Sometimes the partnership is created by the need for money. The poor inventor who goes into business with the wealthy banker is an example.

Like a sole proprietorship, a partnership must usually obtain a license before it can operate as a business. In addition, it is a good idea for the partners to have a written agreement that specifies the terms of the partnership. Such an agreement should list the responsibilities of each partner, the method by which profits will be shared, and the procedures to be used if one partner should die or want to leave the business.

Advantages

The three main advantages of a partnership are as follows:

★ Ease of expansion

★ Shared risk

★ Additional management skills

Ease of Expansion. Growing businesses often need large sums of money. A rich partner or several not-so-rich partners may be able to provide the dollars necessary to allow the business to expand.

Shared Risk. If the business fails, the losses are the shared responsibility of all the partners. One person does not have to bear all the risks of failure.

Additional Management Skills. The partners in a business can use their special skills to make the business successful. It is no longer necessary for a single owner to do all the management tasks. One partner may concentrate on sales while another supervises production. A third partner might be responsible for making sure that the bills are paid and that accurate records are kept.

Disadvantages

The four main disadvantages of a partnership are as follows:

★ Shared profits

★ Unlimited liability

★ Shared decision making

★ Difficulty of dissolving the partnership

Shared Profits. Each owner receives only part of the profit. Sometimes a partner may think that her or his share of the profits is less than what is deserved.

Unlimited Liability. Suppose a partnership consists of the poor inventor and the wealthy banker mentioned earlier. Although both persons are responsible for any losses, the banker has much more to lose. If the inventor cannot repay his or her share of the losses, the banker is legally responsible for the money owed.

In some states this problem can be avoided by agreements that create **limited partners.** The losses of a limited partner cannot be greater than the amount of money that the person put into the business. However, limited partners usually have no right to make decisions about the day-to-day operations of the firm.

Shared Decision Making. Disagreements are not unusual in a partnership. Partners may disagree about ways of producing the firm's product, or about the kinds of new products the firm should sell. Disagreements can occur because one partner wants increased recognition or responsibility. Sometimes one partner may make an important decision without the knowledge of the others. The partnership may be forced to honor such a decision even though it is unwise or perhaps illegal.

Such disagreements can become so serious that the individuals are no longer willing to work together. There are many examples of close friends or relatives who have become so unhappy in business dealings that they no longer speak to one another. In some cases, a partner who feels cheated might actually sue the other partner.

Difficulty of Dissolving the Partnership. If one partner wants to get out of the business, it may be difficult for the firm to continue. One reason is that the departing partner may have special skills that are difficult to replace. Also, the remaining partners may not have enough money to buy out the departing partner. It may be necessary to sell the business or to take out a large loan in order to get the necessary money.

CORPORATIONS

An early Supreme Court decision ruled that legally corporations have the same rights and responsibilities in their business dealings as individuals. Thus, corporations can buy, sell, and own property. They can make contracts and borrow money. They can sue another corporation or an individual. In turn, a corporation can be sued.

There are three important groups in a corporation. They are the officers, the board of directors, and the stockholders. The **officers** of a corporation include the president and vice-presidents. These are the people who make the day-to-day operating decisions in the firm. They are usually selected by the board of directors of the corporation and are responsible for implementing policies approved by the board.

The **board of directors** is a group of three or more individuals who act as the governing body for the business. Usually they have other full-time jobs. For example, a director on the board of General Motors might be a lawyer in New York or a banker in San Francisco. The board meets several times a year to review the performance of the corporation and provide guidance to the managers of the business. As mentioned, the officers usually are selected by the board of directors. If the board does not believe that the officers are doing a good job, it may fire them and find new officers.

Stockholders are the actual owners of a corporation. Their ownership is represented by a document called a stock certificate. A **stock**

Corporate stockholders meet annually to discuss company business, but the board of directors governs the company.

Honeywell, Inc.

certificate contains the name of the owner and lists the number of shares owned. A **share** in a corporation represents one unit of ownership. There may be millions of shares of stock in a large corporation. Some stockholders may own only a single share. Other individuals or organizations may own as many as a million shares. In the United States today, more than 15 million people own stock.

The stockholders' major role is to provide money through their purchase of the firm's stock. They usually have little to do with the overall management of the company. The American Telephone & Telegraph Company has about 3 million stockholders. Clearly, 3 million people cannot be involved in routine decision making. This responsibility is left to the officers and the board of directors. However, stockholders in most companies have a say in electing the board of directors, and sometimes in other decisions as well. The stockholders make these decisions once a year at stockholders' meetings. Each share of stock an investor owns allows one vote, and each stockholder may cast his or her votes by mail or in person at the annual meeting.

To start a corporation, the original investors must obtain a charter from the state in which the business is located. This **charter** lists the name of the corporation, the purpose of the business, the amount of money that is being provided to start the business, and the names of the members of the board of directors. Although the corporation receives its charter from one state, it can easily get permission to operate in other states.

The use of the corporate form of ownership has made large-scale business possible. The reasons should be clear as you learn about the advantages and disadvantages of the corporation.

Advantages

The four main advantages of a corporation are as follows:

★ Increased ease of expansion

★ Limited liability

★ Ease of transferring ownership

★ Increased management skills

Increased Ease of Expansion. Corporations can rely on a large number of people for money. The stockholders of some corporations have provided billions of dollars for use by the firm. If the business needs more money, it can sell additional shares of stock.

Limited Liability. One reason people invest in a corporation is to limit the amount of their liability. No one can lose more than the amount of money he or she invested. No matter how much money the corporation loses, the stockholder's personal possessions cannot be taken to pay the firm's debts.

Ease of Transferring Ownership. When an owner of a partnership dies, her or his relatives may want cash for their shares of the business. The withdrawal of cash may disrupt the operation of the firm. In contrast, stockholders can get their money out of a corporation by selling the stock that they own, which usually is a fairly simple matter. Buying and selling stock is discussed in Chapter 17.

Increased Management Skills. The corporate form of ownership allows a business to become very large. Such large businesses can hire people with the skills necessary to handle the many needs of the business.

Disadvantages

The three main disadvantages of a corporation are as follows:

★ Extra taxes

★ Special government regulations

★ Reduced owner control

Extra Taxes. A charter gives the corporation special rights. In return, a special corporate income tax must be paid on the profits of corporations. This tax does not apply to the profits of sole proprietorships and partnerships. Usually the taxes paid on the profits of a corporation are greater than those paid by a proprietorship or partnership.

Special Government Regulations. To protect stockholders and consumers, corporations must comply with certain government regulations. Many of these regulations do not apply to other forms of business. For example, a corporation usually must receive approval from a government agency called the Securities and Exchange Commission before it can sell shares of stock. This agency makes sure that the information provided by the business is accurate and complete. Its job is to protect investors from dishonest business people.

Reduced Owner Control. Recall that the American Telephone & Telegraph Company has about 3 million stockholders. However, no single person owns as much as 1 percent of AT&T's stock. In fact, about one-half of the company's stockholders own 25 shares or less. As a result, although these stockholders are the owners of the business, they have little to say about the operation of the firm. Like most large corporations, AT&T is controlled by its officers and board of directors.

The Importance of the Corporation

Sole proprietorships, partnerships, and corporations are the three most important forms of business ownership in the United States. Of these three, sole proprietorships are the most common. Figure 7-1 shows that about 70 percent of United States businesses have a single owner. About 10 percent are partnerships and 20 percent are corporations.

Although there are many more sole proprietorships than corporations, corporations make most of the sales. Figure 7-1 shows that about 90 percent of all dollars spent on goods and services go to corporations. The reason is that corporations are usually much larger than sole proprietorships.

Each year, *Fortune* magazine publishes a list of the 500 largest corporations in the United States. These firms are sometimes called the "Fortune 500." Table 7-1 shows the top ten corporations for 1985. General Motors, the automaker, was the largest. This giant corporation sold over $96 billion in cars and automotive products in 1985. If you look carefully at Table 7-1, you will notice that six of the ten largest United States firms were involved in producing either oil or autos. The list indicates the importance of the automobile in our modern society.

FIGURE 7-1

Only about 20 percent of all United States businesses are corporations; yet they receive about 90 percent of all dollars spent on goods and services.

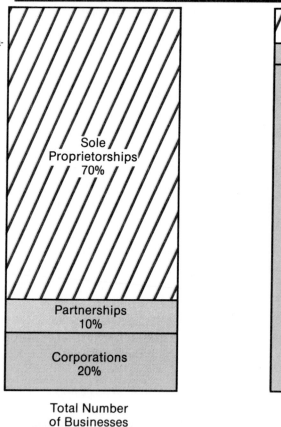

Sole Proprietorships 70%

Partnerships 10%

Corporations 20%

Total Number of Businesses

Sole Proprietorships 6%

Partnerships 4%

Corporations 90%

Total Business Sales

TABLE 7-1

Rank	Company	Sales (billions of dollars)
TEN LARGEST CORPORATIONS IN THE UNITED STATES (1985)		
1	General Motors	$96.3
2	Exxon	86.6
3	Mobil	55.9
4	Ford Motor	52.7
5	International Business Machines	50.1
6	Texaco	46.2
7	Chevron	41.7
8	American Telephone & Telegraph	34.9
9	E. I. du Pont de Nemours	29.4
10	General Electric	28.2

Source: "The Fortune 500," *Fortune*, Vol. 113, No. 9 (April 28, 1986), p. 182.

INSTANT REPLAY

Sole proprietorships are easy to start but difficult to expand. The owner has unlimited liability for losses.

Partnerships allow owners to share the risks and add management skills. Owners still have unlimited liability. Partnerships are difficult to dissolve.

Corporations are owned by stockholders and operated by a board of directors and hired managers. Stockholder liability is limited.

It is easier for corporations to expand and transfer ownership, but corporations are subject to special taxes and government regulations.

About 70 percent of all American businesses are sole proprietorships, but corporations make 90 percent of all sales.

TYPES OF INDUSTRIES

As you learned in Chapter 1, the term *industry* refers to those businesses that produce a similar good or service. For example, when people refer to the garment industry, they are referring to all the firms that make the clothes we wear. Economists call groups of industries that produce similar goods and services **sectors.** You may sometimes hear a newscaster refer to the "manufacturing sector" or the "service sector" of the economy. Usually the name of the industry or sector gives you an idea of what goods and services it produces. Five broad sectors are discussed below.

Extractive

The **extractive industries** are agriculture (farming) and mining. The term *extractive* means that output is "taken out" of the ground. Natural resources such as soil, water, and ore deposits are important to these industries.

In agriculture, food products are produced from the soil. In mining, minerals such as coal, gold, silver, and copper are taken from mines or open pits. Oil and natural gas are produced from wells.

Farming is an extractive industry.

Photo courtesy of New Idea, Coldwater, Ohio

Manufacturing

Most of the output from the extractive industries is not in the form that consumers can use. These products must undergo additional processing to make them useful. **Manufacturing industries** convert unfinished goods into **consumer goods,** which are useful to consumers, or **industrial goods,** which are used by other industries.

For example, at a meat-packing plant, live animals are transformed into steaks, hamburger, and pot roasts for consumers. Ore from iron mines is sent to steel mills where it is converted into sheets and rods of steel that are used by other industries. The auto industry then uses these sheets for fenders, doors, and hoods. Steel rods are used by the construction sector to reinforce concrete.

Construction

Construction industries consist of those businesses that build structures such as roads, buildings, houses, and bridges. There are different types of construction companies. A small firm might consist of an owner and two assistants who build 5 to 10 houses a year. A medium-sized firm might construct 50 to 100 houses or apartment units a year. A very large construction company may build roads, industrial buildings, dams, airports, and thousands of homes all over the world. The Bechtel Group, Inc., with headquarters in San Francisco, has construction projects in many countries. Recently, this company built the world's largest airport in Saudi Arabia.

Trade

Businesses that primarily sell goods to consumers and other businesses are **trade industries.** Firms in retail trade sell goods to consumers. Wholesale trade businesses sell goods to other firms, primarily retail stores. Wholesale and retail businesses often are referred to as **intermediaries** because they are in the middle of a transaction between the manufacturer that produced the product and the consumer. You will learn more about intermediaries in the next chapter.

Service

Firms in the **service industries** do not produce goods. Rather, they provide services directly to consumers or other businesses. For example, a hair stylist cuts your hair, a bus driver transports you from one city to another, and a rock group entertains you. There also are firms that provide services for businesses. A trucking company ships cars from an automobile plant in Michigan to a showroom in Dallas, and a law firm writes the contract for two firms that have just agreed on a big order.

The number of workers in each of the industry categories and their average weekly wage are shown in Table 7-2. In terms of employment, the service sector is the largest, followed by trade and manufacturing. Mining has the fewest employees but the highest average wage. Agricultural workers earn the lowest wages, but often receive free meals and housing as a supplement to their money earnings.

TABLE 7-2

UNITED STATES INDUSTRY CATEGORIES 1985		
Industry Category	Number of Workers (thousands)	Average Weekly Wage
Extractive		
Agriculture	3,200	$180
Mining	866	522
Manufacturing	19,362	393
Construction	4,954	461
Trade	23,939	268
Service	29,033	267

Source: U.S. Department of Labor, Bureau of Labor Statistics, *Employment and Earnings* (Washington: U.S. Government Printing Office).

Service industries provide services to consumers rather than producing products.

The extractive, manufacturing, and construction industries produce goods.

Businesses in the trade sector perform the function of intermediaries in the free enterprise system.

The service sector provides services directly to consumers and other businesses.

S U M M A R Y

A proprietorship is a business owned by one person. Proprietorships are easy to start, do not require sharing of profits, and allow the owner to make all decisions. However, they may be difficult to expand, and they leave the owner with unlimited liability for losses. In addition, the owner may have limited management skills.

Partnerships are businesses owned by two or more people. Partners share the risks, provide money for expansion, and bring more management skills to the business. But partners also have to share the decision making and profits, and each bears unlimited liability for losses. Partnerships are sometimes difficult to dissolve if a partner quits or dies.

A corporation is a business owned by people who buy shares of stock in the company. Stockholders receive propor-tionate shares of the profit and have only limited liability for losses. Corporations can obtain money for expansion by sell-ing stock; the buying and selling of stock allows investors to transfer ownership easily. Corporate owners have little con-trol over business, but corporations can hire people with the specific management skills required. Corporate profits are subject to special taxes, and corporations must adhere to special government regulations.

Industries can be classified into five groups or sectors. The extractive, man-ufacturing, and construction sectors produce goods. The trade sector sells products to consumers and businesses; the service sector provides services to consumers and businesses.

☆ LEARNING ACTIVITIES ☆

Building Your Vocabulary

On a separate piece of paper, write the numbers 1 through 11. Next to each number, write the term that correctly completes the sentence.

✓ sole proprietorship
✓ employees
✓ wage
✓ partnership
  limited liability
✓ officers
✓ stockholders
✓ share
✓ sector
✓ industrial goods
✓ trade industries

1. A business owned by two or more people, each with unlimited liability, is called a _partnership_.

2. _Officers_ are responsible for the day-to-day operations of a corporation.

3. A unit of ownership in a corporation is a _share_.

4. _Stockholders_ are the owners of a corporation.

5. Workers who receive a salary or wage are _employees_

6. A _sole proprietorship_ is a business owned by one person.

7. A _wage_ is an amount paid depending on the time worked.

8. A group of industries that produce similar goods and services is called a _sector_.

9. _Industrial goods_ are products bought by other businesses to be used in making consumer goods.

10. _Trade Industrial_ include businesses that sell goods to consumers and other businesses.

11. _Limited liability_ means that each owner cannot lose more than he or she has invested in a business.

Reviewing the Facts

1. Is it possible that the owners of a corporation may have little to say about the actual operation of the business? Explain.

2. Four types of information must be provided in order for a firm to get a charter as a corporation. What are they?

3. In what ways is a corporation like a person?

4. What is the difference between a corporation's officers and its board of directors?

5. List two advantages of a corporation in comparison to a partnership.

6. List the five industry sectors.

7. What industries act as intermediaries in the economy?

8. As measured by employment, which industry is the largest? Which is the smallest?

Expressing Your Opinion

1. Suppose you were starting a partnership. Would you want the terms of the partnership written down? Why? What things would you include in a written agreement?

2. Why do you think sole proprietorships fail more often than corporations?

3. Do you think it is fair to subject corporations, but not partnerships or sole proprietorships, to special governmental regulations? Why or why not?

4. What factors might explain why the average weekly wage in mining and construction is so much higher than those in the trade and service industries?

Developing Your Attitudes, Values, and Skills

1. Interview two local small business owners. Ask them to explain why they decided to go into business for themselves and how they determined what business to start. Find out whether they are sole proprietors or partners. If they are partners, how many other people own the business with them? Are their partners full partners or limited partners? Question the business owners about what legal steps they had to take before they could start their business.

What managerial skills did they and their partners bring to their business? Think of other questions to ask, and when you complete the interviews, write a report comparing the experiences of the two owners.

2. Suppose that you and a friend enter into a business partnership. You have both invested equal amounts of money in the business and have agreed to do equal work and share equally in the profits. Then the business fails. You are both left with many business debts—money you owe to others. Your partner claims to have nothing of value to help pay off the debts. Under the laws of a partnership, you are legally responsible for all debts—yours as well as your partner's. Do you think this is fair? What would you do? How might this situation have been avoided? Write a short essay explaining your answers.

3. Choose two pages from the yellow pages section of the local telephone book. For every business listed, determine what industry it belongs to— extractive, manufacturing, construction, trade, or service. Some businesses may represent more than one type of industry. Be prepared to compile class totals for each of the five types of industry. Which industry involves the greatest number of businesses in your area?

4. Acquire a copy of a corporation's annual financial report. What kind of information does it contain? How helpful would this information be to a stockholder? What is the major activity of the company? Would it be a good company to invest in? Why or why not? Summarize your findings, and report them to the class.

FOCUS YOUR READING

How can the United States produce 30 percent of the world's total output with only 6 percent of the world's population?

What types of advertising do consumers find most annoying?

Why do some profitable businesses have to raise money by borrowing or by selling part of the business?

CHAPTER 8

BASIC BUSINESS ACTIVITIES

PREVIEW

The standard of living in the United States is one of the highest in the world. Although the United States has only about 6 percent of the world's population, it produces 30 percent of the world's goods and services. Why is production in the United States so great? You might guess that it is because people work harder and longer in the United States, but this is not the case. The average worker in the United States works about 40 hours per week. That number is much less than the number of hours worked per week in many other countries.

There are several reasons for this achieve-ment. First, there are economic rewards for high production. Business owners, managers, and workers are rewarded when production increases. Owners receive higher profits, managers earn higher salaries, and workers are paid higher wages. Another important reason is that American workers have tools, machines, and other equipment that make their jobs easier than the same jobs in some other countries. Finally, emphasis on produc-tion has led to techniques and equipment that have increased the production of goods and services.

In this chapter you will learn about producing and marketing goods and services; you will also learn about financing business operations. When you have completed the reading material and learning activities, you should be able to:

★ Explain how businesses in the United States economy organize labor, land, and capital equipment to produce the most goods and services possible.

★ Discuss the importance of marketing in the modern economic system.

★ Explain the arguments for and against advertising.

★ Explain why businesses often need to borrow money or sell stock.

★ Describe the different ways that businesses obtain money from sources outside the business itself.

PRODUCING

The purpose of business is to organize a society's labor force, natural resources, and capital to produce goods and services. When these factors of production are organized efficiently, more goods and services are produced and the costs of production are decreased. One function of business, therefore, is to seek ways to improve the methods for producing goods and services. The highly industrialized nations of the world, such as Japan, Great Britain, and the United States, have developed efficient methods of production that share certain important characteristics. These characteristics—specialization of labor, mass production, use of capital goods and automation, and interdependence—are discussed below.

Specialization of Labor

Two hundred years ago, a farmer who needed a wagon would go to a wagon-maker, called a wainwright, who would manufacture and assemble each part of the wagon by hand. The wainwright could produce one wagon at a time, and each one took days or weeks to complete. When a wagon needed repairs, the wainwright also had to hand-make the replacement parts.

Imagine the cost and difficulty if automakers made cars the same way today. Each General Motors employee would build one car at a time, making and assembling each part. The task would be difficult and would take a long time. Each car produced this way would also be extremely expensive. Automakers long ago found an easier way to make and assemble the parts of their products. They broke each big job down into hundreds of smaller jobs, and they assigned each worker to one specific task. Some workers make doors, some make fenders, and yet others make steering wheels. Other workers assemble the parts. Some attach doors to the frames, some install the fenders, and so on. This technique is called **specialization of labor.**

Think about the people you see at work. Most of them are specialists. Secretaries concentrate on typing letters and reports, machine operators usually run the same machine each day, bricklayers lay bricks, and electricians do wiring. The economy consists primarily of workers who specialize in doing a few things well. The result is greater production than could be achieved in an economy in which each worker had to perform every part of a complicated job.

However, there are some disadvantages to specialization. Sometimes the jobs are so routine that they are boring and offer little job satisfaction. Some workers who know how to do only one small task have difficulty finding new jobs. Also, it is difficult for some workers to see their contribution to output when they perform only one small task.

Mass Production

The concept of mass production is closely related to the idea of specialized labor. **Mass production** refers to producing goods and services in large quantities using specialized labor. Recall your last visit to a fast-food restaurant. These businesses make large quantities of hamburgers and other food products efficiently. They can serve large numbers of people quickly and at a relatively low cost. In contrast, a full-service restaurant does not use mass-production techniques. Each meal is cooked to order and served to customers at their tables. Of course, this service is costly, and consumers have to pay higher prices than at a fast-food restaurant.

Many firms use an assembly line as their mass-production method. An **assembly line** usually has a number of people working alongside a conveyor belt that moves the product from one worker to another. Each worker performs one or more operations on the product, such as driving screws, spray painting, or inspecting the quality of earlier operations.

Most people are familiar with an automobile assembly line. At one end of the factory, workers place a frame on the conveyor belt. As the process continues, workers add wheels, tires, fenders, seats, and radios until a finished car comes off the end of the line. Usually each worker specializes in one operation. The production of automobiles is efficient because of the use of mass-production techniques and the specialization of labor.

On an assembly line, conveyor belts bring the work to the worker.

Courtesy of Nabisco, Inc.

Adam Smith and the Production of Pins

In Chapter 3 you learned about Adam Smith and his book, *An Inquiry Into the Nature and Causes of the Wealth of Nations.* In his first chapter, Smith teaches the ideas of mass production and specialization of labor by discussing how straight pins are made. A pin is a fairly simple product, but imagine trying to make one. Smith estimates that an unskilled worker without access to the right equipment probably could not make more than about 10 pins each day. But in a pin factory he observed ten workers making 48,000 pins each day, an average of 4,800 per worker. This average is 480 times what each would produce working alone and without the right machines.

Smith described the specialization of labor that he observed:

One man draws the wire, another straightens it, a third cuts it, a fourth points it, a fifth grinds it at the top for receiving the head...the important business of making a pin is divided into about eighteen distinct operations.[1]

Remember that Smith's book was written in 1776. Since then, the business of making pins has been modernized so that workers can make many times more pins each day. But the principle is still valid. By specializing and making large amounts of output, the cost of each unit produced is much less than it would be otherwise.

———————

[1]Adam Smith, *An Inquiry Into the Nature and Causes of the Wealth of Nations,* edited by Edwin Cannan (Chicago: University of Chicago Press, 1977).

Capital Goods and Automation

Recall that capital goods include machinery, tools, vehicles, and most of the things that people use to help them get their work done better and faster. Construction workers almost always use capital goods. These range from hammers and saws to bulldozers and cranes. Secretaries in an office use typewriters, computers, and copying machines. Imagine how difficult it would be to do these jobs without these machines.

An important reason for the growth of the United States economy has been the development of new and better capital equipment. A business that does not have up-to-date capital equipment may have difficulty staying in business, because its competitors will be able to produce more goods and sell them at lower prices.

Automation refers to the replacement of human labor by machines. In most modern economies, the process of producing goods has been automated. For example, on construction jobs, power saws have replaced hand saws; on earth-moving projects, bulldozers have replaced workers with shovels; and in offices, electric typewriters and word processors have replaced mechanical typewriters.

Because machines have taken over some routine and repetitive jobs, some workers can be switched to other more interesting jobs. In some cases, however, automation has caused workers to lose their jobs. Although the job loss poses problems for those workers, the economy benefits from greater production. Usually workers who lose their jobs in one industry are able to switch to jobs in other fields, although sometimes the adjustment is difficult.

Interdependence

When a production system depends on mass production, specialization of labor, capital goods, and automation, the result is a high degree of interdependence. **Interdependence** means that workers and businesses are dependent on one another. For example, if one worker on an assembly line makes a mistake, the entire line may have to be shut down. The result is that the other workers have to stop work until the error is corrected.

Also, each business in the production process may be dependent on other businesses. The automobile manufacturer depends on the tire maker to have tires ready to be put on the cars at the right time and place. If the tires arrive late, the production process may stop until they arrive. Occasionally a labor strike in one industry will cause other indus-

Automation enables machines to perform tedious, repetitive jobs.

Photo courtesy of Cincinnati Milacron, Inc.

tries to close. For example, a strike in the glass industry can result in the closing of an auto plant. If no glass windshields are available, no cars can be finished.

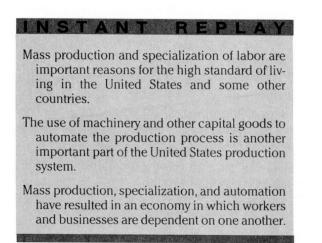

INSTANT REPLAY

Mass production and specialization of labor are important reasons for the high standard of living in the United States and some other countries.

The use of machinery and other capital goods to automate the production process is another important part of the United States production system.

Mass production, specialization, and automation have resulted in an economy in which workers and businesses are dependent on one another.

MARKETING

Consumers satisfy their needs and wants by purchasing the goods and services produced by businesses. But how do consumers obtain these products? They do not line up at the factory gates or on the edge of the farmer's field. Instead, the goods and services are transported to shops and stores where consumers can conveniently purchase them. This process of moving goods and services from the producer to the consumer is called **marketing**.

Marketing activities become more important as economic systems become more complex. In a simple economic system, marketing may not play a large role. Think about a small village where the baker makes flour using wheat purchased from a nearby farm. Orders for pies and cookies are received from people in the village. In such a setting, the baker would have little problem deciding what to bake, and customers would find it easy to complain if the baked goods were not tasty. In this simple economy, the link between the bakery and its customers is very close. Marketing activities are not needed, because producers and consumers deal directly with one another.

In our modern economic system, producers and consumers are not closely linked. Large bakeries buy supplies and equipment from many other businesses. They ship pies, cookies, and other baked goods to stores in many cities. The owners of these large bakeries probably never meet the people who buy their products. In this situation, many people form the link between consumers and producers. Truckers move the goods to the grocery stores. Advertising agencies prepare the ads that are carried in newspapers and on television and radio. Grocery stores display the baked goods to make them appealing to shoppers. These are all marketing activities.

Today, one-third of all workers in the United States are involved in some form of marketing. Fifty cents of each dollar spent by consumers pays for marketing costs. The importance of marketing can be seen in Table 8-1, which breaks down the cost of producing and selling a record album. Marketing costs are marked with an asterisk (*). You can see that marketing expenses are more than half of the total price that consumers pay for records.

Money spent on marketing is the price that consumers pay for choice and convenience. Marketing activities provide consumers with a wide variety of goods and services. Individuals can choose between many brands and styles of clothes, stereo systems, sporting goods, and

TABLE 8-1

COSTS OF PRODUCING AND SELLING A RECORD ALBUM

Vinyl and Pressing	$.48
Record Jacket	1.02
American Federation of Musicians Dues	.09
Payments to Songwriters	.25
Recording Artist's Royalties	.82
*Transportation to Distributor	.07
*Manufacturer's Advertising and Selling Expenses	.70
Manufacturer's Overhead	.69
Manufacturer's Profit	.62
MANUFACTURER'S PRICE	$4.74
*Transportation to Record Store	.03
*Distributor's Advertising, Selling, and Overhead Expenses	.15
*Distributor's Profit	.30
DISTRIBUTOR'S PRICE	$5.22
*Record Store's Advertising, Selling, and Overhead Expenses	.84
*Record Store's Profit	2.33
PRICE PAID BY CONSUMERS	$8.39

*Marketing costs.

other merchandise. Marketing brings products to the consumer for convenient shopping. In a large mall a person can find most items on even the longest shopping list. Marketing informs consumers about new products and good buys. Advertisements in local newspapers emphasize low prices on soft drinks, coats, and school supplies. Cutting back on marketing activities could reduce prices, but as a result, consumers would have less information and a smaller variety of goods and services from which to choose.

Channels of Distribution

Once a good is produced, the firm must decide how to market it. Some products are sold directly to the consumer. An example is fresh vegetables purchased from a farmer's roadside market. This method is called **direct marketing**. Other products pass through various businesses on their way to the consumer. This method is called **indirect marketing**. The path that goods take as they move from the original producer to the final consumer is called the **channel of distribution**.

Businesses involved in marketing activities are called intermediaries. As you learned in Chapter 7, intermediaries provide a useful function by linking the producer with the consumer. Three important types of intermediaries are agents, wholesalers, and retailers.

Agents. **Agents** buy and sell for others. They do not actually purchase goods and services. Rather, they arrange for transfers between owners and buyers. A literary agent, for example, helps bring writers and publishers together. One agent represents several writers. The agent's job is to offer each writer's work to publishers who might be interested in buying it. If a publisher buys a writer's work, the agent helps the writer negotiate a favorable contract. When the purchase is completed, the agent receives a fee as payment for bringing the publisher and writer together. Stockbrokers, who bring buyers and sellers of stock together, and talent agents, who bring producers and performers together, work in much the same way.

Wholesalers. **Wholesalers** buy goods in large quantities from farmers, manufacturers, and other wholesalers. These goods are then sold in smaller lots to others who, in turn, resell them to consumers. Wholesalers are specialists. By buying large amounts of a small number of goods, they are able to purchase goods at lower prices. Also, because the wholesaler repeatedly buys the goods, he or she becomes an expert in judging the quality of the products. The benefits of low prices and good judgment can then be passed on to the wholesaler's customers.

Retailers. **Retailers** buy goods from wholesalers in order to sell the goods to customers. Retailers can be grouped by the type of store, form of ownership, and location.

Wholesalers buy goods in large quantities, then sell them to retailers in smaller lots.

Richard Pasley/STOCK BOSTON

Type of Store. Retailers may sell many types of goods or handle only a few lines of merchandise. A department store sells a large variety of goods, including furniture, appliances, and clothing. Supermarkets provide a broad selection of food and drug items. Specialty stores concentrate on a few products, such as tapes and records or greeting cards. Mail-order houses sell goods through catalogs. Vending machine operations provide snacks and drinks. Although they are very different, all these businesses are retailers.

Form of Ownership. Many retail stores are independently owned. Others are part of a large corporate chain. For example, a J.C. Penney or Sears store in your community belongs to a chain of hundreds of such stores throughout the country. The franchise is a third type of ownership. In Chapter 5 you learned that a franchise is the legal right to sell a product or service in a specific area, and that governments award franchises for some services, such as cable television. Businesses can also sell franchises. In a business franchise, the parent company sells to a local owner the right to use its name and products. The franchise purchases supplies and products from the parent company, but it is not owned by the parent company. Many fast-food restaurants, such as Pizza Hut and Taco Bell, are franchises.

Location. A small grocery store or gas station may be the only business in a neighborhood, but retail stores are usually grouped together. At one time, most stores were found in the downtown business district of a community. Today, suburban shopping centers and malls are important locations for retailers. They allow consumers to shop near their homes. They also provide parking lots, and some offer protection from bad weather.

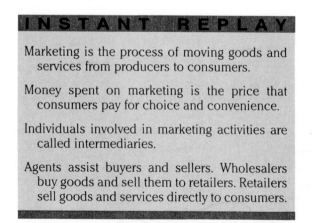

INSTANT REPLAY

Marketing is the process of moving goods and services from producers to consumers.

Money spent on marketing is the price that consumers pay for choice and convenience.

Individuals involved in marketing activities are called intermediaries.

Agents assist buyers and sellers. Wholesalers buy goods and sell them to retailers. Retailers sell goods and services directly to consumers.

ADVERTISING

Advertising is as old as the pyramids. In fact, when some of the slaves who were building the pyramids ran away, their masters posted signs to advertise for their return. That was three thousand years ago in ancient Egypt. Advertising of a more commercial sort was also known to the early Greeks. The following poem was painted on the wall surrounding ancient Athens:

> For eyes that are shining, for cheeks like the dawn,
> For beauty that lasts after girlhood is gone,
> For prices in reason, the woman who knows,
> Will buy her cosmetics of Aesclyptos.

During the Middle Ages criers told people of goods made by local merchants. You may be familiar with the nursery rhyme that goes:

> One-a-penny, two-a-penny, hot-cross buns!
> If you have no daughters give them to your sons.

Repeated by children for hundreds of years, this rhyme originated as a way for bakers to call attention to their products.

When producers and consumers lived and worked in the same community, advertising was simple and not too important. People knew where the bakeries were, who made the best bread and pastries, and how much they charged. But as markets developed, businesses started to sell their goods over a larger area—first in the next town and later in neighboring cities. Today, firms sell goods throughout the world. With growing markets came the need to advertise to make people aware of products.

The Cost of Advertising

In a modern economic system, advertising is an important activity. Each day, you see, hear, or read hundreds of advertisements. Each year, United States businesses spend more than $27 billion on advertising. This amounts to about $100 for every man, woman, and child in the country. Table 8-2 shows the amounts spent in 1985 by the top ten advertisers. It indicates that Procter & Gamble, a large maker of toothpaste, soap, and household products, spent nearly $2 billion on advertising in a single year. Procter & Gamble spent more on advertising in 1985 than some states spent on education.

Advertising makes consumers aware of products and tries to persuade them to buy the products.

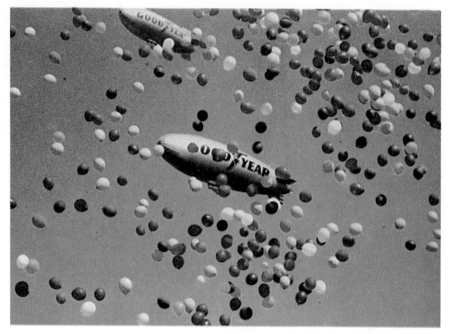

Photo courtesy of Goodyear Tire and Rubber Co.

TABLE 8-2

Rank	Company	Millions of Dollars
TOP TEN ADVERTISERS IN 1985		
1.	Procter & Gamble	$1,600
2.	Phillip Morris	1,400
3.	Nabisco Brands	1,093
4.	Sears, Roebuck	800
5.	General Motors	779
6.	Beatrice	684
7.	Ford Motor	615
8.	K mart	567
9.	McDonalds Corporation	550
10.	Anheuser-Busch	523

Source: *Advertising Age* (September 4, 1986), p.1

Advertising is intended to (1) make consumers aware of a product or service, (2) create a preference for it, and (3) cause people to buy the product or service. There are a number of ways a firm can advertise. Among the most important are newspapers, magazines, radio, and television. Table 8-3 shows the amount of money spent in the United States in 1985 for each type of advertising.

More advertising dollars were spent on television commercials than on the other three forms of advertising combined. Television is an important method of advertising, because consumers can both see and hear the message of the sponsor. The advantages of television are well known to those in the television industry. Although television is an effective medium for advertising, it is also very expensive. Commercial time on a popular show can cost over $150,000 per minute. During the Superbowl or some other special program, the price may approach $1 million per minute.

TABLE 8-3

DOLLARS SPENT IN THE UNITED STATES FOR ADVERTISING, 1985	
Type of Advertising	Millions of Dollars Spent
Newspapers	$ 4,030
Magazines	4,928
Radio	1,883
Television	15,836

Source: *Advertising Age* (September 4, 1986), p. 168.

Advertising: Good or Bad?

Advertising educates consumers about new products and changes in existing ones. Also, although advertising costs money, it can actually reduce the prices of goods and services. This reduction can happen in two ways. First, if the sales of a good increase, the company may be able to use more efficient methods to produce it. The lower cost of producing may more than offset the cost of advertising. Second, advertising can result in lower prices because of greater competition among firms. Eyeglasses are an interesting example. Until recently, many states had laws against advertising the prices of eyeglasses, because legislators feared that advertising would cause some consumers, fooled by low prices, to buy poor quality glasses. But a study showed that prices were much lower in states that allowed advertising and that there was no difference in quality. Clearly, the increase in competition resulting from advertising benefited consumers. Today, all states allow advertising of eyeglasses.

Some people are critical of advertising. They believe that money spent on advertising could be put to better use, such as producing safer and longer-lasting products. They argue that most advertisements provide little useful information for the consumer. Such critics suggest that the typical advertisement is full of half-truths and, sometimes, outright lies. They contend that modern advertisements are designed to appeal to a consumer's emotions.

Table 8-4 shows the results of a survey on advertising. It indicates the percentage of consumers who found advertisements to be informative, enjoyable, annoying, or offensive. You can see that the percentages vary for different products. For example, consumers viewed advertisements for food and food products and for automobiles as more informative and enjoyable than advertisements for tobacco products and alcoholic beverages.

TABLE 8-4

CONSUMER REACTIONS TO ADVERTISEMENTS

Type of Good	Informative	Enjoyable	Annoying	Offensive
Food and Food Products	31%	54%	14%	1%
Toilet Articles	31	35	31	3
Soaps and Cleansers	28	24	45	3
Tobacco Products	8	38	36	18
Soft Drinks	12	69	17	2
Alcoholic Beverages	5	50	22	23
Automobiles	48	31	20	1
Drugs	41	18	36	5

Clearly, advertising can inform the consumer and spark greater competition, thus producing lower prices. However, advertising may also confuse the consumer with conflicting claims about products. Perhaps the best conclusion is that advertising is a useful and necessary activity in a modern economic system, but there is room for improvement in the quality of the information provided.

Another important point about advertising concerns freedom of expression. Free speech is an important right guaranteed by the Constitution. Regulating advertising means restricting this freedom of expression. In the United States most people think that such control should be used only when absolutely necessary.

FINANCING

Producing and marketing goods and services is expensive. Business owners often have to pay their expenses before they can sell their products. Wholesalers have to pay producers when they buy the goods they intend to sell to retailers, and retailers have to replenish the stocks of goods that they sell to consumers. If expenses exceed the amount of money the business owners have available, the owners have to raise the money they need. The process of raising money to meet expenses is called **financing**, and it can be done in two ways. Business owners can borrow the money; this method is referred to as **debt financing**. Or they can sell parts of their business to one or more individuals. Selling a share of a business is called **equity financing**.

Debt Financing

Examples of debt financing include borrowing from a bank and selling bonds. Small firms typically rely on bank loans, whereas large companies borrow from banks and also sell bonds. Banks generally lend money to businesses for periods of one year or less, although loans for three to five years are not unusual. Bonds are usually sold for periods of ten to forty years.

Because a business may not know exactly when it will need the borrowed money, it may arrange for a **line of credit** from a bank. With this arrangement, the business can borrow part or all of a specified amount from the bank as the need arises. The borrower and the bank are saved the time and expense of having to arrange a new loan every time the firm needs money.

A **bond** is a printed promise to repay a certain amount of money, at a specified interest rate, at a certain time. Bonds are sold by corporations, by the federal government, and by state and local governments. The **principal** is the amount of money that the bonds are sold for initially, or the amount of money being borrowed from those who buy the bonds. Bonds usually are issued in $1,000 units and repayment of principal is due after a specified time period. Interest is paid each year. A company will try to sell as many $1,000 bonds as necessary to raise the needed money. For example, a company that needed to borrow $1 million would sell 1,000 bonds.

Bonds sold by firms can be purchased by individuals, banks, and other organizations. A person or organization that owns a bond is a **bondholder**. By buying the bond, the bondholder receives the interest that the bond earns each year. When the bond is due for repayment, the $1,000 principal of the bond is repaid to the bondholder.

Equity Financing

In Chapter 7 you learned that the owners of a corporation are called stockholders. When a new corporation starts up, the stockholders invest their money to get the business going. Later, the firm may need additional money. The managers of the business may decide to obtain that money by selling additional shares of stock. Those who buy this stock are providing money to be used by the business. In return, they receive part ownership of the business.

An individual's ownership in a corporation is determined by the proportion of all the shares of stock owned. For example, suppose Mr. and Mrs. Smith own 100,000 shares of stock in an oil company. If that company has sold 1 million shares of stock, the Smiths own 10 percent of the company.

Unlike bondholders, a stockholder does not receive a guaranteed income from the company. Instead, the stockholder's reward is the dividend paid by the corporation to its owners. A **dividend** is a portion of the corporation's profits that management sets aside for payment to the stockholders. Dividends usually are paid four times a year, or quarterly.

For example, management may decide to pay a dividend of $1 per share. The stockholders will receive $1 for each share of stock they own. The owner of 10,000 shares would receive $10,000. The owner of a single share would receive $1.

The dividend paid to stockholders can change, depending on the success of the company. If the company earns a large profit, manage-

Stocks are shares of ownership in a company.

ment may decide to increase the dividend to $1.25 per share. If the company does poorly, the dividend may be reduced to 75 cents per share. In a particularly bad year, the company might not pay any dividend at all. Some companies earn profits but do not pay dividends. Instead of paying dividends to stockholders, the profits are reinvested in the corporation. Companies that are growing rapidly often need large amounts of money to pay for new factories and increased numbers of employees. These growth companies often pay no dividend.

Stockholders do not get their money back from the company after a stated period, as bondholders do. However, when stockholders sell their shares, they may recover all of their investment plus something extra if the value of the stock has increased. The value of stock increases when a company establishes a good record for earning profits. The stock becomes more attractive to buyers, who are then willing to pay more for it. When stockholders sell shares of stock for more than they paid for them, the difference or bonus is called a **capital gain**. Of course, the value of a stock can also go down if a company does not prosper, and a stockholder who decides to sell shares may receive less than the purchase price. This decrease in stock value is referred to as a **capital loss**. In Chapter 17 you will learn more about how the value of a share of stock is determined and about how stocks are bought and sold.

Differences Between Equity and Debt Financing

Basically, bondholders (or banks) are the lenders to the corporation while stockholders are the owners. Both groups, of course, have provided money to the corporation and expect to earn a return on that money. Bondholders and banks have the first claim to a company's profits. The interest due on bonds and loans must be paid before any dividends can be paid to stockholders. If the money available is just enough to cover interest due bondholders, there can be no dividend paid to stockholders. The result is that bonds are a less-risky investment than stocks.

But bondholders will not receive more than the amount of interest specified by the bond. The corporation has a contract with the bondholders to repay them certain specified amounts on particular dates. However, there is no obligation to pay them any more than this amount. Even if the company is very successful and earns large profits, the interest paid to bondholders will not change. In contrast, stockholders will receive larger or smaller dividends depending on the success of the company.

Another difference between stocks and bonds is that, as owners, stockholders have a voice in the way the company is managed. As you learned in Chapter 7, stockholders can vote at annual stockholders' meetings. Usually the stockholders vote to elect the board of directors and to approve the hiring of an outside accounting firm, who will make sure that all financial reports are accurate. Occasionally, stockholders will bring up, or be asked to decide, issues of company policy or operations. Bondholders do not participate in annual meetings and, except in unusual cases, have no voice in the management of the corporation.

INSTANT REPLAY

Debt financing and equity financing are the two primary ways a business raises money.

Borrowing from a bank and selling bonds are the principal types of debt financing. Selling stock is the principal method of equity financing.

Stockholders are the owners of a business. Their rewards for investing in a business are dividends and capital gains.

Bankruptcy

When a business borrows money, there is a risk that it will not be able to repay the loan. Then the firm may go bankrupt. The term **bankruptcy** refers to a legal procedure that is used when a person or business is unable to repay the money it owes. When a firm declares bankruptcy, it places itself under the authority of a bankruptcy judge. The judge will give the company time to try to become profitable again so it can repay its debts. If it cannot recover, the judge makes sure that the company's remaining assets are divided fairly among its creditors. A **creditor** is someone who is owed money by the business. Creditors may include employees who have not been paid for work done, other businesses that have supplied materials which have not been paid for, and bondholders.

The bankruptcy judge will assign someone called a **trustee**, who will oversee the operation of the business. The trustee will attempt to reorganize the business so that it can become profitable again. Reorganization may mean cutting expenses, dropping unpopular product lines, cutting down on staff, selling equipment, and so on.

Bankruptcy court helps creditors recover some of the debts they are owed.

David Woo/STOCK BOSTON

The trustee also represents the creditors. Creditors provide the trustee with information about the amount owed, and they are reassured that efforts will be made to repay them. In addition, the trustee also keeps the creditors informed of the court's decisions. If a firm cannot become profitable after a reasonable time, it is sold and whatever money is left is paid to the creditors. Often the amount paid is only a fraction of what is owed. You may have heard a statement such as, "The creditors settled for 25 cents on the dollar." This statement means that the creditors received only 25 cents for every dollar owed to them.

The bankruptcy of a large business can affect thousands of people and take years to resolve. When the Pennsylvania Railroad went bankrupt several years ago, it owed millions of dollars to employees, suppliers, and federal, state, and local governments. Attempts were made to keep the railroad running. In fact, the government insisted that the trains keep running to provide service to communities along its tracks. The stockholders and creditors objected to the continuation of service because, by operating, the business lost even more money and reduced its chances of repaying the debts. Finally, the railroad was taken over by the government.

INSTANT REPLAY

The lenders to a business—banks and bond-holders—have first claim to a company's profits.

Individuals or businesses that cannot pay their debts may be forced into bankruptcy.

SUMMARY

Businesses always try to improve the methods and equipment they use to produce goods and services. Specialization of labor, mass production, use of capital goods, and automation are reasons that the United States economy is so productive. In such an economic system, businesses and workers are dependent on one another.

Marketing is the process of moving goods and services from their producers to consumers. Marketing accounts for about one-half the price of goods and services. The path a product takes to go from producer to consumer is called its channel of distribution. Those involved in marketing are called intermediaries. Agents, wholesalers, and retailers are all intermediaries. Agents assist others in buying and selling. Wholesalers buy from producers and resell to retailers. Retailers sell directly to consumers.

Three objectives of advertising are to (1) make consumers aware of a product or service, (2) create a preference for it, and (3) cause people to buy the product or service. If advertising increases the demand for a good, prices may decrease. On the other hand, advertising is costly and sometimes confusing.

Businesses often require money to pay expenses before they can earn a profit on their goods and services. Obtaining additional money is called financing. Borrowing is referred to as debt financing, and selling stock is called equity financing. Debt financing is obtained by borrowing from banks or by selling bonds. Equity financing means selling part of the business in the form of shares of stock. Stockholders are rewarded by receiving a dividend on each share of stock owned. Also, if the company is successful and profits increase, the value of the stock may increase; then stockholders receive a capital gain when they sell their shares. Interest payments on bonds are guaranteed, but dividends are paid only if profits are large enough to warrant the payment. Stockholders are owners of the business, whereas bondholders are lenders to the firm.

If a business fails to meet interest payments when they are due or to pay other debts, it may be forced into bankruptcy. This legal procedure may be necessary to protect the interests of both the bankrupt business and those who are owed money by the business.

================ ☆ LEARNING ACTIVITIES ☆ ================

Building Your Vocabulary

On a separate piece of paper, write the numbers 1 through 12. Next to each number, write the term that correctly completes the sentence.

mass production
assembly line
direct marketing
wholesalers
debt financing
equity financing
line of credit
bondholder
dividend
capital gain
bankruptcy
creditor

1. _____ occurs when a business raises money by borrowing from a bank or selling bonds.

2. A _____ is that part of a corporation's profits that is set aside for payment to the stockholders.

3. _____ occurs when a business sells shares of stock to raise money.

4. By opening a _____ with a bank, a firm may borrow money as necessary without having to take out a new loan each time.

5. The production of goods and services in large quantities using specialized labor is called _____ .

6. _____ occurs when producers sell their goods and services to consumers without the involvement of intermediaries.

7. When a business is not able to pay its debts, its creditors may force the firm into _____ .

8. A person who owns one or more bonds is called a _____ .

9. A person who is owed money by a business is a _____ of that business.

10. When the value of common stock increases, the stockholder has received a _____ .

11. An _____ moves a product under construction from one worker to another.

12. _____ are people who buy goods in large quantities to sell to retailers.

Reviewing the Facts

1. What are three reasons the American economic system can produce so much output?

2. What risks are there in an interdependent production system?

3. What is the difference between an agent and a wholesaler?

4. What are the three objectives of advertising?

5. How can advertising result in lower

prices?

6. What are the two types of financing?
7. What are two ways that a stockholder is rewarded?
8. What are two key differences between

holding stocks and holding bonds?

9. What are the two possible outcomes of a bankruptcy proceeding?
10. What are the duties of a bankruptcy trustee?

Expressing Your Opinion

1. What are some of the advantages of a production system based on specialized labor, mass production, and automation? Can you think of any disadvantages?
2. In this chapter you learned that marketing activities double the price of a record. Is this money wasted? What would happen if there were no marketing activities connected with the record?
3. Are newspapers and magazines more effective than television for some types

of advertising? Why?

4. Should the government provide money or loan guarantees to businesses that are losing money? Why or why not?
5. If you needed $10,000 to start a business, where could you get the money?
6. Do you think it is fair to allow a creditor to force the closing of a business and to take part of the firm's assets if the business has not paid its debts to the creditor? Explain.

Developing Your Attitudes, Values, and Skills

1. Watch half an hour of television. Make a list of the commercials that are shown on the channel you are watching. Note how long each commercial is, what product it advertises, and what audience you think the commercial is aimed at. For example, ads for toys are usually aimed at children. Ads for records try to attract young adults, while ads for insurance are geared to older people. Make a chart similar to Table 8-4, listing each commercial by product, and note whether you found the commercial to be enjoyable, informative, misleading or irritating. Rank the commercials on a scale of 1 to 10 (10 being most enjoyable; 1 would be least), and give your reasons for the rating. Also note whether or not you

already buy the product or think you would buy the product in the future. Do you think the ads have influenced your buying decisions? Why or why not?

2. Look up *bankruptcy* in the *Reader's Guide to Periodical Literature* to identify the name of a company that has recently filed for bankruptcy or has completed bankruptcy proceedings. Then study any magazine or newspaper articles you can find about the company. Try to determine why the company filed for bankruptcy. Did it guess wrong about the popularity of a new product? Did it lose a lawsuit over a product? Did it suffer too many losses during a recession? Who were its major creditors? If the bankruptcy proceedings have been completed, did the company recover its

profitability or were its assets sold? If its assets were sold, how much did its creditors receive on the dollar? Be prepared to give a brief oral report answering these questions in class.

3. Choose one business in your community. Identify all the other businesses this business depends on. For instance, a grocery store relies on banks, delivery companies, distributors, newspapers, farms, manufacturers, and so on. What would happen to the business you chose if one of the businesses it depends on were to fail? Present your conclusions in a short written report.

FOCUS YOUR READING

What is a right-to-work law? Is there such a law in your state?

In addition to higher wages, what other goals do labor unions have?

What percentage of workers receive a paid vacation?

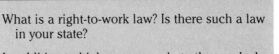

CHAPTER 9

ORGANIZED LABOR

PREVIEW

A *labor union* is a group of workers who have organized to improve their wages and work conditions. About 18 million Americans, nearly one-fifth of all nonfarm employees, are union members. In some large industries such as automobile manufacturing, steel making, and coal mining, almost all the workers belong to a union.

Union supporters argue that unions are necessary to assure that workers are treated fairly by the owners of businesses. Opponents, however, often suggest that unions cause inflation because they force the payment of higher wages and make it difficult for firms to adopt efficient methods of production. Opponents also claim that strikes by union members can cause serious problems in the economic system.

In this chapter you will learn about labor unions in the United States. When you have completed the reading material and learning activities, you should be able to:

★ Discuss the history of organized labor in the United States.

★ List and explain the important laws that affect unions.

★ Describe the organization of labor unions.

★ List the main goals of unions.

★ Explain how collective bargaining works and how workers and employers can be affected by a strike.

A SHORT HISTORY OF ORGANIZED LABOR

Organized labor can be traced to the early 1800s and the Industrial Revolution. The **Industrial Revolution** was the period when machines were first widely used to increase efficiency and cut costs in manufacturing. For example, cloth making was dramatically changed when power-driven looms replaced those run by hand.

With the Industrial Revolution came large factories. Workers in these factories often were required to work 12-hour days, seven days a week. Some of the machines were dangerous, and serious accidents occurred. Wages were low, but workers who complained could easily be replaced by unemployed people eager for jobs.

To improve their working conditions, many of the workers organized to form small unions. These unions greatly increased the bargaining power of their members. However, some union leaders wanted a single labor organization that could speak for all workers. Responding to this

During the Industrial Revolution, many children were required to work long hours for little pay, often around dangerous machinery.

THE BETTMANN ARCHIVE

idea, Samuel Gompers founded the American Federation of Labor (AFL) in 1881. The AFL was an organization of craft unions. A **craft union** organizes workers who have particular skills. For example, one craft union might be made up of carpenters; another, of bricklayers.

For 50 years the AFL was the leading labor organization in the United States. Then, during the depression years of the 1930s, some AFL leaders wanted to broaden the membership by including members of industrial unions. An **industrial union** includes all the workers in an industry. For example, all mine workers, regardless of their particular skill, can belong to an industrial union such as the United Mine Workers.

A bitter disagreement resulted, and in 1938 a competing national labor organization was formed. It was called the Congress of Industrial Organizations (CIO). From 1938 to 1955, the AFL and the CIO existed as rival labor organizations. This rivalry created many problems. Sometimes strikes resulted, not because workers were dissatisfied with their employers, but because there were conflicts between the AFL and the CIO. In 1955 peace was achieved, and the two groups joined to form the **AFL-CIO**. Today, the majority of all union members are part of this organization.

LAWS AFFECTING ORGANIZED LABOR

The owners of businesses often opposed the growth of unions. Many employers believed that it was their right, and theirs alone, to make decisions about their workers. For example, in 1902 during a strike of mine workers, the owners of the mines asserted that

> The rights and interests of the laboring man will be protected and cared for—not by the labor agitators, but by the Christian men whom God in His infinite wisdom has given control of the property interests in this country.

Many employers simply refused to talk with union leaders. When union leaders directed their members to strike, managers accused them of breaking the law. In some cases, the courts agreed that the activities of the labor leaders were illegal. A number of union officials were put in jail. Others lost their jobs because of their involvement with the union. Unions had to fight their employers and the courts. As a result, American organized labor had a difficult time in its early years.

National Labor Relations Act

During the Great Depression, many people were unable to find jobs. As a result, Congress became more aware of the problems of workers and passed laws to help unions. One of the most important was the National Labor Relations Act of 1935. The **National Labor Relations Act**, often referred to as the Wagner Act, guaranteed employees the right to form a union. It also required employers to negotiate contracts with union representatives.

In addition, the **National Labor Relations Board** (NLRB) was set up to enforce the law. Union members can appeal to the NLRB if employers refuse to recognize them or bargain with them. The NLRB also steps in when two rival unions try to organize a company's workers and the company cannot decide which one to recognize. The general purpose of the NLRB is to act as a watchdog over labor-business relations. It assures that neither business nor labor violates the law.

Taft-Hartley Act

In the years just after World War II, there were a number of strikes in important industries. The problems created by these strikes caused many people to think that unions had become too powerful. As a result, the **Taft-Hartley Act** was passed in 1948 to limit the power of organized labor. This act allows the President of the United States to delay a strike if the President thinks the strike would cause serious problems for the nation. For example, a national railroad strike could affect supplies of fuel and food throughout the entire country. The Taft-Hartley Act gives the President the right to order striking workers back on the job for 80 days. This cooling-off period provides time for labor and management to settle their differences. *Strike after 80 days*

Another provision of the Taft-Hartley Act makes closed shops illegal. A **closed shop** is a place of business that hires only union members. This practice is considered to be unfair because it would reduce job opportunities for workers who are not union members.

Only hired if belong to union

Union shops are related to closed shops. In a **union shop**, non-union workers can be hired, but they must join the union within a short time after starting work. Opponents argue that such shops limit the right of individuals to decide whether they want to be a part of organized labor. However, defenders of this system argue that since all workers benefit from union bargaining, all should contribute to the union. Otherwise, they claim, the non-affiliated workers receive benefits without paying for them.

The Taft-Hartley Act did not outlaw the union shop, but it gave individual states the right to outlaw this practice. A state law that outlaws union shops is called a **right-to-work law**. At present, 21 states have right-to-work laws (see Figure 9-1).

Notice that most of the states that have right-to-work laws are in the

South and West. The reason is that states in the Midwest and the East have many union members. These members have succeeded in preventing right-to-work laws from being passed. The debate over passage of these laws often has been a very emotional issue.

FIGURE 9-1
States with right-to-work laws are shown in color on the map. Does your state have such a law?

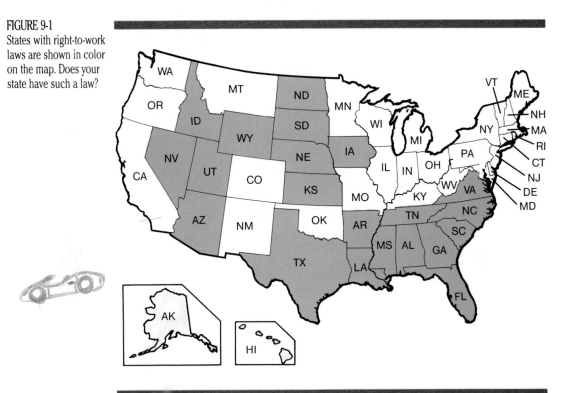

INSTANT REPLAY

Craft unions organize workers with particular skills; industrial unions organize workers by industry.

Most union members in the United States belong to the AFL-CIO.

The National Labor Relations Act gave unions the right to organize, while the Taft-Hartley Act limited the power of unions.

Twenty-one states have right-to-work laws that outlaw union shops. Closed shops were prohibited by the Taft-Hartley Act.

UNION ORGANIZATION IN THE UNITED STATES

Figure 9-2 shows changes in union membership in the United States from 1870 to 1986. Unions grew rapidly between 1935 and 1955. But since 1955, union membership as a percentage of the labor force has declined.

Local Unions

A worker's closest involvement with a union is at the local level. The individual's union membership is with the local union, and dues are paid at this level. Local union members must vote to approve contracts, and the leaders of the local union sign them.

FIGURE 9-2
The percentage of workers who are union members has declined since 1954.

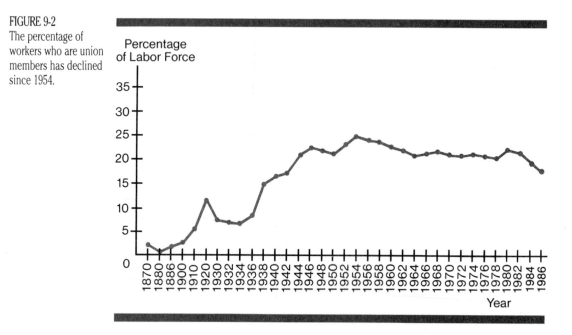

There are about 80,000 local unions in the United States. Some have as few as a dozen members. At the other extreme, employees of the Ford Motor Company in Detroit belong to a United Auto Workers local union with 30,000 members. However, most local unions have between 50 and 1,000 members.

National Unions

National unions represent workers in a particular craft or industry. There are about 200 national unions in the United States. The largest is the Teamsters Union with nearly 2 million members. It consists primarily of workers who drive trucks or other vehicles. There are 12 national unions with at least 500,000 members.

An important responsibility of the officers of a national union is to negotiate contracts. A union contract is a written agreement that lists the terms of work, such as wages, work hours, and job responsibilities.

AFL-CIO

The AFL-CIO acts as a central voice for organized labor. It consists of national unions which, in turn, consist of local unions. Figure 9-3 shows the relationship between the AFL-CIO, national unions, and local unions.

FIGURE 9-3
The AFL-CIO consists of national unions which, in turn, consist of local unions.

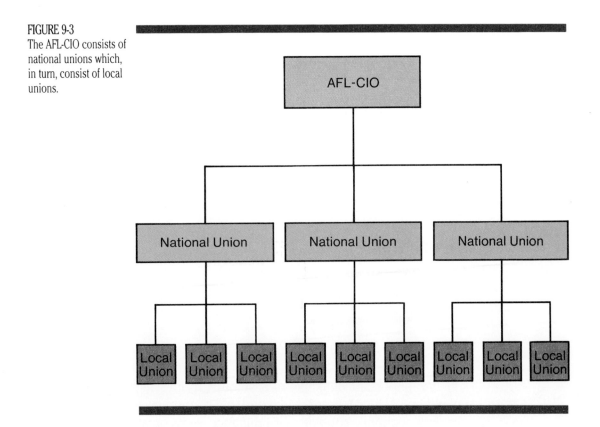

The AFL-CIO coordinates and supports the activities of the national unions. But its direct control over union members is limited. One goal of the AFL-CIO is to improve the image of unions. The organization also works to elect political candidates who are likely to vote for legislation that will benefit union members.

Most national unions are part of the AFL-CIO. However, some large unions, such as the United Mine Workers and the Teamsters, are not. These organizations are referred to as **independent unions**.

> ## INSTANT REPLAY
>
> A worker's membership is with a local union. The national union negotiates contracts that must be approved by the members of the local unions.
>
> The AFL-CIO acts as a national voice for organized labor. It attempts to influence government policies to benefit union members.

GOALS OF UNIONS

The general objective of organized labor is to improve the economic conditions of its members. This broad goal can be separated into six issues that are included in almost all union contracts. Unions attempt to negotiate contracts with the most favorable terms possible in each of the following areas:

KNOW

- ★ Wages
- ★ Fringe benefits
- ★ Work hours
- ★ Work conditions
- ★ Job opportunities
- ★ Grievance procedures

MEMORIZE

Wages

An important objective of a union is to increase the wages of its members. Wage increases depend on a number of factors. One is general economic conditions. During recessions or when a firm's profits

are low, employers may be unable to pay higher wages. Another factor is wages in the geographic area where the union members work. If wages of union workers are lower than those of other workers in that region of the country, then a wage increase can be justified. But if union wages are high compared with the wages of other workers in the region, employers will be less willing to grant an increase.

Fringe Benefits

Fringe benefits are benefits that workers receive in addition to their wages or salaries. Examples of fringe benefits are paid vacation, medical and dental insurance, life insurance, and retirement programs. In many contract discussions there is a trade-off between higher wages and more fringe benefits. Employers will provide more fringe benefits only if the workers are willing to reduce their demands for wage increases.

During the past 20 years, fringe benefits have become more important to union members. In 1960 employers paid 21 cents in fringe benefits for every dollar of wages paid. By 1986 the cost had nearly doubled to 37 cents for each dollar of wages. Table 9-1 shows the proportion of workers who received various fringe benefits in a recent year. It indicates that paid vacations and medical insurance are the most common benefits.

TABLE 9-1

FRINGE BENEFITS FOR WORKERS

Fringe Benefit	Percentage of Workers Receiving the Benefit
Paid Vacation	80%
Medical Insurance	78
Retirement Program	67
Life Insurance Policy	64
Sick Leave	63
Training Programs to Improve Skills	49

Work Hours

A major achievement of unions has been the establishment of the eight-hour work day. Work hours are still of great interest to most unions. Where wages are high, contract discussions involve reducing the number of work hours. In other cases, questions about the timing of

Paid vacations are a common fringe benefit available to workers today.

Florida Department of Commerce

work may be considered. These include when the work day should start and end, the amount of time allowed for lunch, and the number and length of breaks.

Work Conditions

Union leaders are concerned about the health and safety of their members. Contracts negotiated by these leaders may require that the workplace be clean, well-lighted, and neither too warm nor too cold. It may prohibit the employer from using dangerous chemicals or unsafe machines. The contract may also spell out in detail the specific responsibilities of different jobs. For example, the duties of welders and machinists may be carefully defined to prevent disagreements about who should do a particular task.

Job Opportunities

The success of a union is closely related to the number of jobs available for its members. If the demand for union labor declines, some members may lose their jobs. Unions use three main tactics to protect members' jobs. First, they attempt to increase the demand for products made by the union members. Demand may be increased in a number of ways. For instance, you may have seen advertisements that urge consumers to buy union-made products. Unions that represent garment workers have paid for advertisements telling people to "look for the union label." The message is that you should buy clothes that have been made only by union members.

Another way to increase demand for union-made goods is to discourage purchase of nonunion goods. Unions have often urged politicians to pass laws that limit the number of cars, televisions, and other products imported from other countries. If fewer goods are available from other countries, more American-made goods will be bought.

A second tactic for protecting union jobs is to make sure that union members have the first chance at new employment opportunities. Unions can accomplish this goal by negotiating contracts that give preference to union members. For example, union shops give union members an advantage in getting jobs.

Finally, unions protect their members by resisting changes that would reduce demand for union labor. For example, commercial air flights usually include a pilot, co-pilot, and flight engineer in the cockpit. However, airlines are now purchasing new models of aircraft that can fly with two-member crews—a pilot and co-pilot. But the union that represents the engineers argues that three crew members are necessary. The union leaders are probably concerned about safety, but the loss of jobs for flight engineers is also an important concern.

Unions seek to increase job opportunities for members.

H. Armstrong Roberts, Inc.

Grievance Procedures

Grievance procedures are a way of resolving disputes between individual workers and their employers. A worker who has a problem can go to a union officer or representative and make a complaint. This is called *filing a grievance.* The complaint may be that a worker has been fired or disciplined, or that the worker has been asked to make an unwelcome change in hours, shifts, or other working conditions.

Grievance procedures are usually spelled out in union contracts. Sometimes a grievance can be resolved informally at a meeting between the union's representatives and the worker's immediate supervisors. Other times, the grievance procedure requires a formal hearing before a panel consisting of union members and management. For example, employees who have been fired may believe that they lost their jobs, not because they were poor workers, but because their supervisors disliked them. They may ask for a hearing at which the supervisors must explain the reasons for the firing. If the hearing indicates that the employees were treated unfairly, they are likely to get their jobs back. If either union members or employers are not satisfied with the results of the hearing, there may be other grievance procedures they can use. In extreme cases, workers may ask for help from the National Labor Relations Board.

INSTANT REPLAY

Six issues of interest to unions are wages, fringe benefits, work hours, work conditions, job opportunities, and grievance procedures.

Unions try to increase job opportunities by promoting union-made products and resisting changes that would eliminate jobs.

Grievance procedures provide a way for labor and management to work out disputes.

UNIONS IN ACTION

Suppose you work at a place where workers are not represented by a union. After thinking about your wages and work hours, you decide that a union might be able to help you and your co-workers. What would you do to establish one?

To get union representation, workers in a business tell the National Labor Relations Board that they are considering organizing a union.

Officials of the NLRB then supervise an election. Every worker is allowed to vote for or against the proposed union. If a majority of workers favor the union, it then has the right to represent employees in contract negotiations and other discussions with the employer.

Once the union has been approved, the next step is to set a time for negotiating a contract. Discussions about contracts are called **collective bargaining**, because the union leaders negotiate contract terms on behalf of all the members of the union. On the day of negotiations, representatives of the union and of management meet and present their proposals. Typically, the union believes that management's offers are not enough. The management team usually thinks that the union is demanding too much. The two teams then bargain until they can reach an agreement acceptable to both groups.

If the two sides cannot come to an agreement, the union leaders may decide to call a strike. A **strike** occurs when the members of a union decide to stop working in an attempt to force management to negotiate a contract favorable to the union. Often striking workers will set up picket lines around their place of employment. A **picket line** is a group of strikers who march at the company's gates or doors, usually wearing or carrying signs announcing that they are on strike. Picket lines call attention to the strike and attempt to discourage people from doing business with the company. Other company employees who are not members of the union and people who want to do business with the

A picket line calls attention to a strike and discourages others from doing business with the company.

Martin M. Rotker/Taurus Photos, Inc.

company must decide whether to cross through the line of marchers to get to the company's offices or plants.

A strike hurts both the employees and the employer. The workers lose their wages. And although workers may receive money from their union, such funds are limited. At the same time, the owners of the business can no longer produce their products. True, the employer does not have to pay the workers. But payments still have to be made for overhead expenses, such as rent or interest on borrowed money. As a result, an employer can suffer a large loss because of a strike.

A strike is a test of nerves, with both sides contending to see which can hold out longest. The union hopes the company will become desperate and give in to its demands. The employer may be waiting until the union members have used all their savings and must come back to work. Eventually a compromise is reached and a new contract is signed. Often, however, one side will have to compromise more than the other; usually it is the side that has the most to lose if the strike continues.

Discussions between union and management negotiators can be long, complicated, and heated. However, they usually result in an agreement without a strike. In fact, of the 100,000 contracts that are negotiated each year, less than 5 percent involve a strike. During the past 25 years, the time lost from strikes has amounted to only about three minutes per workday. More workdays are lost each year by employees who stay home with colds than from strikes.

Death of a Union

Air traffic controllers are responsible for guiding airplanes in and out of crowded airports. They have a very difficult job because a mistake could cause a collision in which hundreds of lives are lost. Until 1981, these workers had their own union, the Professional Air Traffic Controllers Organization (PATCO).

Air traffic controllers are employed by the federal government. In 1981 PATCO leaders called a strike, because the government would not meet the union's demands for an increase in wages. Strikes by federal employees are illegal, so President Reagan told the controllers that those who did not return to work within 48 hours would be fired. He also took steps to strip PATCO of its right to represent controllers.

Most of the workers stayed on strike and were fired. Their responsibilities were assumed by supervisors and military air traffic controllers. The government rushed to train new controllers. Although the number of airline flights had to be reduced, most airline passengers experienced little inconvenience.

As for PATCO, it was unable to successfully challenge the President's action. As a result, it disappeared as a union.

However, using nationwide averages can be misleading. The impact of a strike on individual businesses and workers can be serious. Some businesses never recover from a long strike and are forced out of business. On the other side, some strikers may spend years trying to regain the income lost during a strike. In most cases, a strike is something that neither the company nor the union wants.

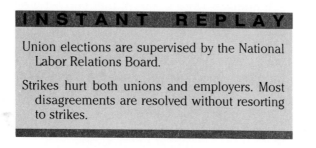

INSTANT REPLAY

Union elections are supervised by the National Labor Relations Board.

Strikes hurt both unions and employers. Most disagreements are resolved without resorting to strikes.

SUMMARY

About 18 million Americans belong to unions. Craft unions organize workers with a particular skill. Industrial unions organize all the workers in an industry. The AFL-CIO acts as a voice for organized labor. It is made up of national unions which, in turn, are made up of local unions.

The National Labor Relations Act gave unions a legal right to exist. It also set up the National Labor Relations Board. The NLRB's job is to make sure that labor and management deal fairly with each other.

The Taft-Hartley Act restricts the power of unions. It allows the President to delay strikes that would cause serious national problems. It also outlaws closed shops and gives states the right to pass right-to-work laws, which prohibit union shops. Closed shops require workers to be union members to get a job in a particular place of business. Union shops require workers to join the union after getting the job.

The general goal of a union is to improve the economic conditions of its members. Wages, fringe benefits, work hours, work conditions, job opportunities, and grievance procedures are areas of importance to unions.

A union gains the right to represent workers in contract negotiations as a result of an election conducted by the National Labor Relations Board. Once a union is approved, the next step is the negotiation of a contract. If labor and management cannot agree, the union may call a strike. Striking workers sometimes picket the place where they work. Most contract disagreements are settled without a strike, but a long strike can cause serious problems for both employers and union members.

★ LEARNING ACTIVITIES ★

Building Your Vocabulary

On a separate piece of paper, write the numbers 1 through 11. Next to each number, write the term that correctly completes the sentence.

Industrial Revolution
craft union
industrial union
AFL-CIO
National Labor Relations Act
Taft-Hartley Act
union shop
right-to-work laws
collective bargaining
strike
picket line

1. A law that prohibits closed shops is the _____.

2. The _____ is an organization made up of national unions.

3. Machines became widely used in manufacturing during the _____.

4. A union consisting of workers with a particular skill is called a _____.

5. State _____ prohibit union shops.

6. When workers agree to stop working, a _____ occurs.

7. A _____ is the name given to a group of workers marching in front of a business to call attention to their demands.

8. A workplace where new employees must agree to join a union soon after beginning work is called a _____.

9. A union that includes all the workers in a given industry is called an _____.

10. Another name for contract negotiations between management and representatives of a group of workers is _____.

11. The _____ is a law that gave unions the right to represent workers.

Reviewing the Facts

1. What was the Industrial Revolution, and how did it affect the development of unions?

2. Is the United Auto Workers Union a craft union or an industrial union?

3. Which law gave unions the right to exist and to bargain with employers?

4. What are the two major provisions of the Taft-Hartley Act that limit the power of unions?

5. What is a union shop, and how do right-to-work laws affect it?

6. What role does the AFL-CIO play in the labor movement?

7. What are the six common objectives of unions?

8. Why do unions sometimes picket businesses?

Expressing Your Opinion

1. Should public employees such as police officers and fire fighters be allowed to strike? Why or why not?
2. Unions often argue that promotions should be based on seniority. Do you agree? Why or why not?
3. If a business is losing money, should union members be willing to work for lower wages? Why or why not?
4. Should people buy goods and services from a business that is being picketed? Would you cross a union picket line?
5. Are right-to-work laws fair? Why or why not?
6. How do you think workers and employers determine salaries, fringe benefits, and work conditions at a company that has no labor unions?

Developing Your Attitudes, Values, and Skills

1. There are many arguments both for and against organized labor. Assume that you have been appointed to a debate team that is to argue either the pro or con side of the issue: Resolved, labor unions have outlived their usefulness in the United States. Choose the side of the issue you prefer, and read recent books and magazine articles to locate points to bolster your argument. Try to anticipate the points that the opposing side might present. If you have difficulty locating information, the AFL-CIO and National Right-to-Work Committee can provide supporting details from their respective viewpoints. The AFL-CIO is located at 815 16th Street, NW, Washington, D.C. 20006, and the National Right-to-Work Committee is located at 8001 Braddock Road, Springfield, VA 22160. Be prepared to present at least one argument for or against organized labor in class discussion.
2. The history of the labor movement in the United States has been at times exciting, colorful, and violent. It has added the names of many influential and controversial labor leaders to the pages of American history. A few of these include Eugene V. Debs, Samuel Gompers, John L. Lewis, Walter Reuther, Mary Harris "Mother" Jones, George Meany, Bessie Abramowitz Hillman, and Cesar Chavez. Pick one of these labor leaders to study. Find out what conditions or events caused the workers to unionize or what contribution the labor leader made to organized labor. Write a brief biography of the labor leader you have chosen.
3. You can find out a great deal about labor unions by interviewing one or two union members. Find out what company or industry employs them and what unions they belong to. How many members belong to their local union? Were they required to join the union, or did they choose to join? What do they do in their union meetings? If their union has recently participated in contract negotiations, ask them what issues divided management and labor, and how those issues were resolved. How much are monthly union dues? Have

they ever filed a grievance? How was it resolved? What do they think are the benefits and drawbacks of belonging to a union? Have they ever participated in a strike? If so, how long did it last? How did they pay their bills and take care of their families during the strike? Did they take part in picketing? How did they react when people crossed the lines? Which side gave in first to end the strike? Do they feel they benefited from the strike, or would they rather avoid a strike over similar issues in the future? Prepare a brief written report based on your interviews.

UNIT 4

★ **Government, Business, and the Individual**

★ **Banking and the Federal Reserve System**

★ **Taxes**

★ **Government and the Economy**

Washington D.C. Convention and Visitors Association

Government plays an important role in the United States economic system. In this unit you will learn about government regulation of banking and the organization and function of the Federal Reserve System. You will identify how government protects consumers, workers, and the environment. You will also learn about different taxes, examine the government's budget, and evaluate monetary and fiscal policies.

Your neighbors will not pay you the $25 they owe
you for work that you did for them. How could
a small claims court help you get your money?

Who decides how much your family will have to
pay for electricity?

How are consumers protected against false
advertising?

CHAPTER 10

GOVERNMENT, BUSINESS, AND THE INDIVIDUAL

PREVIEW

In most circumstances, the free enterprise system does a good job of meeting people's needs and wants. But there are situations in which government can improve the operation of the economic system. For example, in a free enterprise system a business may find that the least expensive way to produce products is to dump wastes into a nearby lake. The result may be water so filthy that nothing can survive in it. Government can help preserve the quality of this natural resource by forcing the firm to reduce its pollution of the lake.

Government affects businesses and individuals in hundreds of ways. Only a few are discussed here.

In this chapter you will learn about some of the most important functions of government. When you have completed the reading material and the learning activities, you should be able to:

★ Discuss how government acts as a referee in the economic system.

★ Define what is meant by antitrust and public utility regulation.

★ Explain how government protects consumers from unsafe products and false advertising.

★ Describe how government protects workers against unsafe and unfair working conditions.

182

★ Explain why government help may be needed to protect the environment.

★ Discuss the benefits and costs of government regulation.

GOVERNMENT AS A REFEREE

Imagine being in a boxing match without a referee. Although you would undoubtedly fight within the rules, your opponent might use illegal tactics, such as gouging, kicking, and biting. Without a referee to enforce the rules, you would be at a serious disadvantage.

It is equally important to have a referee in the economic system. Someone or some group must have the power to set and enforce rules of fair behavior. Otherwise, people would spend much of their time and money protecting themselves against unfair practices.

Government acts as a referee in the economic system. Laws are passed stating what individuals and businesses can and cannot do. Once these laws are passed, judges, the police, and other officials make

The government acts like a referee, enforcing the rules and settling arguments.

H. Armstrong Roberts, Inc.

sure that they are enforced. The following are examples of government's role as a referee.

Protecting Individuals Against Theft and Violence

Suppose that some people come to your house and steal your car. You ask them to return it, but they refuse. At this point, if there were no governmental referee, you could either let them have the car or try to get it back by force. Although you have a right to your car, force is not a good solution. If everyone tried to solve problems by force, our society would become a war zone.

An important duty of government is to protect people against theft and violence. Laws have been passed making activities such as car theft illegal. The police can enforce those laws and help you get your car back. A judge and jury have the power to decide how to punish the thieves.

Enforcing Contracts

Another of the government's referee functions is to enforce contracts. A **contract** is an agreement between two or more people. It specifies that one person or group will do certain things and that another person or group will do other things in return. Sometimes the contract may be nothing more than an oral agreement between two people. For example, if you offer to mow your neighbor's lawn for $10 and the neighbor accepts, a contract exists between you and that person.

If the terms of a contract are complicated or if large sums of money are involved, a written contract usually is used. A written contract includes the date, the specifics of what is to be done, and the amount of money to be paid. Once the parties agree on all these matters, they complete the contract by signing it.

For example, the managers of an airline might enter into a contract to buy four airplanes from a manufacturer for $100 million. Based on the signed contract, the manufacturer proceeds to build the airplanes. This decision would involve spending a great deal of money to purchase materials and to pay workers.

Suppose that the airline decides that it no longer wants the finished planes. The manufacturer would be left with four unsold airplanes and millions of dollars in bills. Unless there is some way to require the airline to honor the contract, the manufacturer could face serious financial losses.

Government also makes sure that businesses and individuals abide by the contracts that they sign. The manufacturer could take the airline to court. If the manufacturer proves its case, the judge can then issue a court order compelling the airline to honor the contract. Then the airline would have to pay the manufacturer for the planes. The court could also require the airline to pay all the costs of bringing the matter to court.

Resolving Honest Disagreements

In a boxing match, a referee may be necessary to prevent biting, which is clearly against the rules. However, sports referees also must make more difficult decisions. For example, the difference between a blocking foul and a charging foul in basketball is sometimes hard to determine. Each player may sincerely believe that it was the other player who fouled. The role of the referee is to make a fair decision based on what he or she sees.

Honest disagreements occur in the economic system as well as in sports. Usually the people involved can work out the problem by themselves. But sometimes they may be unable to come to an agreement. In these cases, government can serve as a referee and resolve the dispute.

Consider the developer of computer software who believes that another company has unfairly copied its program. The other business may argue that its product is much different from that of the first company. The managers of both businesses may honestly believe that they are right. As a result, it may be impossible for the two firms to resolve their disagreement. The only solution may be to take the matter to court and to let a judge or jury decide. Once the verdict is issued, the court must make sure that both parties abide by the court's terms. Those who violate a court order may be fined or put in prison.

Resolving honest disagreements in the court system can be expensive. A large corporation may spend millions of dollars on lawyers and research before a case is finally decided. However, many of the disagreements between individuals involve relatively small amounts of money. When the amount is less than $1,000 (the exact limit differs by state), there usually is an easy and inexpensive way to settle disputes. The disagreeing parties can take the matter to a small claims court.

In a **small claims court** the parties to the disagreement present their arguments before a judge. Usually no lawyers are involved and there is only a small fee for bringing the case to court. The judge makes a decision and issues an order that both parties must abide by. This order may involve paying a sum of money, completing a job, or delivering a product that has been purchased.

The Case of Marshall Vs Clemente

John Marshall bought a used trampoline from his neighbor, Marsha Clemente. The agreement called for Marshall to pay $150 when he took the trampoline and another $150 a month later. After two months, Marshall still had not made the second payment. Clemente went to his house and asked for her money. Marshall told her that the mat on the trampoline had ripped and that he had no intention of making the second payment on a defective product.

Clemente then asked Marshall to return the trampoline. Marshall said that he would when he got his $150 back. But Clemente argued that she should keep the money to pay for repairing the mat. Unable to get either the trampoline or the second $150, Clemente paid a $15 filing fee and took the case to small claims court.

At the trial, Marshall and Clemente presented their sides of the story to the judge. The judge asked questions, looked at photographs of the trampoline, and then announced a decision. Because Marshall had an opportunity to inspect and use the trampoline before he took it, the judge's verdict favored Clemente. Marshall was given the choice of paying the second $150 or returning the trampoline. The total time spent in court was about 20 minutes.

INSTANT REPLAY

Government acts as a referee in the economic system. This service reduces the need for people to spend time and money protecting their lives and property.

A contract is an agreement between two or more people. The courts can compel individuals or firms to abide by the terms of a contract.

The courts can be used to settle honest disagreements. Small claims courts are designed to help individuals settle problems involving small amounts of money.

GOVERNMENT AND COMPETITION

In Chapter 5 you learned that the benefits of competition include lower prices, a greater variety of goods and services, and products of a higher quality. In contrast, if firms do not face competition, the consumer usually does not receive the best service or value for the money. An important role of government is to promote competition between businesses. Antitrust laws are used for this purpose. But where competition is not possible, government may protect the consumer by regulating the activities of firms in an industry.

Antitrust

Antitrust laws are designed to increase the amount of competition between firms. They also prevent companies from dealing unfairly with consumers or other companies. Some antitrust laws focus on the size of firms; others deal with the way firms conduct their businesses.

Antitrust and Size. In Chapter 5 you learned that companies that have market power have little need to compete. Monopolies have considerable market power. As the single seller of a good or service, a monopoly is free from the need to compete at all. As a result, consumers usually pay a high price for the product. Even when a firm is not a monopoly, it may be so much larger than the other firms in an industry that it controls the market for that industry. The other companies in the same industry simply cannot compete with it. Antitrust laws allow the government to break up large corporations that do not face much competition.

A recent example is the American Telephone & Telegraph Co. For many years AT&T provided both local and long distance telephone service to most of the United States. But in 1982 the federal government announced that the firm was to be split into several smaller companies. The parent company, AT&T, would continue to provide long distance telephone service, while the other firms would supply local service in their geographic areas.

It is much easier to prevent a firm from becoming too large than it is to break one up. Mergers are one way that firms grow. A **merger** occurs when two or more firms combine to form a new company. Antitrust laws can be used to prevent mergers. If the government decides that a merger would result in a new firm that has too much market power, government lawyers can go to court to stop the merger. If the courts agree, the merger will not be allowed.

Antitrust and Conduct. Competition keeps prices low as firms try to win sales from one another. However, the managers of some companies try to avoid competing. They get together with the other firms in the industry and decide to set the same price for the good or service. This tactic is called **price fixing.** Consumers are the losers, because they must pay more than they would if the firms were actively competing.

People have a greater choice of long-distance telephone service now that the government has split up AT&T.

Philip John Bailey/Jeroboam, Inc.

Price fixing is illegal. Firms that engage in this practice can be fined, and the managers involved can be sent to jail. In addition, people who pay high prices for the product can sue the guilty parties. In some cases, firms convicted of price fixing have been required to pay millions of dollars in damages to consumers and to other firms.

Regulation

In most cases, competition between firms is good for consumers, because it keeps prices down. However, there is at least one situation in which society may be better off without competition. In Chapter 5 you learned that economies of scale sometimes allow larger firms to produce at a lower cost. In some industries the advantage of economies of scale may be so great that a single firm is the most efficient choice.

The electric utility industry is a good example. Suppose that two electric companies provided electricity in your community. Each would have to string wires to serve its customers. Two sets of wires would run down many streets. Since there would be duplicate wiring, the total cost would be much greater than if just one electric company served the city. Thus, in most cities a single firm is responsible for providing electricity.

The problem with having just one electric company in a community is that the business faces no competition. There are no other firms to force its prices down. And since electricity is necessary in a modern society, consumers would have no choice but to pay high electric bills.

A single firm is the most efficient way of producing electricity. But the efficiency advantage may be lost if the firm sets a high price because of a lack of competition. How can this dilemma be solved?

The United States addresses the problem by regulating public utilities. A **public utility** is a business that provides an important good or service and for which economies of scale allow a single firm to be most efficient. Local telephone, natural gas, water, and electric companies are examples of public utilities.

In most states public utility regulation is the job of the state **public service commission,** or **public utility commission.** The members of these commissions are either appointed by the governor of the state or elected by the voters. The most important responsibility of the public service commission is to set the prices that public utilities are allowed to charge. The goal is to provide a fair profit to stockholders while keeping prices as low as possible. The utility, consumers, and other groups are allowed to present evidence to the commission when it is determining prices. The members of the commission must then examine the evidence and determine a fair price.

INSTANT REPLAY

Antitrust laws are used by government to increase competition between firms. They can be used to break up monopolies, prevent mergers, and punish price fixers.

Public utilities are firms that provide an important good or service and for which economies of scale allow a single firm to be most efficient.

Prices of electricity, natural gas, and local telephone service are regulated by state public service or public utility commissions.

GOVERNMENT AND CONSUMER PROTECTION

The operation of the free enterprise system offers consumers protection against shoddy or unsafe products. Competition forces firms to provide high quality goods and services. Companies that consistently supply inferior products soon go out of business. In contrast, firms that build a good reputation are likely to do well. However, in some situations government may need to protect the consumer.

Unsafe Products

The federal government protects consumers from unsafe products in a number of ways. In the case of automobiles, the *National Highway Traffic Safety Administration* requires that all vehicles sold in the United States have certain safety equipment such as shatterproof windshields, adequate headlights, turn signals, padded dashboards, and seat belts. The agency also has the power to require automobile manufacturers to correct problems in vehicles that have already been sold. You probably have read about cars being recalled to have brake, steering, or transmission problems repaired.

The *Consumer Product Safety Commission* is another federal agency that protects consumers. The commission collects information on injuries caused by various products. This information is used to determine which products are most dangerous. The commission can require that unsafe products be improved or withdrawn from the market.

A recent example involved baby cribs. The commission determined that a number of babies had been injured or killed because their heads became stuck between the slats on the sides of cribs. As a result, an

The National Highway Traffic Safety Administration sets safety standards for all vehicles sold in the United States.

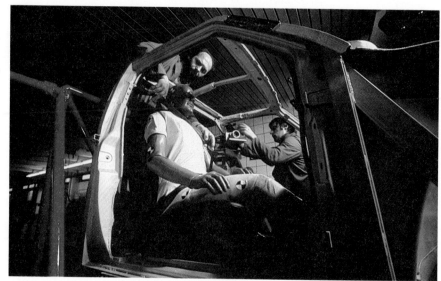

TRW, Inc.

order was issued requiring that the slats be put closer together so that a baby's head could not fit between them.

The *Food and Drug Administration* performs a similar function. This agency requires that drugs be carefully tested before they are put on the market. Any food or drug that may cause illness or death can be removed from the market by the Food and Drug Administration. The Food and Drug Administration's insistence on careful, long-term testing has protected American consumers from experiencing the serious side effects of many untested drugs. Clearly, the employees of this agency are faced with difficult decisions that have important consequences for consumers.

False Advertising

Consumers depend on advertising to obtain information about goods and services. But some advertisements contain misleading information or outright lies. Often, the consumer is not in a position to evaluate the truth of advertising claims.

The *Federal Trade Commission* has the responsibility for detecting false advertising. When members of the commission become aware of a problem, they can order the firm to change its advertising.

False Advertising: Seeing Is Not Believing

A few years ago a glass company used television commercials to show that its glass was clearer than that of other firms. Unfortunately, the company was less than honest. In the commercials, petroleum jelly was smeared on the glass of competitors. In addition, the company took the glass out of the window frames that were supposed to contain its glass. The effect was to make it appear as though its glass was so clear that looking through it was like looking through nothing at all. That, of course, was exactly the case!

Television viewers had no way of knowing that the glass company was not playing by the rules. But the Federal Trade Commission investigated the commercial and determined that the firm was guilty of false advertising. As a result, the commission issued an order that required the company to stop using the commercial.

In some cases, the commission has required a firm to advertise that it had been untruthful in the past. For example, one company claimed that its mouthwash would kill germs and protect users from the common cold. The Federal Trade Commission found that this was not true

and ordered the company to advertise that for cold protection its mouthwash was no more effective than gargling with warm water.

GOVERNMENT AND WORKER PROTECTION

Government helps workers by making workplaces safer. Government also protects workers from being treated unfairly while on the job.

Worker Safety

Certain occupations are known to be risky. Stunt riders and football players, for example, know that their jobs involve risk of injury. Their salaries reflect the dangers they face. Most workers, however, do not expect to suffer injury or illness on the job. They expect their employers to follow safety procedures and to provide safe working conditions.

Unfortunately, companies do not always operate safely, and every year thousands of people are injured on the job. Other people suffer serious health problems, such as cancer, because they are exposed to harmful chemicals in the workplace. In some cases, the harmful effects of these chemicals do not appear until long after the person has quit working for the company.

The *Occupational Safety and Health Administration* is a federal

Government agencies protect workers on the job against hazardous materials and unsafe working conditions.

Alcoa

agency established to maintain safety standards and improve working conditions. Employees of the agency inspect businesses to make sure that unsafe situations are corrected. A firm found to have safety problems can be fined, or, if the hazard is especially dangerous, it can be required to close until the problem is corrected.

Discrimination

Job opportunities and salaries in a free enterprise system should be determined by a worker's contribution to the business. Someone who is especially good at a job has the right to expect a promotion and more money than someone who cannot perform the tasks as well.

Unfortunately, job opportunities and pay sometimes depend on race, sex, age, or religion. When decisions are based on these factors rather than performance on the job, the employer is said to be practicing **discrimination.**

If just one employer discriminates against a class of workers, those workers may be able to find other jobs where they are treated more fairly. But if many employers practice discrimination, the workers may have difficulty finding good jobs.

There are laws against discrimination in the workplace. Firms that violate these laws can be fined by the government and sued by workers. Firms practicing discrimination may be prohibited from doing business with the government until they change their policies. Efforts by government have not eliminated discrimination in job markets, but they have made the practice less common.

INSTANT REPLAY

Consumers are protected against unsafe products by agencies such as the National Highway Traffic Safety Administration, the Consumer Product Safety Commission, and the Food and Drug Administration.

The Federal Trade Commission is responsible for preventing false advertising.

The Occupational Safety and Health Administration inspects working conditions to make sure that they are safe.

Firms that practice discrimination can be fined, sued, or prevented from doing business with the government.

GOVERNMENT AND ENVIRONMENTAL PROTECTION

In producing goods and services, some businesses have damaged the environment. Some rivers and lakes have become so polluted that neither fish nor people can swim in them. Severe air pollution in some cities has significantly reduced air quality and has forced some people to move to protect their health.

Why are some businesses unconcerned about the damage being done to the environment? The answer is that a free enterprise system does not always reward those who work to preserve natural resources.

The basic objective of a business is to earn a profit. Profits are the difference between dollars received and dollars spent. Thus, in making a product, a firm must use costly resources sparingly. A manager can be less concerned about using resources that are not so expensive. And resources that are free to the firm can be used freely.

Air and water are resources used by many businesses. A steel mill uses the air to get rid of smoke coming from its furnaces. A paper mill may dump waste materials into a river. Since the air and water are free to these businesses, there is no reason to conserve them.

Company profits usually are not affected if a river becomes polluted or if the air becomes unpleasant to breathe. In fact, any attempt to reduce the pollution of the water and air requires the use of other costly resources, which reduces profits. Thus, in some cases managers have little incentive to protect the environment.

Even though dirty air and water do not affect a company's profits, they do affect the people living near the plant or factory where the pollution is occurring. What should these people do? Possibly they could threaten to boycott the company's products if it continues to pollute the air and water. However, a business may sell most of its goods to people who live hundreds of miles away from the plant and who, therefore, are unaware of the pollution problem. Thus, there really is no way, in a pure free enterprise system, to compel a firm to change its methods of operation.

This problem suggests that there is a need for government to protect the environment. Government has the power to make firms pay for the costs of their actions. This power can be used in a number of ways. First, laws can be passed to prohibit or limit the amount of pollution. Second, the firm may be required to buy equipment that reduces the level of pollution. Finally, a company may be fined if it continues to pol-

It is the government's job to make sure that businesses do not pollute the environment.

H. Armstrong Roberts, Inc.

lute. If the fine is large enough, the company will have a reason to change its behavior.

The *Environmental Protection Agency* is the federal agency responsible for protecting the environment. This agency uses all the methods mentioned above. Clean air laws empower the Environmental Protection Agency to shut firms down under certain conditions. Another way the government has cleaned up the air is by introducing laws concerning auto emissions.

BENEFITS AND COSTS OF GOVERNMENT REGULATION

Many government regulations have beneficial effects. Consumers save billions of dollars every year as a result of antitrust laws that prevent companies from charging high prices for their goods. We all benefit from pollution control regulations that keep our lakes and rivers clean and ensure adequate air quality. Government regulations save lives, too. Accidental poisonings of small children have been reduced by 90 percent since a new law was introduced a few years ago. This law requires all medicines to be packaged in bottles that children cannot open easily.

Although government regulations provide benefits, they can also impose significant costs on the business community. Some industries spend billions of dollars each year on pollution control equipment. Others spend large sums of money to meet government standards for safe products and workplaces. It is estimated that compliance with all the governmental regulations now in effect may cost business as much as $150 billion per year. This is about $700 for each person living in the United States.

The benefits of government actions must be evaluated relative to their costs. For example, the required use of childproof bottles can be defended because it provides great benefits to the public at little cost to the firms who make the medicines. In contrast, some government regulations are very expensive in comparison to the benefits they provide. In such cases, it would be better if the free enterprise system were allowed to operate without government interference.

INSTANT REPLAY

Since air and water are free, businesses have little incentive to preserve the environment.

The Environmental Protection Agency is the federal agency responsible for environmental protection.

Evaluating government actions involves comparing the benefits of individual regulations with the costs.

SUMMARY

Government acts as a referee in the economic system by protecting individuals against theft and violence, by enforcing contracts, and by resolving honest disagreements. A small claims court can be used for disagreements involving relatively small amounts of money.

The government uses antitrust laws to promote competition and reduce the market power of large companies. The government can break up large firms, and it can prevent smaller firms from merging into one large company. The government can also take action against price fixing.

A public utility is a firm that has been granted the exclusive right to provide an important good or service in a geographic area. Government agencies called public service commissions or public utility commissions regulate public utilities by determining the prices that the utilities can charge.

Government protects consumers by requiring that unsafe products be changed or removed from the market. It can also prevent companies from using false advertising. Various government agencies protect workers by requiring safety in the workplace and by enforcing laws against discrimination.

Government has a role in protecting the environment. Because air and water are free, businesses have little reason to conserve these important natural resources. By setting standards, requiring pollution control devices, and using fines, the Environmental Protection Agency can force firms to reduce the amount of pollution they cause.

In an evaluation of government actions, the benefits of individual regulations should be compared with the costs.

☆ LEARNING ACTIVITIES ☆

Building Your Vocabulary

On a separate sheet of paper, write the numbers 1 through 8. Next to each number, write the term that correctly completes the sentence.

antitrust laws
small claims court
merger
price fixing
discrimination
public utilities
contract
public service
   commission

1. Firms that provide electricity, local telephone service, and natural gas are called _____.

2. Paying an older worker less than a younger one for the same job is an example of _____.

3. An agreement between managers of different firms to charge the same price is called _____.

4. A _____ occurs when two firms join to form a new firm.

5. Disagreement involving small amounts of money can be resolved in _____.

6. Prices to be charged for electricity, natural gas, and local telephone service in a state are set by a _____.

7. _____ are used to increase competition among firms.

8. A _____ is an agreement between two persons or groups of people.

Reviewing the Facts

1. Give two examples of how government acts as a referee in the economic system.
2. Why is small claims court useful in resolving disagreements involving small amounts of money?
3. How can antitrust laws be used to increase competition?
4. How does government control the price of electricity?
5. How does the Consumer Product Safety Commission protect consumers against unsafe products?
6. Give an example of false advertising.
7. What can the Occupational Safety and Health Administration do if it determines that a firm's workplace is unsafe?
8. How has the federal government reduced automobile pollution?

Expressing Your Opinion

1. Why is the price of electricity regulated but not the price of electric refrigerators?
2. Could a merger between two firms ever benefit consumers?
3. Are there any disadvantages involved in taking a disagreement to small claims court?
4. Should the government examine all advertisements to make sure that they are not misleading? Why or why not?
5. What would happen if the government prohibited *all* pollution?

Developing Your Attitudes, Values, and Skills

1. In recent years there have been many mergers of large companies. Choose one example of a merger from newspaper and magazine indexes. Read the relevant articles about the merger. Were the companies involved in totally unrelated activities, or did they have similar interests? Did people think the merger would damage competition or create a more efficient company? What was the outcome of the merger? Write a brief report summarizing the history of the merger and the development of any controversy the merger provoked.
2. Newspapers frequently carry stories about requests for rate hikes by local public utilities. Choose a local public utility—electricity, gas, water, telephone, taxicab—and research newspaper articles, or telephone the utility's public information office, to find out if the utility is currently requesting a rate hike. Find out the amount of the request, the reason for it, and how it would affect the average consumer's monthly bill if granted. If you cannot obtain all the information you need from newspaper articles, choose a class representative to contact your state public utility commission and find out the status of the request. Is the request under investigation? Will it come up for a vote soon? When was the last time the utility received a rate hike and how much was it?

Are any consumers protesting the current request? If an organized group of consumers is opposing the rate hike request, you may be able to contact the group's leader to find out the reason for its opposition. When you have completed your research, suppose that you are an investigator for the public utility commission and write a report recommending that it grant or deny the utility's request for a rate hike. What is the basis for your conclusions?

3. Interview the manager of a local manufacturing company to find out what government agencies regulate the firm and what regulations it must meet. Does the company have to submit forms and reports to the government? How often? How much time does it take to process the paperwork? How do the company's owners, managers, and workers feel about the regulations? Do they think that the regulations are necessary or unnecessary? How much do they estimate that regulation has added to the cost of manufacturing the company's products? Do the workers handle any toxic substances or dangerous machines? How does the company ensure safety for the workers? What is it required to do to protect consumers from defective products and residents near the plant from pollution? If it is not possible to interview a plant manager, choose a case to research in the periodical guides by looking under Consumer Product Safety Commission, Occupational Safety and Health Administration, or Environmental Protection Agency. Be prepared to discuss your research in class. You should indicate whether you believe the government regulations are justified in the case you studied and to defend your conclusions.

4. Investigate the history of one of the government agencies mentioned in this chapter. What led to the creation of the agency? Has the agency's scope of powers changed since it was first organized? How does the agency enforce its regulations? What problems does the agency face? Outline your findings, and prepare a short presentation to the class.

FOCUS YOUR READING

What would happen if all the depositors at a bank wanted their money at the same time?

How long is the typical dollar bill in use?

In terms of economic decisions, who is the second most powerful person in the United States?

CHAPTER 11

BANKING AND THE FEDERAL RESERVE SYSTEM

PREVIEW

The rich and powerful King Ammon came one day to the Temple of the Moon. To Omni, the High Priest, he said, "I am about to depart for a far country. Wilt thou keep my gold for me?"

Hiding his joy at the prospect, Omni replied, "It is a great responsibility, but I will do it." King Ammon brought 10,000 rupees of gold to the temple. In return, Omni gave King Ammon a receipt for the gold.

As soon as King Ammon was gone, the clever Omni said to the other priests of the temple, "Go thee now to the merchants of the town, and say to each that we have gold for lending."

Soon a great merchant came to borrow part of the gold of King Ammon. From the merchant, Omni received a promise to repay the gold plus a little more. Looking at the gold he had borrowed, the merchant said to Omni, "I have no place to store so much gold. Keep it safe for me, and give me a receipt that I can use as money."

The next day, other merchants came to the Temple of the Moon. Omni lent part of the gold of King Ammon to each. Each promised to repay the amount borrowed plus a little more. All the merchants left the gold they had borrowed in the possession of Omni. Each was given a receipt that could be used as money.

Soon Omni had given out notes for the entire fortune of King Ammon. But Omni still had all the gold. Omni thought about what had happened and said to himself, "They neither know nor care how much gold I possess. They want only the notes that they can use as money. I have one grand idea."

More merchants came, and Omni showed them the gold of King Ammon. He lent a portion of the gold to each, although he had already lent the gold to those who came before. Soon he had written receipts for more than 10,000 rupees. And still he had all the gold.

Then Omni called his fellow priests together and said, "I have discovered the greatest secret of all time. I have learned the magic

200

of making money out of nothing. In a few years we will build a fortune that will make King Midas look like a beggar."

Omni's work spread rapidly until it occupied the whole Temple of the Moon. To celebrate his success, Omni renamed the temple, calling it the First National Bank. The name comes from an ancient language and means, "the place of imaginary money."

Most people view banking as a mysterious business. The activities of banks and the importance of banking in the economic system are not well understood. To many, banks really do seem like the "place of imaginary money" discussed in the fable above.

In this chapter you will learn about banking and the Federal Reserve System. When you have finished the reading material and learning activities, you should be able to:

★ Explain how banks function as financial intermediaries.

★ Discuss how banks earn a profit.

★ Describe what is meant by fractional reserve banking.

★ Explain the purpose of the Federal Deposit Insurance Corporation.

★ List and discuss the major responsibilities of the Federal Reserve System.

★ Describe the basic organization of the Federal Reserve System.

BANKS AS FINANCIAL INTERMEDIARIES

The managers of grocery stores buy food from farmers, meat packers, canneries, and other suppliers. They then sell these goods to consumers. Grocers act as intermediaries between the producers and consumers of products. As you learned in Chapter 8, an intermediary is a person or business whose job is to bring buyers and sellers together. The advantage of having an intermediary in a market is that the transaction costs of trade are reduced. That is, less time and effort are needed to make exchanges than if buyers and sellers had to search for each other.

In many ways, a bank is like a grocery store. The grocery store buys and sells food. Banks buy and sell money. The money purchased by the bank comes from individuals and businesses. They are willing to provide money to the bank for two reasons. First, the bank can keep their money safe. The vaults of the bank provide protection against fire and theft. Second, the bank will pay them interest for their money. **Interest** is a payment for the temporary use of another person's money.

Banks "sell" most of the money that is deposited with them. But the term *sell* is a bit misleading. Banks do not actually sell money. They sell the right to use a sum of money for a period of time. Sometimes the period may be as short as a few days. In other cases, it can be up to 30 years. In return for the use of the bank's money, borrowers pay interest to the bank.

Why are banks necessary in the economic system? Why do buyers and sellers of money go through a bank instead of trading directly with each other? The answer is that in this case a bank serves the same function as a grocery store. By bringing buyers and sellers together, the bank acts as an intermediary and reduces transaction costs. Because banks operate in money or financial markets, they are referred to as **financial intermediaries.**

An example will help to explain the role of banks as financial intermediaries. Mr. Jones wants to build a new house. He has $10,000 and needs to borrow $50,000 to pay the builder. At the same time, there are 50 people in his community who each have $1,000 that they would like to save. If Mr. Jones knew who these people were and how much money they had available, he could go to each one of them and try to borrow their money. However, it would be very unlikely that he would know who they were. People who keep large amounts of money in their homes usually do not tell anyone except their immediate family about it.

If Mr. Jones knew the names of the money holders, he would still find it difficult and costly to borrow from each one of them. Those who

Banks act as intermediaries to bring lenders and borrowers together.

did not know him would be reluctant to risk their money. Even his close friends would probably want IOUs or some other form of notes stating how and when they would get their money back. Even if all this could be arranged, Mr. Jones would still be faced with the inconvenience of making payments on 50 different loans.

Similarly, the 50 savers would need to find out who wanted to borrow money. This search would be a difficult task. The transaction costs necessary to find the right borrower could be quite high. In many cases, lenders might simply decide that they would rather spend their money than save it.

The bank brings borrowers and savers together by continually accepting deposits and making loans. A bank can efficiently accept deposits of $1,000 each from the 50 savers. These savers are willing to give the bank their money, because they have confidence that they can get it back when they want it, and they can earn interest. Putting money in the bank is easy, because the bank is always in the same place and always ready to take and return their money. Thus, transaction costs of saving are greatly reduced because of banks.

The bank can also help Mr. Jones get the money he needs to build his house. The bank can take the $50,000 deposited by the 50 savers and combine those funds into one loan. Mr. Jones no longer has to search for a large number of people who are willing to lend him money. He does not have to worry about writing many IOUs and making payments to several people. The bank has done the searching for him and has reduced the transaction costs of borrowing.

Every day banks accept many small deposits of money and a few large deposits. These funds are then combined to form a pool of money from which loans can be made. Some of these loans may be for only a few hundred dollars. Others may be for several million dollars. It is not necessary to match individual buyers and sellers of money. Indeed, borrowers and lenders usually have no contact whatsoever with each other. It is the bank's responsibility to match their needs. When the bank performs this function, both buyers and sellers of money benefit.

Why would the owners of a bank want to be in the business of acting as financial intermediaries? Like other entrepreneurs, the goal of the banker is to earn a profit. Bankers earn a profit in the same way as the grocer. They mark up the price of the good that they sell. That is, the banker buys money at one interest rate and sells it at a slightly higher interest rate. For example, a bank might pay 7 percent for funds deposited in the bank and lend those funds at 10 percent. In this way, the bank earns a 3 percent profit on all the money lent out.

INSTANT REPLAY

Banks act as intermediaries. They reduce transaction costs by bringing buyers and sellers of money together.

Banks receive money from depositors and then use this money to make loans.

Banks can profit by charging borrowers a higher interest rate than they pay to depositors.

FRACTIONAL RESERVE BANKING

Banks receive money from depositors. When a depositor places money in a bank, she or he is given a receipt. The receipt may take the form of an entry in a book, indicating that the person has a certain amount of money in a savings account. Or it may be a printed slip, indicating a deposit to a checking account. Checking account receipts cannot be used as money, but depositors can write checks that are then used as money. As you have already learned, these demand deposits are an important form of money in the economic system.

Managers of banks do not expect all depositors to withdraw their money at the same time, so banks do not have to keep all the money that is deposited with them on hand. However, at any one time, some depositors will want to withdraw their funds. The funds the bank keeps on hand to meet this need are called **reserves.**

A bank's reserves are usually only a small part of the total amount of money that people have deposited there. For example, suppose that the people in your community deposited $100 million in the local bank. If you went to the president of the bank and asked to count all the money in the building, how much would be there? You might find the reserves totaled less than $1 million.

What happened to the other deposits? The bank has lent most of them to people who need money. Some of it may have gone to a family that wants to add another bedroom to their house. Someone may have borrowed money to buy a car. An entrepreneur might have received a loan to start a new business. The bank may also have lent money to the government in return for government bonds.

How can the bank operate with only $1 million in its vaults when a total of $100 million has been deposited? The answer is that experience has shown that only a very small percentage of depositors will want their money at any moment. Therefore, the managers of the bank believe that

A bank's reserves are usually only a small part of the total amount of money that people have deposited there.

John Coletti/Stock Boston

$1 million should be enough to meet the day-to-day withdrawal requests of depositors.

Banks earn their profits from the interest they receive on loans. Thus, if they kept all deposits in their vaults, they would have no money to lend and they would earn no profits. The practice of lending most of their funds and keeping only a fraction of their deposits in reserve is called **fractional reserve banking.**

COMMERCIAL BANKS AND OTHER FINANCIAL INTERMEDIARIES

Commercial banks are owned by private citizens. They accept deposits from, and make loans to, individuals and businesses. But not just anyone can decide to start a bank. Those desiring to be bankers must first obtain a charter from the state or federal government, stating that the business has the legal right to operate as a bank. Those who are granted charters are selected with care. They are required to demonstrate that they have the knowledge and experience necessary to run a bank. They also must be willing to invest a considerable amount of their own money in the bank. If their own money might be lost as well as that of the depositors, the owners will be especially careful.

Banks that receive their charter from the federal government are called **national banks.** Those approved by the state are called **state**

banks. Although these two types of banks receive the right to operate from different government agencies, there is little difference between them. Presently there are about 5,500 national banks and about 9,000 state banks in the United States.

Commercial banks are not the only financial intermediaries in the economic system. **Savings and loan associations** perform a similar function. Like commercial banks, they accept deposits. However, many of the loans made by a savings and loan association are mortgages to assist home buyers. Until recently, savings and loan associations were not permitted to offer all the services provided by commercial banks. For example, a depositor could not open a checking account. Today, customers can get almost the same services at a savings and loan association as they can at a bank. In the United States there are nearly 5,000 savings and loan associations.

Credit unions are another type of financial intermediary in the economic system. Credit unions are usually formed by people who have a similar interest. Often the common interest is work-related. For example, teachers in a school district or the employees of a large automobile manufacturer may start a credit union.

The services of a credit union are similar to those of a bank. Credit unions pay a certain interest rate on deposits and lend money at a slightly higher interest rate. An important difference is that a credit union is owned by its depositors. Thus, the profits of the credit union go to its depositors. There are over 20,000 credit unions in the United States today. However, most credit unions are much smaller than commercial banks and savings and loan associations.

FEDERAL DEPOSIT INSURANCE CORPORATION

Fractional reserve banking works only if people have confidence in the banking system. If depositors think they can withdraw their money at any time, they will leave their deposits in banks. Reserves will take care of the small number of customers who want to make withdrawals each day.

One way to increase confidence in the banking system is for the government to guarantee depositors that they will not lose their money. In 1934 Congress created the **Federal Deposit Insurance Corporation (FDIC),** which insures all deposits up to a maximum of $100,000. To be covered by this plan, a bank must pay one half of 1 percent of its deposits to the FDIC each year. Today, almost all banks are part of this insurance plan. Other federal agencies insure deposits in savings and loan associations and credit unions.

Today, nearly all bank deposits are insured by the FDIC.

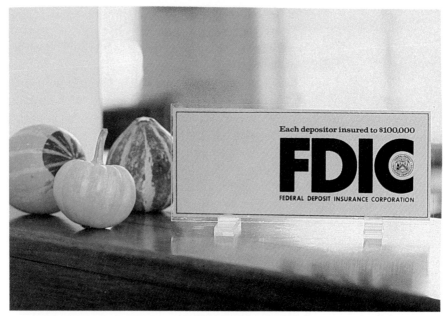

Each depositor insured to $100,000

FDIC

FEDERAL DEPOSIT INSURANCE CORPORATION

INSTANT REPLAY

Modern banks keep only a small proportion of total deposits in their vaults at any given time. This is called fractional reserve banking.

Anyone who wants to open a bank must first obtain a charter from the state or federal government.

Savings and loan associations and credit unions are also financial intermediaries in the economic system. Their operations are similar to those of a commercial bank.

The Federal Deposit Insurance Corporation insures all bank deposits up to a maximum of $100,000.

THE FEDERAL RESERVE SYSTEM

If a local florist went out of business, its customers would probably have to travel further to buy flowers. The store's customers would be inconvenienced, but they would not suffer any substantial harm. However, a bank closing would be different, because banks are in a special position of trust and responsibility. If a bank closed, its customers would not only have to find a new place to do their banking, but they might also lose all their savings and deposits. The failure of a local bank, then, can have serious consequences for its customers.

Because banks play a special role in the economy, it is generally agreed that there is a need for some type of government control of the banking system. In countries with command economies, the government actually owns and operates the banks. In mixed economies, such as the United States, the banks are privately owned, but the government sets rules that must be followed. Usually, there is some kind of central bank to set and enforce these rules. A **central bank** is an organization responsible for all the banking in the country. In the United States, the central bank is the **Federal Reserve System,** often called the "Fed" for short. It was established by Congress in 1913 to assist and supervise the nation's commercial banks.

Functions of the Federal Reserve System

The Federal Reserve System is sometimes called a bank for bankers. It provides many of the same services for commercial banks that those

The Federal Reserve System was created by Congress in 1913 to assist and supervise commercial banks.

Federal Reserve

banks provide for individuals and businesses. However, the most important functions of the Fed are the following:

★ Provides currency to banks.

★ Acts as a clearinghouse for checks.

★ Sets the reserve ratio and holds reserves.

★ Supervises banking activities.

★ Makes loans to member banks.

★ Regulates the supply of money.

Provides Currency to Banks. Each Federal Reserve District provides coins and currency to the banks in its area. The need for such money changes from month to month. For example, some stores make up to 40 percent of their total annual sales during the Christmas season. As a result, the need for coins and currency at that time of year is much greater than during other months. To assist the banks, the Fed sends extra coins and currency to banks in November and December. At other times it stores the extra money.

Coins can be used for many years, but currency wears out quickly. For example, the average dollar bill stays in use for only about 18 months. When paper money becomes worn, a bank can send it back to the district Federal Reserve Bank. The district bank will destroy the old bill and send the bank new currency. Every year the Fed shreds billions of dollars of worn currency.

Acts As a Clearinghouse for Checks. Suppose Nancy Cohen buys a new bicycle. She writes a check to be paid by her bank, the First National Bank. The check is then deposited in the Jackson State Bank by the owners of the bike shop. At this point, the bicycle store account has more money in its checking account than before, but Nancy Cohen has no less money. The reason is that the First National Bank does not yet know that Nancy has written the check.

Now the clearinghouse service of the Federal Reserve System comes into play. The Jackson State Bank sends the check to the district Federal Reserve Bank. The Fed then sends the check to the First National Bank, which deducts the amount from Nancy Cohen's account. Because there is a central clearinghouse, the commercial banks do not have to send their checks directly to one another. Instead, all checks are cleared by the Fed.

Each year the Federal Reserve System clears about 25 billion checks, using high-speed check-sorting machines. The numbers on the lower left-hand side of a check provide a key for these machines. These numbers identify the bank and the person who wrote the check. They are printed using magnetic ink. By reading these numbers, the check-processing machines of the Fed can sort checks into groups at the rate of 60,000 per hour.

Sets the Reserve Ratio and Holds Reserves. Earlier you learned that banks set aside part of their deposits in reserve to meet their customers' immediate needs. But how much should be kept in reserve? If a bank holds only a small amount of its total deposits in reserve, it can lend the rest and earn high profits. However, if it lends too much of its total deposits, it may not have enough reserves on hand to meet the withdrawal demands of its customers.

The Federal Reserve System is the agency that decides how much money each bank must keep as reserves. This amount is determined by the reserve ratio. The **reserve ratio** is the proportion or percentage of each bank's total deposits that it cannot lend. That is, it is the fraction of deposits that must be kept in reserve. For example, if the reserve ratio is 15 percent, the bank must keep on reserve 15 cents out of every dollar deposited.

The reserve ratio for demand deposits is usually greater than the reserve ratio for savings accounts. People are less likely to withdraw money from their savings accounts than from their checking accounts. Thus, the needs of savings account customers can be met with less money in the vault. The reserve ratios for savings and demand deposits

Each year the Federal Reserve clears about 25 billion checks, using high-speed sorters.

Federal Reserve

are shown in Table 11-1. The lower percentages apply to small banks; the higher percentages apply to the country's largest banks.

TABLE 11-1

RESERVE RATIO ON SAVINGS AND DEMAND DEPOSITS	
Type of Deposit	Reserve Ratio
Demand	3–12%
Savings	0–3%

Not all of a bank's reserves must be kept in its own vaults. Part of the reserve requirement can be kept on deposit with the district Federal Reserve Bank. However, a bank does not earn interest on these reserves.

Supervises Banking Activities. The Federal Reserve System supervises the day-to-day operations of banks. For example, officers of the Fed enforce the reserve ratio requirement. They also join other government agencies in unannounced inspections of banks. The purpose of these inspections is to make sure that the banks are following good banking practices. The inspections help identify and correct any problems before they become serious.

Makes Loans to Member Banks. Although banks are required to maintain a minimum reserve ratio, they can sometimes run out of money temporarily. This situation happens when several of their customers make unusually large withdrawals at about the same time. One service of the Federal Reserve System is to make loans to banks during such periods. The banks are charged interest on the money that they borrow. The interest rate charged by the Fed is called the **discount rate.** The discount rate serves as a signal in the economy. When it goes up, other interest rates are likely to increase. If the Federal Reserve System reduces the discount rate, then other rates are likely to decline, too.

Regulates the Supply of Money. Regulating the amount of money in the economic system is the most important responsibility of the Federal Reserve System. Officers of the Fed must make sure that there is enough money so that the economy can grow. But it is also necessary to avoid having too much money available. Too much money chasing too few goods and services can cause inflation.

The Federal Reserve System controls the money supply by changing the amount of demand deposits. Demand deposits are altered by the Fed's use of open market operations. **Open market operations** refers to the buying and selling of bonds by the Federal Reserve system.

When the Federal Reserve System wants to reduce the amount of demand deposit money, it sells bonds that it owns. These bonds are purchased by individuals and businesses. They usually are paid for by check. When the check is sent to the proper bank, the amount of demand deposits at the bank is reduced. Thus, by selling bonds, the Fed can reduce the supply of money.

If the Federal Reserve System wants to increase the amount of demand deposit money, it buys bonds that are owned by individuals or businesses. One way the Fed pays for these bonds is by giving the owner new currency. When the owner takes this money to the bank and deposits it into a checking account, the demand deposits in that bank increase. Hence, by buying bonds the Fed has put additional money into the economic system.

Control of the supply of money is very important in an economy. You may recall the inflation problems of Germany in the 1920s and Hungary in 1946, which are described in Chapter 6. In those countries, so much currency was in circulation that it became worthless. Whenever there is a large increase in the supply of money, there is likely to be a corresponding decrease in its value.

Too much of a decrease in the supply of money can also cause problems. During the 1930s, the Federal Reserve System allowed the supply of money in the United States to decline. Many economists believe that this action was a serious mistake and that the Great Depression would have been less serious if the Federal Reserve System had prevented the decrease in the money supply. These examples show that changes in the supply of money can significantly affect economic conditions.

INSTANT REPLAY

The Fed provides currency to commercial banks and acts as a clearinghouse for checks.

The Fed sets the reserve ratio. This ratio is the proportion of deposits that must be kept on reserve.

The discount rate is the interest rate charged by the Fed for loans made to banks.

The most important function of the Fed is controlling the supply of money. By buying and selling bonds, called open market operations, the amount of demand deposits in banks can be changed.

Organization of the Federal Reserve System

The legislation that created the Federal Reserve System divided the country into 12 districts. A Federal Reserve Bank was established in each district, and each Federal Reserve Bank is owned by its member banks. See the map in Figure 11-1.

National banks are required to be members of the system; state banks can join if they wish. Currently about 5,500 banks are members. Although this is only about 40 percent of all the banks in the United States, most of the nation's large banks are included. The Fed's member banks currently hold almost three-fourths of all deposits.

Although each district Federal Reserve Bank is owned by the member banks, these banks do not have the right to make decisions about the policies of the Fed. Actually, the reverse is true. The Federal Reserve System makes the rules under which the member banks must operate.

The Board of Governors of the Federal Reserve System. The officers of each of the 12 Federal Reserve Districts supervise banking in their areas. How-

FIGURE 11-1
Each of the 12 Federal Reserve Districts is responsible for banking in its area.

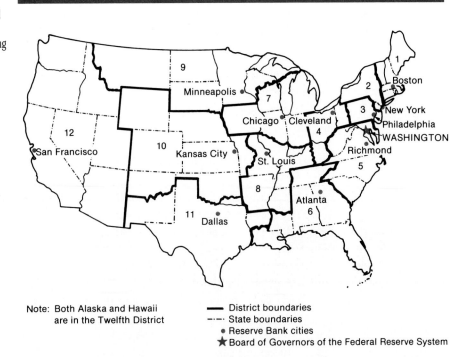

Note: Both Alaska and Hawaii are in the Twelfth District

— District boundaries
—·— State boundaries
• Reserve Bank cities
★ Board of Governors of the Federal Reserve System

ever, the overall responsibility for banking in the United States has been given to the Fed's Board of Governors. The **Board of Governors** consists of seven persons who are appointed by the President of the United States and approved by the Senate. Each person on the Board of Governors serves for 14 years.

The members of the Board of Governors supervise the operation of the entire Federal Reserve System. They are also involved in making decisions about the amount of coins, currency, and demand deposits that are available in the United States. Because money and banking are so vital in the economic system, these seven persons are among the most important in the entire country. Often, their decisions have a greater effect on the economy than the decisions of any representative or senator.

The chairperson of the Board of Governors announces important decisions that have been made by the Fed and makes frequent comments about the condition of the economy. These statements are widely reported on television and in newspapers. Many people consider the chairperson to be the second most important person in America, with respect to economic decisions. They believe that only the President has more power to change economic conditions.

Independence of the Federal Reserve System. The Federal Reserve System is different from most of the organizations discussed in this book. Clearly, it is not part of the private enterprise system. Yet, it is not really a part of the federal government either, even though Congress created it and has the power to change it.

The reason that members of the Fed's Board of Governors are appointed is to give them the independence to make wise, but not necessarily popular, decisions without having to worry about facing angry voters or special interest groups. The members serve 14-year terms and can be removed from their position only for certain, specific reasons. For example, they could be removed if they broke the law or if they became mentally incapacitated. These provisions allow board members to concentrate on their responsibilities without having to worry about losing their jobs.

Another source of the Federal Reserve System's independence is that Congress does not provide any money to operate the system. In fact, each year the Fed earns substantial profits, which it returns to the federal treasury. Since it does not rely on Congress for funding, the Fed does not have to please Congress with its decisions for fear that its funding could be cut off.

Sometimes the independence of the Federal Reserve System results in disagreements. For example, the President may believe that certain policies should be followed, while the members of the Board of Governors have a different view. Because the Fed is not part of the federal government, it is not required to follow the President's orders. However, remember that the Federal Reserve System was created by Congress. Therefore, Congress could change the powers of the Fed or even abolish it.

Identifying Federal Reserve Notes

By looking at the black numbers and the black seal on the front of a bill, you can tell which Federal Reserve District issued the note. The number *1* and the letter *A* indicate Boston; *2* and *B*, New York; *3* and *C*, Philadel- phia; *4* and *D*, Cleveland; *5* and *E*, Richmond; *6* and *F*, Atlanta. This sequence continues through to *12* and *L* for San Francisco. For example, the bill pictured here was issued by the Cleveland district.

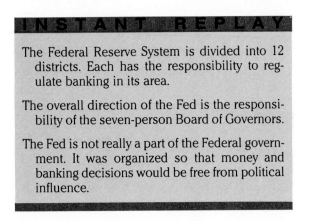

INSTANT REPLAY

The Federal Reserve System is divided into 12 districts. Each has the responsibility to regulate banking in its area.

The overall direction of the Fed is the responsibility of the seven-person Board of Governors.

The Fed is not really a part of the Federal government. It was organized so that money and banking decisions would be free from political influence.

SUMMARY

Banks act as financial intermediaries in the economic system. By bringing together buyers and sellers of money, they reduce the transaction costs of saving and borrowing. Banks earn a profit by charging a slightly higher interest rate on loans than they pay on deposits.

Bank managers realize that it is unlikely that all depositors will want to withdraw their money at the same time. So banks keep only a small portion of total deposits in their vaults. This practice is called fractional reserve banking.

You must obtain a charter before starting a bank. A commercial bank with a charter from the federal government is a national bank. A bank with a charter from the state government is a state bank.

Savings and loan associations and credit unions also act as financial intermediaries. Savings and loan organizations concentrate on making loans to home buyers; however, they also offer many of the services of most commercial banks. Credit unions are usually formed by people with a common interest. Unlike commercial banks and savings and loans, credit unions are owned by their depositors.

Commercial bank deposits up to a maximum of $100,000 are insured by the Federal Deposit Insurance Corporation. Deposits in savings and loan associations and credit unions are insured by other government agencies.

Banks are in a special position of trust in the economic system. Therefore, almost all countries have some kind of central bank that is responsible for regulating banking and the supply of money. The Federal Reserve System is the central bank of the United States.

Important responsibilities of the Federal Reserve System include (1) providing coins and currency to banks, (2) acting as a clearinghouse for checks, (3) setting the reserve ratio and holding reserves, (4) supervising banking activities, (5) making loans to member banks, and (6) regulating the supply of money.

The Fed divides the nation into 12 districts. Each district bank is owned by the member banks. All national banks must be members; state banks can join if they choose.

A seven-person Board of Governors directs the operations of the Fed. To preserve its independence, the Federal Reserve System was set up so that it is not part of the federal government.

☆ LEARNING ACTIVITIES ☆

Building Your Vocabulary

On a separate sheet of paper, write the numbers 1 through 8. Next to each number, write the term that correctly completes the sentence.

commercial bank
savings and loan
  association
central bank
reserve ratio
discount rate
Board of Governors
open market
  operations
Federal Deposit
  Insurance
  Corporation

1. A _____ is responsible for all banking activities in a country.

2. A _____ is a bank owned by private citizens.

3. A financial intermediary set up to make loans for home building is a _____ .

4. The agency that insures bank deposits is the _____ .

5. The group that heads the Fed is called the _____ .

6. The percentage of deposits that a bank cannot lend is the _____ .

7. The buying and selling of bonds to change the money supply is called _____ .

8. The _____ is the interest rate charged for money lent by the Fed.

Reviewing the Facts

1. How do financial intermediaries reduce the transaction costs of lending and borrowing money?
2. How do banks make a profit?
3. How can a bank operate successfully while keeping only a small portion of total deposits in its vaults?
4. What must a person do to get a bank charter?
5. Why do almost all countries have some sort of central bank?
6. Why does fractional reserve banking work only if people have confidence in the banking system?
7. In which Federal Reserve District do you live?
8. Why was the Fed not made part of the federal government?
9. Why is the reserve ratio for savings accounts less than it is for demand deposits?
10. How does the clearinghouse operation of the Fed make banking more efficient?

Expressing Your Opinion

1. How do the managers of a bank decide what interest rate they will pay on deposits and how much to charge for loans?
2. What are some of the possible problems with fractional reserve banking?
3. Should all the officials of the Fed be bankers? Why or why not?
4. Why might people want to put their money in a credit union rather than a commercial bank?
5. Should the government have some control over the banking system? Why or why not?
6. How does the existence of the Federal Deposit Insurance Corporation make bank failures less likely?

Developing Your Attitudes, Values, and Skills

1. Most banks offer a wide variety of services to customers. Visit the bank where you or your parents have an account, and investigate the services it offers. Then visit another nearby bank, and explore its services. Make a chart that compares each bank's services. Which offers the highest rates on savings accounts and certificates of deposit? Which offers the highest rate on interest-bearing checking accounts? Which bank charges less for safety deposit boxes? What interest rates do the banks charge for mortgages, car loans, and home improvement loans? Summarize your findings in a brief report. State which bank you would choose to patronize and why. Keep in mind that other factors such as location, automatic teller service, and hours of operation may figure in your decision.

2. The news media often print or broadcast stories about the Fed; yet its chairperson and activities remain a mystery to most people. Choose one of these assignments: Prepare a biography of the chairperson of the Fed's Board of Governors. Or, find out what decisions the Fed made over a recent one-year period. If you choose the biography, research the chairperson's educational and occupational background, and be sure to answer the following questions. How much of the chairperson's term on the Fed remains, and which President appointed him or her? During the chairperson's tenure, what major decisions has the Fed made that have had a significant impact on the economy? Does the chairperson usually agree or disagree with the President and Congress on economic issues? For either project, you can begin by looking up Federal Reserve System in the periodical guides. If you choose to study the Fed's economic decisions, be careful when researching articles to distinguish between those that predict what the Fed is going to do and those that report on what it has done.

3. The Federal Deposit Insurance Corporation was established in 1934 at the height of the Great Depression. In the early years of the Depression, people lost faith in fractional reserve banking and withdrew their deposits from their local banks. When many customers showed up at once to withdraw money, the situation was called a "run on the bank." In most cases, the result was the closing of the bank. Interview your grandparents or any older adults about this period, and ask them what they remember about these bank runs. Did they ever participate in one? If so, what did they have to do to try to get their money back? Did they get their money back or lose their savings? What did they do with their money after that? What made them lose faith in the banks? Prepare a summary of your interviews, and compare them with those of your classmates.

4. In 1984 the Continental Illinois National Bank and Trust Company, one of the nation's largest banks, collapsed and had to be taken over by the federal government. Conduct a case study of this event or of any other recent bank failure, and determine what caused the

bank to fail. What role did the FDIC play in protecting the bank's customers? What actions did it take, and how much money did it have to provide to protect depositors? Did depositors stage a run on the bank? What happened? Did the bank stay in business, or did it close? If it went into bankruptcy, how much on the dollar did stockholders and creditors receive? Do you think that federal government should have taken over the bank? Why or why not? Write a one-to-two page report summarizing your findings.

FOCUS YOUR READING

How can taxes be used to discourage consumers from purchasing a good or service?

How could a tax on income cause a person to reduce his or her work effort?

How does the Internal Revenue Service check for mistakes and cheating on tax returns?

CHAPTER 12

TAXES

PREVIEW

"The art of taxation consists of plucking the goose so as to obtain the largest amount of feathers with the least amount of hissing."

Jean Baptiste Colbert
Seventeenth century French statesman

To the poet, spring is the time when a young person's fancy turns to thoughts of love. But for the typical worker in the United States, spring is not very romantic. It is a time for gathering records and finding money to meet the government's April 15th deadline for payment of income taxes.

Taxes are payments that individuals and businesses are required to make to the government. They differ from other uses of money in that the taxpayer has no choice about paying taxes. You can choose whether or not to spend your money on a piano, motorcycle, or house. But tax payments are not a matter of choice. The government has a legal right to force you to pay the taxes that you owe.

More than $1.4 trillion ($1,400,000,000,000) in taxes are paid in the United States each year. This figure represents approximately $1 out of every $3 earned. Two-thirds of these taxes go to the federal government. The remainder are paid to state and local governments.

In this chapter you will learn about the tax system in the United States. When you have completed the reading material and learning activities, you should be able to:

★ List four purposes of taxation.

★ Explain how taxes can be used to change the mix of goods and services people consume.

★ Discuss the difference between a progressive tax and a regressive tax.

★ Describe the basic features of the personal income tax.

★ Explain how social security, sales, excise, and property taxes are determined.

PURPOSES OF TAXATION

There are four main reasons that individuals and businesses are required to pay taxes. Taxation is used by the government for these reasons:

★ Finance government activities

★ Change consumer decisions

★ Redistribute income

★ Manage the economy

Finance Government Activities

The government, like a business, needs money to purchase goods and services and to pay its employees. The main purpose of taxation is to provide government with the income it needs to function. Taxes pay for tanks, missiles, and soldiers. They provide the money to build roads, dams, and bridges. They pay school teachers, finance building construction, and buy fire engines. Tax money is also used to help poor countries, to explore space, and to provide medical care.

Change Consumer Decisions

Taxes can be used to change consumer decisions. Sometimes a government's objective is to reduce consumption of a good or service. For example, faced with congested roads and the need to buy large quantities of oil from other nations, the leaders of many European countries decided to reduce gasoline consumption by making use of the law of demand. They imposed high taxes on gasoline to make it much more expensive and to cause people to cut back on their driving. In these European countries the price of a gallon of gasoline is at least twice the price charged in the United States.

Cigarettes and alcohol are other examples of goods that are heavily taxed. These taxes help finance the activities of government, and they discourage the use of these products by increasing their prices.

Taxes can also be used to encourage consumption. This goal is

Taxes pay for defense and other activities of government.

U.S. Department of the Navy

accomplished by providing tax advantages to purchasers of certain goods. Solar water heaters are a good illustration. The sun is a clean and plentiful source of energy. The government wanted to encourage people to use the sun to heat the water in their homes. So Congress passed a law that allowed the buyers of solar water heaters to reduce their income taxes.

Suppose a person paid $1,000 for the solar water heater. The law stated that income tax payments could be reduced by 40 percent of the purchase price, or $400. Thus, the effect of the law was to reduce the cost of the water heater from $1,000 to $600. Once again, the law of demand came into play. At the lower price, more people bought solar water heaters.

Redistribute Income

In the United States some people are rich, but many others are poor. By imposing heavier taxes on the wealthy, the government can use taxes to equalize the distribution of income. Some of the tax money collected may be used to assist low-income groups.

Manage the Economy

Taxes are used as a tool for managing the economy. Changing the amount of taxes paid by individuals and businesses may increase the number of jobs, reduce the inflation rate, and increase the rate of growth of GNP. This use of the money collected by taxes is discussed further in Chapter 13.

INSTANT REPLAY

Taxes are payments that individuals and businesses are required to make to the government.

Taxes are used to (1) finance government activities, (2) change consumer decisions, (3) redistribute income, and (4) manage the economy.

PROGRESSIVE AND REGRESSIVE TAXES

The total amount of money paid as taxes is determined by the tax base and the tax rate. The **tax base** is the number of dollars to be taxed. The **tax rate** is the proportion of each dollar in the tax base that must be paid as taxes.

For example, consider a tax based on the total amount of money earned by a person. Such a tax is called a **personal income tax.** Suppose a person's income is $20,000. This income is the *tax base*. Also suppose that 20 percent of each dollar of income is to be paid as tax. Thus, 20 percent is the *tax rate*. The total tax is determined by multiplying the tax base by the tax rate. For example, in this case the tax would be $20,000 × .20, or $4,000.

Progressive Taxes

In the United States the tax rate varies for different levels of income. As a taxpayer's income rises from one level to the next, the taxpayer has to pay a higher tax on the additional income. The rate at which income is taxed at each level is called the **marginal tax rate.** An example of some hypothetical marginal tax rates for a progressive income tax is given in Table 12-1. The table indicates a 10 percent tax rate on the first $10,000 of income earned. For income between $10,000 and $20,000, the rate is 20 percent. For income above $20,000, the rate is 30 percent.

TABLE 12-1

EXAMPLE OF A PROGRESSIVE TAX	
Income	Marginal Tax Rate
$0–$10,000	10%
$10,001–$20,000	20
$20,001 and above	30

Using the rates from Table 12-1, determine how much tax would be paid by someone with an income of $40,000. A rate of 10 percent on the first $10,000 would be $1,000. A rate of 20 percent on the next $10,000 would be $2,000. The 30 percent rate would apply to the final $20,000 of earnings and would be $6,000. Thus, the total tax is $1,000 + $2,000 + $6,000, or $9,000.

Table 12-1 illustrates a progressive tax. A **progressive tax** is one that has increasing marginal tax rates. That is, people pay a higher tax rate on extra dollars of income as their incomes increase. You can see in Table 12-1 that the marginal tax rate increases as income rises. It goes from 10 percent on the first $10,000 to 30 percent for incomes above $20,000.

Progressive taxes are based on the idea that those with higher incomes are able to pay more taxes. Thus, the proportion of high-income dollars taken by the tax is greater than the proportion of low-income dollars. The personal income tax used by the U.S. federal government is an example of a progressive tax.

Regressive Taxes

A **regressive tax** imposes decreasing marginal tax rates on higher levels of income. Table 12-2 is an example of a regressive tax. In this example the tax rate is 10 percent on the first $10,000 of income. The next $20,000 is taxed at 5 percent. On all additional dollars of income the tax is 2 percent.

TABLE 12-2

EXAMPLE OF A REGRESSIVE TAX	
Income	Marginal Tax Rate
$0–$10,000	10%
$10,001–$20,000	5
$20,001 and above	2

With regressive taxes, high-income dollars are not taxed as heavily as low-income dollars. Thus, payment of a regressive tax may be difficult for low-income earners. A good tax system should avoid regressive taxes as much as possible.

INSTANT REPLAY

Progressive taxes are based on the idea that those with higher incomes are able to pay more taxes. Such taxes use increasing marginal tax rates.

Regressive taxes have decreasing marginal tax rates. They may impose a heavy burden on low-income groups.

PERSONAL INCOME TAX

As the name suggests, the personal income tax is a tax on the money that people earn as income. It is a tax on wages, salaries, tips, investment income, and in some cases, pensions and retirement benefits. The personal income tax raises more revenue than any other tax imposed by the federal government. Most states and some cities also tax personal income. Because the income tax systems of the states and cities vary widely, only the federal personal income tax is discussed here.

Income Tax Rates

The federal personal income tax is a progressive tax. Thus, the marginal tax rate is greater for high incomes than it is for low incomes. Table 12-3 shows the marginal tax rates set by Congress for a married couple in 1988.

TABLE 12-3

FEDERAL PERSONAL INCOME TAX FOR A MARRIED COUPLE, 1988

Taxable Income	Marginal Tax Rate
0–$29,750	15%
Above $29,750	28

In Table 12-3, the marginal tax rate increases as income rises. Rates go from 15 percent for the first $29,750 in taxable income to 28 percent on taxable income above $29,750. In 1986 changes in the tax law greatly simplified the tax table. Prior to these changes, there were 14 marginal tax rates ranging from 11 percent on the first $2,000 of taxable income to 50 percent on income above $150,000.

Some people do not understand how the marginal tax rates of the personal income tax are used. You may have heard individuals say that if they get a raise it will put them in a higher tax bracket, and they will have less money after taxes than before the raise.

That is not true. Marginal tax rates apply just to extra dollars—not all dollars of income. It is true that a raise could put a person in a higher marginal tax bracket, but only the extra dollars resulting from the raise would be taxed at the higher rate. The rest of the person's income would be taxed at the same rates as before. For example, as shown in Table 12-3, the marginal tax rate on the first $2,000 of taxable income would be 15 percent, whether the total amount of taxable income is $2,000 or $200,000.

Taxable Income, Deductions, and Exemptions

Look again at Table 12-3. Note that the first column is labeled taxable income. **Taxable income** is the income on which taxes must be paid. A person's taxable income is not the same as the total amount of money earned. In determining your income tax, you may be allowed to subtract certain expenses. These include some interest payments, money given to charity, medical bills, and certain other items. These expenses are called **deductions.** Extra deductions can also be claimed if the taxpayer is over 65 or blind.

Taxable income is also reduced depending on the number of **exemptions** that are claimed. A taxpayer receives an exemption for each person in the family.

As an example, suppose that a husband and wife earn $30,000 each year, that there are four people in their family, and that each exemption results in a $2,000 decrease in taxable income. In computing their taxes, the couple would be able to claim four exemptions, or $8,000. Also, suppose that they have $6,000 in deductions. Thus, their taxable income would be $16,000. They would pay personal income taxes on this amount.

Tax Withholding

Employers are required to withhold a portion of their employees' wages and send it to the Internal Revenue Service (IRS), the agency responsible for collecting the federal personal income tax. This payment system is referred to as **tax withholding.** Its purpose is to assure the government that the taxes will be paid, and to make paying taxes easier for the taxpayer. It also provides a year-round flow of revenue to the government.

Employers use tables provided by the government to determine the right amount to withhold. Usually, the amount withheld is different from the total amount of taxes owed by the person for the year. If too much money has been withheld, the taxpayer can get a refund from the government. If too little has been withheld, the taxpayer must pay additional taxes.

Problems with the Federal Personal Income Tax

There are some problems with the federal income tax. One is that the tax system is complicated. A tax return for a wealthy person with many sources of income could be 10 to 20 pages long. Even a *simple* tax return is not always simple. About half of all taxpayers hire someone else to prepare their tax forms. Over $1 billion a year is spent on tax preparation.

A second problem with the income tax is that it may reduce the incentive to work. Think about a person whose taxable income is $200,000. Suppose that person is offered $10,000 to do a job that would be very useful to society—supervise the building of a bridge, for example. Table 12-3 shows that person is in the 28 percent marginal tax bracket. Thus, only 72 percent or $7,200 of the $10,000 would be left after paying income taxes. Because the government takes such a large part of additional income, the person may decide not to take the job.

Tax rates are not as high as they used to be. At one time the top marginal rate was more than 90 percent. That is, a person with high income kept less than 10 cents of each additional dollar earned. Under such a system, there was not much incentive for those with high incomes to continue working. Even with today's top rate of 28 percent, the income tax may reduce the work effort of some high-income people.

Tax Cheaters and the Internal Revenue Service

Each year the Internal Revenue Service receives about 100 million tax returns. Clearly, there are some people who do not pay all the taxes they owe. Faced with so many returns, can the IRS catch all those who are cheating?

The answer is no. Some tax cheating goes undetected. The Internal Revenue Service estimates that cheating costs the government about $90 billion in unpaid income taxes each year. Of this total, about two-thirds is owed on income that people did not report. For example, some workers are paid in cash for jobs. Part of this income may not be reported as income at tax time. Because no record of the payment exists, it is difficult for the IRS to detect this type of tax cheating.

The government also loses taxes because people claim more exemptions than they should or because deductions are overstated. By doing so, they reduce their taxable income. For example, a person might claim to have given $4,000 to charity, when only $2,000 was actually donated.

Although the process is not perfect, the IRS does have ways of catching those who cheat on their taxes. It also has methods for catching honest mistakes made by a taxpayer. When a tax return comes to an IRS office, it is first checked for obvious mistakes. Then the information is fed into a computer. The computer has been programmed to look for arithmetic mistakes and suspicious entries. If something looks wrong or strange, the computer marks that tax return as needing further examination.

These marked returns then are examined by IRS employees. If the worker has a question about the return, the taxpayer may be asked to bring her or his records to an IRS office. Each year over a million taxpayers are called in for such meetings. In four out of five cases, the person ends up paying more taxes. The average amount of extra taxes paid is over $2,000. If the problem is cheating rather than an honest mistake, the person may also be fined or even sent to prison.

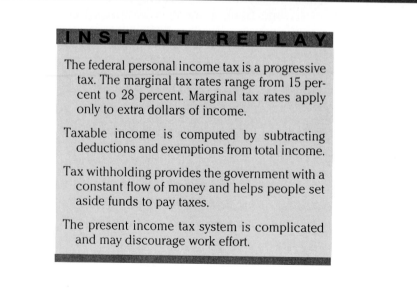

INSTANT REPLAY

The federal personal income tax is a progressive tax. The marginal tax rates range from 15 percent to 28 percent. Marginal tax rates apply only to extra dollars of income.

Taxable income is computed by subtracting deductions and exemptions from total income.

Tax withholding provides the government with a constant flow of money and helps people set aside funds to pay taxes.

The present income tax system is complicated and may discourage work effort.

OTHER TYPES OF TAXES

Dozens of different taxes are collected in the United States. There is a tax on money that is inherited and a tax on large gifts. Profits of corporations are taxed. Some states tax the use of hotel rooms. Other states tax production of coal and oil. However, in addition to the personal income tax, these are three other taxes that you are most likely to pay:

★ Social security taxes

★ Sales and excise taxes

★ Property taxes

Social Security Taxes

In 1935 Congress passed the **Federal Insurance Contribution Act (FICA),** which created the Social Security system. Its purpose is to provide income for workers who are retired or disabled and for dependents of those workers.

Under this act, employed people pay **social security taxes** throughout their working years. Self-employed workers pay the entire tax. Those employed by others pay half and their employers pay the other half. Employers deduct the tax from the worker's earnings. The employer then matches this amount and sends the tax payment to the federal government. The government places the tax payments in a special fund from which benefits are paid. This fund is supervised by the Social Security Administration.

Congress sets the rate and the base of the social security tax. In 1986 the rate was 7.15 percent. The tax base for each worker was all wages and salaries up to $42,000. That is, the employee paid 7.15 percent of the first $42,000 that was earned. No tax was paid on wages or salary above that amount. Each year the maximum earnings tax base is increased. Thus, in 1986 the maximum social security tax paid by employees was 7.15 percent of $42,000, or $3,003. In addition, the employer pays the same amount; therefore, the total tax on a worker with $42,000 in income is $6,006.

When a worker reaches retirement age, the Social Security Administration sends a monthly social security payment. The monthly payments are intended to replace part, not all, of the worker's lost income to assure the retired person of at least a minimal standard of living. Many retired persons also receive other pension payments.

Disabled workers, handicapped people who cannot work, and the families of workers who die or become disabled before reaching retirement age are also eligible for social security benefits.

The amount that a retired person receives each month from social security comes from the taxes paid by those who are still working. That is, income is redistributed from current workers to retired workers. In turn, the social security income for current workers is to be provided by those who will be working in future years. The amount of the monthly payment is set by Congress and reflects the average wage earned by the individual while employed, the rate of inflation, and other factors.

Sales and Excise Taxes

A **sales tax** is a tax on the goods and services a consumer purchases. Sales taxes are a major revenue raiser for most states. They apply to virtually all purchases, but many states exempt a few items such as clothing, restaurant meals, public utility services, food, and medicine. These exemptions vary from state to state. The sales tax rate is set at a percentage of the selling price. For example, a state may have a 5 percent sales tax. This figure means that for every dollar spent on

Sales tax is a percentage of each purchase.

goods and services, the seller collects 5 cents in sales tax and sends it to the state.

Unlike a sales tax, an **excise tax** is a tax on the purchase of a specific good or service. The federal government does not use a general sales tax, but it imposes excise taxes on several goods and services such as alcoholic beverages, tobacco, gasoline, tires, movies, and airline tickets. For example, the federal government currently imposes an excise tax of 11 cents on every gallon of gasoline sold. State governments also levy excise taxes on some items. Every state government has an excise tax on gasoline. The tax ranges from 4 cents to 15 cents per gallon.

Property Taxes

A **property tax** is based on the value of the property a person owns. In most cases, taxed property includes real estate such as buildings and land, but in some places, other kinds of personal property, such as vehicles, stocks and bonds, and jewelry, are also taxed. State and local governments have relied on property taxes as an important source of revenue for many years. For example, the operation of most public schools depends on property tax revenues.

To compute property taxes, government workers first assess the value of the property. The **assessed value** is the tax base of the prop-

Property taxes are based on the assessed value of the taxpayer's real estate and other property.

erty tax. In some cases, the assessed value might be the full market value of the property; that is, the amount that the owner could actually get for the property if it were to be sold. Usually, however, the assessed value is less than the full market value. In many states it is set at 20 percent of market value. Thus, a house that could be sold for $100,000 would have an assessed value of $20,000.

The tax rate of the property tax is usually expressed in mills. A **mill** is one-tenth of one cent or $.001. As an example, a county government might set the property tax rate at 50 mills. A 50-mill tax rate means that the tax would be 5 cents on each dollar of assessed value of the property. Thus, the property tax on a house with a $20,000 assessed value would be .05 $\times$ $20,000, or $1,000.

INSTANT REPLAY

The social security tax is collected from workers to provide income for retired persons and others who are unable to meet their own financial needs.

A sales tax usually applies to almost all the goods and services that a consumer purchases. Excise taxes apply to purchases of specific goods and services.

The property tax is a tax on land, buildings, and other kinds of property. The tax rate is usually expressed in mills. The tax base is the assessed value of the property.

SUMMARY

Taxes are payments that individuals and businesses are required to make to the government. They are used to finance government activities, to redistribute income, to change consumer decisions, and to manage the economy.

The marginal tax rate is the percentage of extra dollars of income to be paid as taxes at each income level. Progressive taxes have increasing marginal tax rates. A regressive tax has decreasing marginal tax rates. Regressive taxes may be especially difficult for low-income groups to pay.

The federal personal income tax is a progressive tax. Its marginal tax rates range from 15 percent to 28 percent of taxable income. Taxable income is computed by subtracting deductions and exemptions from total income. Tax withholding is used to provide the government with a year-round flow of revenue and to help taxpayers put aside money for taxes. Problems with the federal personal income tax include its complexity and high marginal rates that may discourage work effort.

The social security tax is used to provide income to retired people and others who have difficulty earning enough income for their own needs. Sales and excise taxes are imposed on the purchase of goods and services. Property taxes are based on the assessed value of land, buildings, and other kinds of personal property, such as vehicles and jewelry. The rate of the property tax is usually expressed in mills.

☆ LEARNING ACTIVITIES ☆

Building Your Vocabulary

On a separate sheet of paper, write the numbers 1 through 10. Next to each number, write the term that correctly completes the sentence.

tax base
marginal tax rate
progressive taxes
regressive taxes
exemptions
tax withholding
social security
sales tax
excise tax
mill

1. Taxes with decreasing marginal tax rates are called _____.

2. The proportion of extra dollars paid in taxes is the _____.

3. The number of dollars to be taxed is called the _____.

4. Taxes with increasing marginal tax rates are called _____.

5. Reductions in taxable income allowed for each member of a family are called _____.

6. The _____ system provides income for retired and disabled workers and for their dependents.

7. A _____ is a tax on almost all goods and services purchased.

8. One-tenth of a cent is called a _____.

9. The practice of deducting income taxes from an employee's paycheck is known as _____.

10. A tax on the sale of a specific kind of good or service is an _____.

Reviewing the Facts

1. How can taxes be used to change the demand for goods and services purchased by consumers?

2. Give an example of a progressive tax.

3. Why is taxable income usually less than total dollars earned?

4. Why does the federal government use tax withholding?
5. What is the purpose of the social security tax?
6. What is the difference between a sales tax and an excise tax?
7. How could the personal income tax discourage work effort?
8. Suppose the property tax rate is set at 60 mills. What would be the tax on a house with an assessed value of $10,000?

Expressing Your Opinion

1. Do you think that blind people and those over 65 should be given extra deductions in computing their taxable income? Why or why not?
2. A few years ago, during a severe oil shortage, the government gave home-owners a special tax deduction if they would add insulation to their homes as a way to conserve fuel oil. Do you think this deduction was fair? Why or why not?
3. Should the Internal Revenue Service carefully check every tax return for cheating and mistakes? Why or why not?
4. Social security taxes apply to wages only up to a specified level of income. Do you think this system is fair, or do you think that workers should also pay social security taxes on income above that level? Explain.
5. Why do you think some states exempt food and medicine from their sales taxes? Do you think these items should be taxed? Why or why not?

Developing Your Attitudes, Values, and Skills

1. Survey five to ten family members, neighbors, or friends who pay taxes to find out what their thoughts are about the federal income tax laws. The class will need to formulate a set of questions beforehand, so that you all ask the same questions in your surveys. You can ask people if they think the tax laws are fair, if they think the government should allow more or fewer deductions and exemptions, if the tax law is too complicated, and so on. Do they think there is too much cheating on taxes? Do they think the rich pay their fair share? How would they change the laws if they could? When you have completed your survey, compile your results with those of your classmates for an overall view of what the people you know think about the federal tax system.
2. How is an individual's income tax determined? Find out the answer to this question by obtaining copies of tax forms and filling them out. Create a reasonable scenario for the income you could produce and the exemptions you could claim. As you fill out the forms, observe what the tax is based on, how the tax rate is determined, what deductions people are allowed, and anything else that is important in the determination of an individual's income tax. Summarize and explain your findings to the class.
3. Before 1913 the United States did not have an income tax. Read about the

origins of the income tax in a history book. Focus your reading on the reasons the tax was established. Summarize your findings, and report to your class on the conditions that led to the establishment of the income tax in the United States.

4. In 1986 the federal government enacted sweeping reforms to the income tax laws. These changes were designed to simplify the law and place more of the tax burden on people avoiding income taxes and on corporations. Use magazine and newspaper articles to determine what specific changes the government made and what results those changes were expected to produce. Make a chart to summarize your findings.

FOCUS YOUR READING

What can government do about inflation and
unemployment?

Why is government willing to pay for most of the
cost of your education?

What is your share of the U.S. national debt?

CHAPTER 13

GOVERNMENT AND THE ECONOMY

PREVIEW

Most economic decisions in the United States are made by individuals and businesses. However, certain decisions are made by people in government. For example, Congress decides the amount of resources that will be used for national defense. Local government leaders decide how much to spend for schools. Leaders at all levels of government determine the amount of money that will be used to help the poor.

Government also tries to influence the levels of GNP and employment by changing the amount of money it spends and the amount of money created by the Federal Reserve System. The federal government generally spends more each year than it receives in taxes and other payments. The result is a large and increasing national debt. In one recent year, spending was $200 billion more than revenue. In that year, the national debt increased by more than $800 for every person in the United States.

In this chapter you will learn about some of the important activities of government in the United States economic system. You will also learn about the government's sources and uses of money. When you have completed the reading material and learning activities, you should be able to:

★ Explain how fiscal and monetary policies are used by government to reduce the rates of inflation and unemployment.

★ Explain why government produces certain goods and services, such as national defense and education.

236

★ Explain how local, state, and federal governments obtain the money they spend and what they spend that money on.

★ Discuss some of the problems created by a large national debt.

GOVERNMENT AND INFLATION/UNEMPLOYMENT

Two important goals of any economic system are to keep inflation and unemployment at acceptable levels. As you have learned, the government collects data on price changes and unemployment rates. These data tell how well the government is meeting its economic goals, and they help people in government make decisions that will improve economic performance. The methods used by the federal government in dealing with inflation and unemployment, called fiscal policy and monetary policy, are complicated. However, this section should help you understand the basic ideas.

Fiscal Policy

Fiscal policy refers to government action to increase GNP or reduce unemployment and inflation. Each year, the federal government spends billions of dollars. It buys submarines and missiles; it pays for dams, bridges, and interstate highways; it builds federal courthouses and mints; it purchases furniture and supplies for federal offices, and so on. Advocates of fiscal policy argue that by increasing or decreasing this spending, the government increases or decreases the total demand for goods and services in the economy. They argue that each new submarine or highway or mint the government finances creates new jobs, which give more money to workers to spend on consumer goods.

On the other hand, each time the government decides not to build a new ship or dam, the demand for goods and services drops because workers are laid off and they have less money to spend on consumer goods. Thus, government spending can affect GNP, inflation, and unemployment. For example, advocates of fiscal policy argue that when the economy is in a recession, government spending should be increased to raise the GNP and lower the unemployment rate.

Alternatively, the government may keep the level of spending unchanged, but may change the amount of taxes it collects from individuals and businesses. As you learned in Chapter 12, if taxes are reduced, people have more money to spend. Thus, GNP should increase and the unemployment rate should decline. If inflation is a problem, a tax increase should reduce the amount of money people have to spend and thus reduce the rate of inflation.

According to fiscal policy advocates, when the government spends more money, the GNP rises.

The Asphalt Institute

Monetary Policy

Monetary policy involves changing the supply of money available for consumption and production. The Federal Reserve System changes the total supply of money in the economy by buying or selling bonds. These functions of the Federal Reserve System were explained in Chapter 11.

Many economists think that changes in the money supply can have a significant effect on both inflation and unemployment. As you learned in Chapter 6, demand-pull inflation results from too much money chasing too few goods and services. Thus, one cure for inflation is to reduce the amount of money people have to spend. An example of an anti-inflation monetary policy would be the Federal Reserve System reducing the amount of money in the economy.

Monetary policy also can be used to lower the rate of unemployment. If the unemployment rate is too high, it can be reduced by increasing the demand for goods and services. Greater demand can be created by increasing the amount of money in the hands of businesses and individuals. When more money is available, people will demand more goods and services and more workers will be hired to produce them.

Evaluation of Fiscal and Monetary Policies

There is considerable debate among economists about the effectiveness of fiscal and monetary policies. Advocates of fiscal policy argue that the level of GNP and employment can be changed by changing income tax rates or government spending. For example, during a recession the government could spend money borrowed from banks and individuals to buy goods and services. Such action, it is argued, would increase GNP, create jobs, and reduce the unemployment rate.

Critics of fiscal policy argue that when government borrows from banks and individuals, the latter have less money to spend. That is, government will spend more, but the amount will be offset because individuals will have less to spend and banks will have less money to lend. Therefore, total demand and GNP would be unchanged.

Others argue that although fiscal policy may be effective in changing GNP, such policies take too long to put into effect. Suppose the economy is in a recession; that is, GNP has declined and the unemployment rate has increased. Federal officials may decide to borrow money to build new interstate highways, thus creating demand for workers and materials. But it may take as long as a year for Congress to pass the legislation approving the program and for construction work to begin. By that time the recession could be over and the expansion phase already started.

There also is debate about the effectiveness of monetary policy in influencing the economy. **Monetarists** are people who claim that changes in the rate of growth in the money supply can affect the level of GNP, the unemployment rate, and the rate of inflation. Some experts say, however, that the lag time between the change in money supply and its effect on the economy is unpredictable. This lag may be as short as three months or as long as two years. Because the lag is so variable, these experts oppose using monetary policy to combat economic problems. Rather, they argue that the money supply should be increased at a steady rate of perhaps 3 to 4 percent per year. In their opinion, this increase would allow steady growth of GNP.

Some economists believe that the primary cause of inflation in the United States has been that the Federal Reserve System allows the money supply to increase too rapidly. For example, there have been periods when GNP increased 2 or 3 percent per year while the amount of money increased at 10 to 15 percent annually. These economists claim that during such periods, too much money chasing too few goods resulted in inflation.

There is no general agreement about these issues. The relative merits of monetary and fiscal policies are still being debated. However, certain economists now agree that monetary and fiscal policies probably are not good tools for managing the economy. Within this group, some believe that these tools are ineffective and others believe that these tools have effects but that the effects are too unpredictable to be useful.

Supply-Side Economics

Another way to encourage growth in GNP and employment is supply-side economics. Supporters of **supply-side economics** argue that the government should assist economic growth by using policies that promote maximum production. These supporters suggest, for example, that rules should be designed to encourage work, production, and investment in capital goods. Environmental and safety rules should be reasonable so that they do not hinder the production of goods and services. Finally, government should regulate business only when absolutely necessary.

In the 1980s, supply-side economics attracted considerable interest in the federal government. Congress passed laws that reduced tax rates and provided greater incentives for companies to invest in machinery and other capital goods. Some environmental rules were relaxed, and regulations were reduced in several industries. During this period, there was general agreement that the climate for investment, production, and consumption had improved, although the growth rate of GNP was slightly below expectations.

Supply-side economics calls for government to promote production and investment.

Photo courtesy of Alcoa

INSTANT REPLAY

Fiscal policy involves changes in government spending or taxation in order to improve the performance of the economic system.

Monetary policy uses changes in the supply of money as the tool for managing the economy.

Some critics of fiscal and monetary policies argue that these tools are either ineffective or too unpredictable to be useful in managing the economy.

Supply-side economics involves creating an economic environment that encourages production and investment.

GOVERNMENT AS A PRODUCER OF GOODS AND SERVICES

Most of the goods and services consumed in the United States are produced by privately owned firms. The widespread use of private enterprise in the United States is based on the belief that it is better to separate economic and political power. That is, those who have the power to make political decisions should not have direct control over economic decisions.

Although private enterprise is responsible for producing most goods and services, various departments of government also produce them. A complete listing of the goods and services provided by government would require many pages. Here are just a few examples:

Water	Garbage collection
National parks	Libraries
Highways and roads	Museums
Hospitals	Education
Buses and trains	Sewers
Postal service	Airports
Housing	Electricity
National defense	Flood control
Swimming pools	

The government provides low-cost recreation to its citizens.

Courtesy Michigan Travel Bureau

Reasons for Government Involvement

Government provides goods and services for many reasons. In some cases, a project may be too costly or risky for individual firms to undertake. An example is the launching of satellites. Rockets used for this purpose were developed by the federal government as a part of defense and space exploration programs. Private firms soon realized that satellites could be valuable for communications, oil exploration, and many other uses. But the cost of developing and building rockets to launch satellites could be billions of dollars. No private business could afford this amount. As a result, private firms own satellites but depend on the federal government to build the missiles that launch the satellites into space. The firms pay fees to the government for this service.

Some government projects are started because government officials want to provide citizens with cultural and recreational opportunities at a low cost to each individual. Examples include libraries, museums, and parks. Other government projects are designed to help a community or region grow. Airports, harbors, and roads all serve this purpose. Improvements to a transportation system make an area a better place to live and attract new firms and workers.

Some government businesses exist because private enterprise in a particular industry is not profitable. In 1970 Congress created Amtrak to provide railroad passenger service. The private railroads had been losing money on passenger service and wanted to get out of the business. Now the government provides passenger service, and any losses by Amtrak are made up by federal subsidies paid for with tax dollars.

In some cases there is no clear reason why an enterprise is run by government instead of by private enterprise. Many goods and services that are provided by government in one city are supplied by private firms in another city. For example, in most places the local government provides garbage collection. But some cities have contracts with private businesses for the collection of garbage. Often, the private firm can do the job at a lower cost.

Government and National Defense

Each year the federal government spends billions of dollars on national defense. This money goes to pay soldiers, to purchase new weapons and equipment, and to repair existing weapons and equipment. Some people argue that too much money is spent on defense, but almost everyone agrees that defense is important.

Why is national defense the responsibility of the federal government? Why is it not possible for private firms to sell protection to individual citizens? Clearly, one reason is the enormous cost. Another is that national defense is a public good. **Public goods** are goods that everyone can consume, whether each individual pays for them or not.

Think about a situation in which a private firm sells national defense. Suppose a salesperson comes to your house and offers to install missiles in the area around your community. These missiles are supposed to provide your family with complete protection against an attack from a foreign country. The price for your family is $1,000 per year. Your parent agrees and writes out a check for the full amount.

The salesperson then goes next door to your friend's house and makes the same offer, but your friend's parent decides not to participate. This response is a wise business decision. If your family receives protection from the missile attack, there is no way that the company can avoid providing protection for your neighbors as well. Any system that protects your house will also protect the house next door. Even though your neighbors do not pay, they cannot be prevented from consuming the service offered by the firm. Thus, there is no reason for them to pay the $1,000.

You and your family soon realize that if others have paid, you will still receive the benefits. As a result, your parent probably would stop making the payments to the firm. So would everyone else, and the firm would quickly go out of business. Unless there is a way to make everyone pay, few will pay.

The reason government provides national defense is that only the government can make everybody pay. It can force people to pay taxes, which then can be used for national defense. No private firm has this power. Only government can adequately provide public goods such as national defense.

Government and Education

Federal, state, and local governments spend large amounts of money on education. The government pays almost all the costs of educating those who attend public schools from kindergarten through high school. You may have to spend money on books, supplies, and extracurricular activities, but these represent only a small fraction of the total cost of your education.

Why does government pay the cost of your education? Would it not be fairer if each person or family paid the cost? There is a good reason that government pays. Education involves a positive externality. A **positive externality** is a benefit received by someone other than the person who buys the good or service.

In the case of education, the positive externality is that all members of society benefit from having educated citizens. The successful opera-

Education involves a positive externality.

tion of the democratic system requires that citizens be able to understand the issues on which they vote. Also, an educated society usually has lower rates of crime and disease.

If each person had to pay the entire cost of his or her education, many would drop out of school. By paying most of the costs of education, government lowers the price to the individual. The law of demand holds for education just as for any other good. Because the price is lower, more people complete their education. Society benefits because of the positive externality associated with education.

INSTANT REPLAY

Government is involved in producing many types of goods and services.

Public goods such as national defense are provided by government because only government can require everybody to pay a fair share.

Government pays for most of the costs of education to take advantage of the positive externality resulting from education.

GOVERNMENT BUDGETS

In addition to the federal government, there are 50 state governments, more than 3,000 county governments, and about 36,000 city governments. Each of these units collects and spends money. In this section you will learn about government budgets at the federal, state, and local levels.

Revenue

Figure 13-1 shows the most important sources of revenue for the federal government. **Revenue** is the income a government receives from all sources, including taxes, fees, and fines. The personal income tax is the main source of federal government revenue. Almost half of all dollars received come from this tax. Social security taxes are the next most important source, composing over one-third of all federal revenues. About 12 percent comes from the corporate income tax, which is a tax based on the profits of corporations. About 4 percent is derived from excise taxes on goods such as gasoline and liquor.

FIGURE 13-1
These are the estimated
sources of revenue for
the federal government
in 1987.

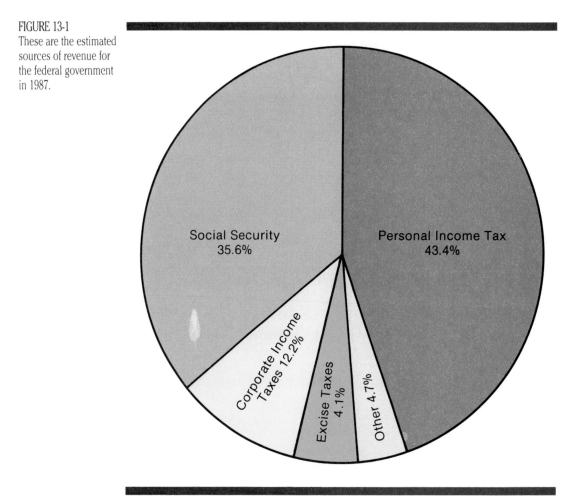

Source: Council of Economic Advisors, *Economic Report of the President* (Washington: U.S. Government Printing Office, 1986), p. 341.

Figure 13-2 indicates where the dollars come from to support state and local governments. An important source of revenue is money given to state and local governments by the federal government. Almost one-fifth of their revenue comes from this source. Sales and excise taxes are the most important sources of tax revenue, and property taxes are almost as important. Personal and corporate income taxes represent about 15 percent of total revenues but are not nearly as important as at the federal level. The "other" category includes money from selling electricity and water and from providing services such as collecting garbage, operating liquor stores, and selling licenses for automobiles, hunting, and fishing.

FIGURE 13-2
These were the sources of revenue for state and local governments in 1984.

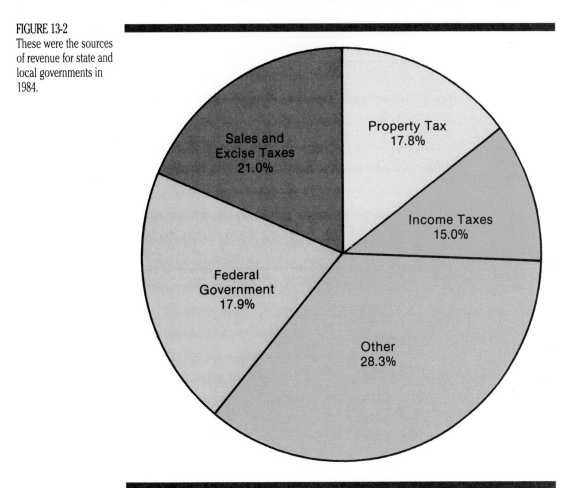

Source: Council of Economic Advisors, *Economic Report of the President* (Washington: U.S. Government Printing Office, 1986), p. 347.

Expenditures

In 1987 the federal government spent a total of $994 billion ($994,000,000,000). It is difficult to comprehend such a large number, but you can understand it better if you look at the following comparisons. If you had $994 billion you could:

★ Spend $1 million a day for over 2,000 years.

★ Buy a new Cadillac for everyone in the state of Texas.

★ Make a path of dollar bills nearly 600 feet wide that would encircle the earth at its equator.

Table 13-1 shows how the federal government spends its money. The largest single category is income security. This category includes all the federal government's programs to provide a minimum income to unemployed, disabled, and retired people. Most of this money is paid in social security payments, but these payments include unemployment compensation and welfare benefits as well. About 30 percent of total expenditures is used for national defense. Interest on the national debt is nearly 15 percent of the total and represents interest payments to those who have lent money to the federal government.

TABLE 13-1

ESTIMATED FEDERAL GOVERNMENT EXPENDITURES, 1987

Category	Percentage of Total Expenditures
Income Security	39.9%
National Defense	28.4
Interest	14.9
Health	3.5
Education and Employment	2.8
Veterans' Benefits	2.7
Transportation	2.6
Natural Resources	1.2
Other	4.0

Source: Council of Economic Advisors, *Economic Report of the President* (Washington: U.S. Government Printing Office, 1986), p. 341.

State and local governments spent $435 billion in 1984, about one-half the amount spent by the federal government. Table 13-2 shows how these dollars were used. The spending pattern is much different from

TABLE 13-2

STATE AND LOCAL GOVERNMENT EXPENDITURES, 1984

Category	Percentage of Total Expenditures
Education	34.9%
Public Welfare	13.2
Highways	7.8
Other	44.1

Source: Council of Economic Advisors, *Economic Report of the President* (Washington: U.S. Government Printing Office, 1986), p. 347.

that of the federal government. State and local governments spend the largest part of their money on education, highways, and public welfare (such as money for hospitals and assistance to the poor).

INSTANT REPLAY

The income tax is the most important source of revenue for the federal government.

State and local governments rely heavily on the property tax and on sales and excise taxes. A part of their revenue comes from the federal government.

Income security programs, such as social security payments, represent about 40 percent of federal expenditures. About 30 percent of federal expenditures are for national defense.

Most state and local dollars are used for education, highways, and public welfare.

THE NATIONAL DEBT

In the last section you learned that the federal government spent $994 billion in 1987. But revenues that year were only $850 billion. Thus, the federal government spent nearly $150 billion more than it collected. When government expenditures exceed revenues, the difference is known as a **deficit.** Deficits are not an unusual occurrence for the federal government. In fact, the federal budget has had a deficit in 23 of the last 24 years.

When individuals spend more than they earn, they must borrow money to make up the difference. The same is true for the federal government. If government expenditures exceed revenues, the government must borrow money. These dollars are lent by firms and individuals in the United States, investors from other countries, and other government agencies. The total amount of money owed by the federal government is called the **national debt.**

Size of the National Debt

Each year that the federal budget has a deficit, the national debt grows by the amount of that deficit. For example, the 1987 deficit caused the debt to increase by nearly $150 billion. Table 13-3 shows the growth in the national debt. The table indicates that the total debt was more than five times as great in 1945 as in 1940, because the government had to borrow large amounts of money to pay the cost of fighting in World War II. The national debt often increases rapidly during wartime.

TABLE 13-3

NATIONAL DEBT IN SELECTED YEARS	
Year	National Debt (billions)
1929	$ 16.9
1940	50.7
1945	260.1
1955	274.4
1965	323.2
1970	382.6
1975	544.1
1980	914.3
1985	1,827.5
1987	2,320.6

Source: Council of Economic Advisors, *Economic Report of the President* (Washington: U.S. Government Printing Office, 1986), p. 339.

Since the early 1970s the United States has been at peace, but the national debt has continued to climb. The debt was four times as great in 1987 as it was in 1975. In 1987 the total was $2,320.6 billion, amounting to about $9,400 for every man, woman, and child in the United States.

Misunderstandings About the National Debt

Many people are worried about the national debt. Some of these concerns are justified, but others are the result of not fully understanding the facts. Two common misunderstandings are considered here.

The Federal Government Is Going Bankrupt. One concern is that the national debt is becoming so large that the federal government may go bankrupt. A federal bankruptcy is unlikely to occur. The government is different from a private firm in that it has the power to tax. Thus, the government has a means of getting the dollars needed to make the interest payments on the national debt. Increased taxes may cause problems for individuals and businesses, but the government will not go bankrupt.

The National Debt Is Too Large. The national debt is a huge amount of money. Indeed, it may be too large. But it is misleading to evaluate the national debt only in terms of its total size. A more useful measure is the debt as a percentage of gross national product. At present, the national debt is about 46 percent of a year's GNP, meaning that the debt is less than one-half of one year's output. In these terms it does not seem so large.

It would not be unusual for a family to have a home mortgage debt that is two or three times the amount of income that the family earns in a year. Families are not unduly burdened by this amount of debt. Hence, the federal government probably can function with a debt that is less than one-half its annual income. The best protection against problems resulting from the national debt is a growing economy. The reason is that as GNP increases, the amount of taxes collected by the government also increases.

Valid Concerns About the National Debt

There are some serious problems caused by a large and growing debt. Some of the problems associated with a large national debt are identified here.

Redistribution of Income. About one-third of the national debt is owed to other government agencies, such as the Federal Reserve System. The remainder is held by private individuals. Most of this privately owned debt is held by United States citizens. Thus, the national debt really consists of dollars that we owe to ourselves. Taxes are collected from taxpayers and then used to pay interest to bondholders.

The problem is that the redistribution of income caused by the national debt may result in the rich getting richer. The people who receive interest payments from money they have lent the federal government are likely to have above-average incomes. Thus, the tax system collects dollars from all taxpayers and redistributes them to high-income investors.

Waste. Many people believe that much of the money spent by the federal government is wasted. They cite examples such as expensive weapons that do not work, workers who have little work to do, and research studies that are not important. If the national debt increases as a result of such waste, a burden is placed on future generations who must pay the interest on that debt. That is, future taxpayers will be forced to pay for goods and services that do not provide any benefits.

High Interest Rates. Interest rates are determined by supply and demand. When the federal government has to borrow money because of a budget deficit, the demand for money increases and interest rates for all borrowers may rise. One result is that private firms may cut back on borrowing for the purpose of purchasing capital goods. But capital goods are necessary if the economy is to grow. Thus, one consequence of deficits and a large national debt may be a slowing of the rate of economic growth.

INSTANT REPLAY

When government expenditures exceed revenues, the difference is called a deficit. The total amount of money owed by the federal government is the national debt.

Currently the national debt amounts to about $9,400 for every man, woman, and child in the United States.

The national debt may be a problem if it redistributes income to the rich, results from waste in government, or causes high interest rates.

SUMMARY

Fiscal and monetary policies are used by government to increase economic growth and decrease inflation and unemployment. Fiscal policy involves changes in taxes and government spending. Monetary policy refers to changes in the supply of money. There is considerable debate about the effectiveness of fiscal and monetary policies.

Government is an important producer of goods and services. Electricity, water, garbage collection, roads, parks, and museums are a few of the goods and services provided by government.

The government must provide public goods such as national defense because private firms cannot profitably provide such goods. Education is largely financed by government because of the positive externality associated with this service.

The personal income tax is the most important source of revenue for the federal government. State and local governments rely on money from the federal government and on property, sales, and excise taxes. Over half of federal expenditures are for national defense and social security payments. The most important uses of money at the state and local level are for education, highways, and public welfare.

A deficit occurs when the government spends more money than it takes in. The national debt is the result of budget deficits. The debt has grown rapidly in recent years and now is over $2,300 billion. Possible problems caused by the debt include a burden on the future that results from wasteful spending, a redistribution of income from the poor to the rich, and high interest rates.

☆ LEARNING ACTIVITIES ☆

Building Your Vocabulary

On a separate sheet of paper, write the numbers 1 through 7. Next to each number, write the term that correctly completes the sentence.

deficit
fiscal policy
monetary policy
supply-side
  economics
public good
national debt
positive externality

1. Changes in taxes and government spending designed to achieve economic goals are known as _____.

2. Changes in the money supply designed to achieve economic goals are known as _____.

3. A _____ is something everyone consumes whether the individual pays for it or not.

4. The _____ is money owed by the federal government.

5. A _____ occurs when expenditures exceed revenues.

6. A _____ is a benefit received by someone other than the purchaser of a good or service.

7. Supporters of _____ believe that government policies should promote maximum production and investment.

Reviewing the Facts

1. How could fiscal policy be used to reduce the rate of unemployment?
2. How could monetary policy be used to combat inflation?
3. Describe two reasons why government provides goods and services.
4. What is the most important source of revenue for the federal government? For state and local governments?
5. What causes the national debt to increase?
6. How does a large national debt affect interest rates?
7. What are the federal government's three largest categories of expenditures?

Expressing Your Opinion

1. Do you think it is a good idea to use fiscal policy to promote economic growth? Why or why not?
2. Should the federal government be in the business of operating buses and trains, paying for sewers and flood control, and running hospitals? Justify your answer in each case.
3. Why is the personal income tax such an important source of revenue for the federal government? Do you think it is the fairest kind of tax for the government to impose? Why or why not?
4. Should the federal government be required to have a balanced budget each year? Explain your answer.
5. Why does the United States have such a large national debt? What do you think can be done to reduce it?

Developing Your Attitudes, Values, and Skills

1. In the mid-1980s, the federal government enacted the Gramm-Rudman-Hollings Act to sharply reduce the national deficit. Research this law to find out why it was enacted. What did it require the President and Congress to do to curb spending? How did the act get its name? What were the results of implementing the act? How did it affect domestic and defense programs? What did its opponents say about it? Were there any legal problems with it? Write a brief report summarizing your findings, and state whether you believe Gramm-Rudman-Hollings was a beneficial or harmful law. Be prepared to defend your opinion.
2. In 1929 the national debt per person was only about $137; in 1987 it was about $9,400. Has the national debt per person increased slowly and steadily throughout this period, or has it suddenly increased? Using *World Almanac* or census figures, write down the population of the United States for each of the years listed in Table 13-3. Divide the national debt for each year by the population for that same year to get the per capita amount. Do the figures show a rapid or a gradual increase? Make a simple chart or graph that shows this information in pictorial form. What are some reasons you can think of that would explain these figures? Present your data to the class.
3. The Social Security Administration provides benefits to retired and disabled workers and their families in accordance with complicated regulations and guidelines. To examine these regulations, suppose that you are one of these people—a worker who has just reached his or her 65th birthday, a woman with two small children whose husband was recently killed in an industrial accident, a blind person, a 35-year-old disabled worker, or the divorced spouse of a retired worker. Consult almanacs, magazines, or social security publications available at your local library or Social Security Administration office. Or as a class, interview an employee of the Social Security Administration. Find out what benefits you can expect to receive

and what you have to do to qualify for those benefits. How much can you expect to receive each month? How many years would you have had to pay into the system before you qualify for benefits? What documents do you have to present to the Social Security Administration? How long do you have to wait before the benefits begin arriving? What medical benefits do you qualify for? Will you receive a cost-of-living adjustment and if so, when? Summarize your findings, and be prepared to present them to the class.

UNIT 5

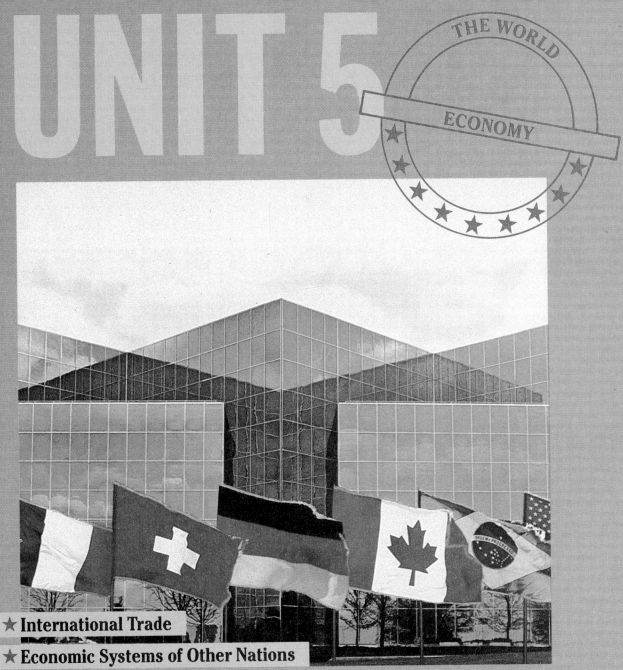

R.J.R. NABISCO, INC.

★ **International Trade**

★ **Economic Systems of Other Nations**

The United States is part of an international trading system. Many of our trading partners have economic systems that are not based on free enterprise principles. In this unit you will learn about the purposes, extent, and the impact of world trade on the United States' economy and how the economic systems of many of these trading partners differ from that of the United States.

CHAPTER 14

INTERNATIONAL TRADE

PREVIEW

Goods produced in the United States are sold throughout the world. Chinese airlines use planes assembled in Washington. Cattle in the U.S.S.R. are fed on grain grown in Kansas. Skyscrapers in Mexico City are built with steel manufactured in Pennsylvania. Canadian grocery stores sell California oranges.

At the same time, United States citizens use goods made in other countries. American highways are crowded with Hondas, Toyotas, Mazdas, and Subarus manufactured in Japan. Millions of gallons of gasoline used by those cars come from the oil fields of Saudi Arabia. The coffee that gets people going in the morning is purchased from Brazil and Colombia. This trading of goods and services links the world together.

In this chapter you will learn about the advantages and problems of trade between nations. When you have completed the reading material and learning activities, you should be able to:

★ Explain how nations can benefit by trading with each other.

★ List the main imports and exports of the United States.

★ Define what is meant by balance of trade and balance of payments.

★ Explain the difference between fixed and floating exchange rates.

★ Discuss what tariffs are and how they reduce the demand for imports.

258

BENEFITS OF INTERNATIONAL TRADE

Trading is one of the most important activities in a free enterprise system. As you have learned, workers trade their labor for wages so that they can buy goods and services. Business owners trade the products produced by their firms in order to pay workers and earn profits. People trade goods and services when they expect to be better off as a result of the exchange. By giving up something of lesser value, they get something that they value more.

When goods and services produced in different countries are exchanged, that activity is called **international trade.** Trade between nations enables people to buy things that they might otherwise have to do without. No country can provide everything that its citizens want. For example, most of the world's diamonds are found in Africa. If trade were stopped between the United States and the African diamond-producing nations, few Americans would have diamond jewelry. Without international trade, many other items that make life more pleasant would be unavailable or at least more expensive.

The Principle of Absolute Advantage

Human, natural, and capital resources are necessary to produce goods and services. But these resources are not distributed equally among nations. Some countries have abundant natural resources but few capital goods. Other countries have plenty of human resources, but few natural resources. International trade allows nations to concentrate on the activities for which they are best suited. Countries with many workers can produce goods that require a lot of labor, while countries with valuable natural resources can focus on developing and selling those resources.

When a country can produce a good or service at lower cost than another country, it is said to have an **absolute advantage.** For example, Colombia, in South America, possesses more than 90 percent of the world's supply of emeralds, a gemstone that exists in small quantities in a few other nations. Thus, Colombia is said to have an absolute advantage in producing emeralds. In contrast, the capital goods owned by automakers in the United States allow vehicles to be produced at a much lower cost than they could be produced in Colombia. Hence, the United States has an absolute advantage in manufacturing cars.

Colombia, S.A., enjoys an absolute advantage in emerald production, because it possesses more than 90 percent of the world supply.

© George Roos/Peter Arnold, Inc.

Usually, countries should specialize in making those goods and services for which they have an absolute advantage. This specialization allows an economic system to operate more efficiently, and it results in the production of more goods and services. A simple example will help you understand this idea. Suppose Country *A* has few people but many valuable natural resources, such as oil and iron ore. In contrast, suppose Country *B* has a large population but is short on natural resources, except for good farmland.

If Country *A* is not involved in international trade, its citizens may find it difficult to obtain certain goods. There may be plenty of gasoline available, but a lack of skilled workers may limit the number of cars that can be manufactured. This country also may be unable to produce enough food to feed its people, because it has few workers and unsuitable land for agriculture.

With its excellent farmland, Country *B* can produce more food than its people need. This nation also has plenty of workers to manufacture automobiles. But there is not enough iron ore to make steel for automobile parts. Country B may also be unable to produce enough gasoline to meet the demands of its citizens.

The people of both countries could have more goods and services if they were to trade with each other. Then each nation could produce those goods for which it has an absolute advantage. Country A would concentrate on using its natural resources to produce oil and steel. Country B's large population would be employed to manufacture goods such as cars and to grow food.

The oil and steel produced in Country A can be traded for automobiles and food produced in Country B. By specializing in what they do best, the citizens of both countries are better off. People in Country A now receive the benefits of the human resources in Country B. Those in Country B are able to share the natural resources of Country A.

The Principle of Comparative Advantage

It is not surprising that both trading partners can benefit by specializing in those products for which they have an absolute advantage. But what if one nation is more efficient at producing both of the goods to be traded? For example, suppose that both beef and computers can be produced at lower cost in the United States than in Taiwan. Table 14-1 shows the hypothetical opportunity cost (in terms of American dollars) of producing both of these goods in each country. Note that both a pound of beef and a computer cost less to produce in the United States than in Taiwan. That is, the United States has an absolute advantage in producing both beef and computers. In this situation, is there any reason the two countries might benefit by trading with each other? The answer involves the concept of **comparative advantage,** which means that a country benefits from specializing in the production of those products at which it is relatively most efficient.

TABLE 14-1

COSTS OF PRODUCING BEEF AND COMPUTERS IN THE UNITED STATES AND TAIWAN		
Country	Beef	Computers
United States	$2 per pound	$500 each
Taiwan	$5 per pound	$750 each

Suppose in this example that beef and computers are the only two goods produced in both Taiwan and the United States. To determine which country has the comparative advantage in producing computers, you have to determine how much it would cost each country—its opportunity cost—to switch its resources from producing beef to making computers. In this case, according to Table 14-1, the United States would have to give up 250 pounds of beef ($500 ÷ $2) to produce one computer. But in Taiwan, the opportunity cost of producing one computer is only 150 pounds of beef ($750 ÷ $5). Therefore, since the opportunity cost is less for Taiwan than the United States, Taiwan would have a comparative advantage in producing computers.

The same principle of comparative advantage holds true for trading computers and beef between the two countries as for producing them. Suppose that an importer suggests trading one Taiwanese computer for 200 pounds of American beef. In Taiwan the computer can be traded for only 150 pounds of beef, so this trade is good for the Taiwanese. At the same time, the opportunity cost of providing a computer in the United States would be 250 pounds of beef, but the cost of getting a computer by trading with Taiwan is only 200 pounds of beef. Thus, the trade also benefits people in the United States.

Whenever nations have a comparative advantage, they can benefit from trade even if one of the nations has an absolute advantage in both goods. Each country should specialize in the production of the good for which it has the comparative advantage. Thus, Taiwan will produce computers and the United States will produce beef.

Babe Ruth's Comparative Advantage

Babe Ruth was one of the greatest baseball players of all time. He managed to hit 714 home runs at a time when few home runs were hit. His lifetime batting average of .342 is one of the highest in baseball history.

Although Ruth spent most of his career playing right field, he started out as a pitcher. During three years of full-time pitching he was one of the best in the American League, winning 65 games and losing only 31. In World Series play, he once pitched nearly 30 consecutive innings without giving up a run.

In 1919 Babe Ruth switched from pitching to become a full-time outfielder. His skill as a pitcher had not decreased, but he was such a good hitter that his manager wanted him in the lineup every day.

Ruth had an absolute advantage over most players both as a pitcher and as a hitter. But his comparative advantage was as a hitter. That is, compared with other players he was even better as a hitter than he was as a pitcher. Thus, Ruth specialized in his comparative advantage and spent the rest of his career hitting baseballs for home runs.

INSTANT REPLAY

The exchange of goods and services between nations is called international trade.

International trade allows countries to specialize in those things which they can produce most efficiently, thus making everyone better off.

Even if a country has an absolute advantage in producing several kinds of goods, it can benefit from international trade by specializing in those goods for which it has a comparative advantage.

IMPORTANCE OF INTERNATIONAL TRADE

The goods that a nation sells to other countries are called **exports.** Goods purchased from other countries are called **imports.** Exports and imports represent less than 10 percent of all business activity in the United States. This percentage may seem small, but the number of workers and dollars involved is very large. In 1984 businesses in the United States exported $212 billion worth of goods, and the value of imports was $326 billion. Nearly 4 million workers in the United States have jobs that depend on international trade.

Table 14-2 shows the dollar value of imports and exports for selected countries in 1984. It indicates that the United States was the largest trader in the world. Other nations with large amounts of imports and exports are West Germany, Great Britain, France, and Japan. To-

TABLE 14-2

	INTERNATIONAL TRADE IN SELECTED COUNTRIES, 1984		
Country	International Trade As a Percentage of GNP	Imports	Exports (billions of dollars)
Hong Kong	49%	$ 25	$ 22
West Germany	25	152	171
Great Britain	19	105	94
France	17	103	93
Japan	15	136	170
United States	7	326	212

Source: U.S. Bureau of the Census, *Statistical Abstract of the United States: 1986*, 106th edition (Washington, D.C., 1986), pp. 842 and 856.

gether, these five nations account for about 40 percent of world trade. In contrast, although almost half of the earth's population lives in China, India, and the U.S.S.R., these three nations account for only about 5 percent of all international trade.

Although international trade in countries such as Japan and the United States involves billions of dollars, these nations are much less dependent on international trade than are many other countries. For example, Table 14-2 shows that about half of all business activity in Hong Kong is tied to imports and exports. This proportion compares with 15 percent in Japan and only 7 percent in the United States. The explanation is that Hong Kong is a small place with many workers and few natural and capital resources. Thus, Hong Kong has specialized in making goods that require much labor, such as clothing. These goods are exported throughout the world. In turn, Hong Kong imports food, fuel, and the materials necessary for making goods.

Exports of the United States

Countries export goods for which they have an absolute or a comparative advantage. Figure 14-1 shows the most important exports of the United States. They fit into three main categories. First, the United States

FIGURE 14-1
These were the most important exports of the United States for 1984.

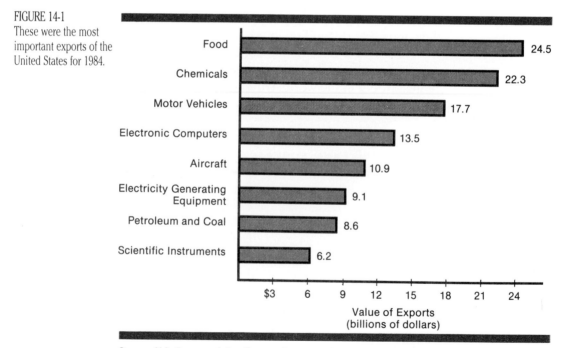

Source: U.S. Bureau of the Census, *Statistical Abstract of the United States: 1986*, 106th edition (Washington, D.C., 1986), pp. 814-815.

has more capital goods than any other country. As a result, it is a leader in exporting products that require a lot of capital goods to produce. These goods include airplanes, motor vehicles, scientific instruments, computers, and equipment for generating electricity. Second, the United States has many valuable natural resources that are needed in other nations. Coal is one of the most important. Other exports in this category include chemical products, especially those used as fertilizers. Finally, the United States is the world's largest producer of food. Each year, American farmers produce far more than is used in the United States. This extra food, especially wheat and corn, is sold to countries that are unable to grow enough to feed their citizens.

Imports of the United States

Countries import products they cannot produce or for which other nations have a comparative advantage. Some products are not produced at all in the United States. For example, virtually all the bananas, cocoa, diamonds, and natural rubber used in the United States are imported. The United States also has to import most of its supply of certain metals and metal ores. These include about 90 percent of the ore used to make aluminum and over 80 percent of the tin. Although the United States produces most of its own oil, the dollar value of oil imports is still very large. In 1984, nearly $56 billion worth of petroleum was purchased from the Middle East and other parts of the world. Figure 14-2 shows the most important imports of the United States.

Multinational Firms and International Trade

Multinational firms are businesses that make and sell products in many different countries. These firms are important to the worldwide economic system. The 400 largest multinational firms account for about one-third of all the goods produced in the western industrialized nations.

Almost all large United States firms are multinationals. General Motors, IBM, Coca-Cola, and Exxon all have operations in other countries. Exxon, a seller of petroleum products, is one of the world's largest multinational firms, with some 400 units doing business in more than 100 nations. The company's activities take place in so many countries that when the name "Exxon" was chosen in 1972, a computer checked that the new name did not have an obscene or negative meaning in the language of any of these countries.

Basically, corporations become multinational in the quest for additional profits. Sometimes they are trying to obtain valuable natural

FIGURE 14-2
These were the most important imports of the United States in 1984.

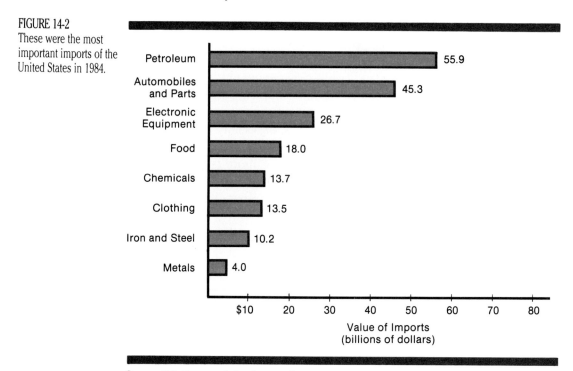

Petroleum — 55.9
Automobiles and Parts — 45.3
Electronic Equipment — 26.7
Food — 18.0
Chemicals — 13.7
Clothing — 13.5
Iron and Steel — 10.2
Metals — 4.0

$10   20   30   40   50   60   70   80

Value of Imports
(billions of dollars)

Source: U.S. Bureau of the Census, *Statistical Abstract of the United States: 1986*, 106th edition (Washington, D.C, 1986), pp. 816-817.

resources, such as metals or petroleum. In other cases, the company sees an opportunity to serve a new market. For example, Coca-Cola has proved to be very popular in China. A third explanation is comparative advantage. A business may set up a mining operation in a country with valuable natural resources, refine the resources in another country where wages are low, and engage in manufacturing in a third country that has plenty of capital resources.

By making use of the comparative advantage of each country, multinational firms enable the economic system to operate more efficiently. Additional jobs are created, and more goods are produced. However, such businesses can also cause problems. Sometimes multinational corporations remove natural resources without providing any real benefits to the country in which the resources were found. In other cases, workers are brought in so that few new jobs are created for the citizens of the host country. Also, there is a danger that the multinational corporation will use its power to force changes in the customs or politics of the country in which it operates.

Many American companies have become multinational in their quests for additional profits.

© Tom McHugh, 1979/Photo Researchers, Inc.

INSTANT REPLAY

Exports are goods sold to other countries. Imports are goods purchased from other countries.

Important United States exports include food, airplanes, machines, fuels, and chemicals. Petroleum and automobiles are among the most important United States imports.

Multinational firms are businesses that make and sell goods in many countries. By using the principle of comparative advantage, they help the economic system operate more efficiently.

INTERNATIONAL FINANCE

Suppose that each state had its own money. This situation would make buying goods and services much less convenient. Purchases in Texas could be made using only Texas money. Texans who traveled into Oklahoma would need to get Oklahoma money.

Of course, only one kind of money is used throughout the United States, and this fact makes buying and selling very easy anywhere in the nation. In international trade, however, each country has its own form of money, which complicates the process of buying and selling among countries. For example, Japan has its yen, Great Britain has its pound, and West Germany has its mark. Usually people must use a country's money to purchase goods and services in or from that country. Therefore, there must be some means of exchanging one form of money for another. The process of paying for goods and services in international trade is called **international finance.**

Suppose an American importer goes to Japan to buy cameras to sell in the United States. Japanese firms do not want to be paid in dollars, because workers and owners cannot spend dollars in Japan. Thus, the American importer first trades dollars for yen in the **foreign exchange market.** This market consists of banks and other firms that specialize in trading money. For a fee, persons in this market will take United States dollars and provide yen that can be used to buy the goods.

Exchange Rates

The price of one currency in terms of another is called the **exchange rate.** For example, in September 1986, the number of yen that could be bought for $1 was 155. The number of West German marks that could be bought for $1 was 2.05. Thus, a $10,000 car would cost 1,550,000 yen or 20,500 marks.

Many countries use a **floating exchange rate;** that is, the price of that nation's money can change (or float) from day to day or even from hour to hour. For example, $1 bought 155 yen in September 1986. In contrast, 227 yen could have been purchased for $1 in 1984.

One factor that determines the exchange rate between two currencies is the demand for a country's goods and services. Suppose that

The exchange rate determines how different currencies can be exchanged to carry out international trade.

G. Schachmes/Sygma

Americans decide to buy more Japanese products. To buy Japanese goods, United States buyers will have to obtain more yen. As the demand for yen increases, the price of yen will rise. That is, a dollar will buy fewer yen. In contrast, if Americans import fewer goods and services from Japan, the demand for yen will drop and the price in terms of dollars will decrease.

Some countries use a **fixed exchange rate;** that is, the government sets or fixes the rate at which its money may be traded. This rate may be in terms of gold or another currency. For example, until 1971, the United States government set the exchange rate between the dollar and gold at $35 per ounce. During this period, the government was willing to pay people in other countries one ounce of gold for each $35. Since 1971, the value of the dollar has been allowed to float in terms of gold and other currencies.

When a fixed exchange rate is too low, a nation may have to **devalue** its money. Devaluation is accomplished by raising the rate of exchange. For example, suppose that when the dollar was fixed at $35 per ounce of gold, the rate would have been $75 if it had been allowed to float. In this case, no one would want to trade gold for dollars. Devaluation would have involved setting a new fixed exchange rate near the floating rate of $75 per ounce.

Balance of Trade and Balance of Payments

When a country exports goods, it receives money from other countries. In contrast, imports require that payments be made to other countries. The difference between money received from exports and money spent for imports is called the **balance of trade.** In 1984 imports exceeded exports in the United States by $114 billion. When imports are greater than exports, a country is said to have a negative or unfavorable balance of trade. The balance of trade for the United States has been unfavorable in recent years.

A nation can improve its balance of trade by devaluing its currency. By reducing the cost of its money in comparison to the money of other countries, its exports become cheaper. Suppose that the Mexican peso is devalued so that a dollar will buy twice as many pesos as before. The devaluation would allow an American tourist to buy for $10 a blanket that would have cost $20 before the devaluation. At the same time, devaluation makes it more expensive for the citizens of a country to buy imported goods. Thus, Mexicans would have to use twice as many pesos to buy an American-made television set.

The reason devaluation helps improve a nation's balance of trade is that the law of demand works the same way in international trade as it does within a free enterprise system. In the example above, you learned that an American tourist could buy a $20 blanket for $10 in devalued pesos. More people in the United States would want to buy these blankets at $10 than at $20. Thus, the demand for blanket exports would rise as the price decreased, and more money would flow into Mexico. On the other hand, since Mexicans would have to pay twice as much for goods imported from the United States, fewer people would buy imported goods (demand decreases as prices rise) and less money would flow out of Mexico. As a result, with more money coming in and less going out, Mexico's balance of trade would improve.

In addition to exports and imports, other factors affect the flow of money in and out of a country. For example, the federal government of the United States pays for military operations in many places around the world. The government also provides money to help nations in need. Both of these activities send dollars out of the United States. However, at the same time, investments in other countries by individuals and multinational corporations yield profits that bring money back into the United States. The total of all money received from other countries minus the amount spent in other nations is called the **balance of payments.** Usually these profits are sufficient to make up for the unfavorable balance of trade and the money spent by the federal government.

INSTANT REPLAY

Goods and services usually are paid for with the currency of the country producing them. Foreign exchange markets exist to trade currencies.

The price of one country's money in terms of another's is called the exchange rate.

Floating exchange rates change from time to time. A fixed exchange rate may require a country to devalue its money periodically.

The dollar value of exports minus imports determines a country's balance of trade. The balance of payments is the difference between all money received from other nations and all money spent in other nations.

RESTRICTIONS ON INTERNATIONAL TRADE

You have learned that international trade allows people to have goods and services that would not otherwise be available. Free trade between nations has other advantages as well. One is that competition between businesses may increase. The calculator industry is a good example. To avoid losing sales to Japanese manufacturers, American calculator makers have been forced to be more competitive. The result is that United States consumers pay lower prices and can choose from a greater variety of calculators.

Another benefit of international trade is that it can link nations together socially and politically. As business people work together, they come to understand one another. This understanding makes them more tolerant of lifestyles and customs in other nations. Trade also provides a reason for the leaders of nations to cooperate. Countries that depend on the goods of their neighbors are more likely to seek peaceful solutions to their differences. Great Britain, West Germany, Canada, and Japan are the most important trading partners of the United States. It is not surprising that they are also America's strongest political allies.

International trade
fosters cooperation and
links nations together
socially and politically.

USDA Photo/Russell Forte

Problems Created by International Trade

The links created by trade between nations also can cause problems. Sometimes international trade can be used as a weapon to achieve political goals. The oil embargo of the Arab nations in the 1970s is a good example. Arab nations cut off oil exports to the United States in an attempt to force the United States to abandon its support of Israel. In 1980 the United States cut off sales of wheat to the U.S.S.R. as a protest against that nation's invasion of Afghanistan.

However, neither attempt was very successful, because international trade works so well. The United States was able to buy oil from other countries. The U.S.S.R. had little trouble getting grain from Canada and South America.

The increase in competition resulting from international trade can also cause problems. Japanese manufacturers have captured a large share of the American automobile market. The sales lost by General Motors, Ford, Chrysler, and American Motors forced these companies to lay off workers. In communities such as Detroit, where automobile manufacturing is very important, many workers have had difficulty finding other jobs.

Managers and union leaders in the automobile industry have suggested that the government limit imports to protect American jobs. Such policies may save jobs in one industry but hurt workers in other industries. If fewer Japanese cars are sold in the United States, less money will flow from the United States to Japan. Japanese citizens will not be able to buy as many American goods. As a result, there will not be as many jobs for United States workers who make goods for export. Thus, jobs of some United States workers may be saved at the expense of other workers' jobs.

Another problem with international trade is that it may make it difficult for new industries to develop. For example, if United States televisions are sold at low prices in Mexico, it may be impossible for Mexican television manufacturers to get started. Such firms might be very efficient if they were allowed time to develop, but the presence of American competition may cause the Mexican firms to fail.

Finally, international trade can cause problems in times of war. Before World War II, all the natural rubber used in the United States was imported. When the war started, the rubber supplies were cut off. This situation could have resulted in serious problems in producing military equipment and supplies. Fortunately, American scientists developed methods that enabled the United States to produce synthetic rubber.

Next time the United States might not have good substitutes. As you have learned, some important metals are obtained almost entirely from other countries. A war might interrupt these supplies. Other countries could face even more serious problems. For example, Japan must import almost all its coal and petroleum. If these sources are cut off, that country's economy could be crippled.

Tariffs

One way of limiting imports is the use of tariffs. A **tariff** is a tax placed on imported goods. This tax increases the price and reduces the demand for such goods. Tariffs in varying amounts can be placed on different goods, depending on how much the government wants to reduce imports. Some goods have a very low tariff, or no tariff at all. But if a government wants to protect one of its industries from competition or to keep a product out of the country for other reasons, the tariff may be more than 100 percent of the price of the good. For example, a car that sells for $10,000 in the United States might cost the equivalent of $20,000 in another country that has a high tariff.

Although tariffs may protect the jobs of some workers, they can create additional problems. First, imported goods become more expensive. Second, tariffs invite retaliation. A tariff placed on imports into the United States may result in tariffs set by other countries on goods made in the United States. This action would reduce production worldwide. Finally, tariffs may cause protected firms in a country to become inefficient. Freed from the need to compete against foreign businesses, managers may devote less attention to keeping costs down and developing new products.

INSTANT REPLAY

International trade links nations together socially and politically. It can also benefit consumers by increasing competition between firms.

Problems that may result from international trade include its use as a weapon to achieve political goals, loss of jobs at home, difficulty for new industries to develop, and cutoff of supplies during wartime.

Tariffs can be used to reduce imports. However, they hurt consumers, invite retaliation, and promote inefficiency.

SUMMARY

The exchange of goods and services between nations is called international trade. A country has an absolute advantage when it can produce a product more efficiently than another country can. A comparative advantage exists when the opportunity cost of a product in terms of other goods is less than in other countries. International trade causes the economic system to operate more efficiently by encouraging nations to specialize in those products for which they have an absolute or comparative advantage. Multinational firms use the principle of comparative advantage in setting up operations in various countries.

Exports are goods sold to other countries. Imports are goods purchased from other countries. The United States exports aircraft, food, machines, fuels, and chemicals. Imports include petroleum and automobiles.

The money of different countries is traded in foreign exchange markets. The price of money in terms of the currency of another country is called the exchange rate. Many nations allow the exchange rate to float in response to market conditions. Other countries use fixed exchange rates, which sometimes require that the country devalue its money.

The balance of trade is the difference between the value of exports and imports. The balance of payments includes all flows of money between nations. The balance of trade for the United States has often been unfavorable, but the difference is made up by profits received by Americans from investments in other countries.

By linking countries economically, international trade can create social and political ties. Trade also benefits consumers by increasing competition. Possible disadvantages include the use of trade as a weapon in political disputes, jobs lost by workers in certain industries, harm done to developing industries, and the possible cutoff of supplies of important products. Imports can be restricted by tariffs. However, tariffs result in higher prices to consumers, invite retaliation, and may promote inefficiency.

Building Your Vocabulary

On a separate piece of paper, write the numbers 1 through 10. Next to each number, write the term that correctly completes the sentence.

absolute advantage
comparative
  advantage
imports
multinational firms
international finance
foreign exchange
  market
floating exchange rate
balance of trade
balance of payments
tariff

1. A tax placed on certain imports is called a _____.

2. When a country can provide a product at a lower cost than another country, it is said to have an _____.

3. The ability to provide a product relatively more efficiently than another country can is called _____.

4. A place where different currencies are traded is a _____.

5. The value of exports minus imports is the _____.

6. Goods purchased from other countries are _____.

7. Businesses that operate in many countries are _____.

8. The process of paying for goods and services bought in international trade is called _____.

9. An exchange rate that changes with market conditions is called a _____.

10. Total money received by a country minus money paid to other countries is the _____.

Reviewing the Facts

1. What does it mean for a country to have an absolute advantage? Give an example.
2. How can two countries benefit from trade even though one nation has an absolute advantage in producing all goods?
3. What resources does the United States have that allow it to be an important exporter of aircraft?
4. Why is Hong Kong so dependent on international trade?
5. How do multinational firms use the principle of comparative advantage?
6. How can devaluation help a country improve its balance of trade?
7. Suppose that a dollar buys 200 yen. What would be the price of 1 yen in terms of dollars?
8. How do tariffs reduce imports?

Expressing Your Opinion

1. Some athletes have had the opportunity to play two or more professional sports. How might the principle of comparative advantage help them decide which sport to choose?
2. What effect would a cutoff of American

grain sales to the U.S.S.R. have on United States farmers? How could the government assist farmers?

3. How can political situations affect the amount of money that people in other nations are willing to invest in a country?

4. Should the United States government set high tariffs on automobiles produced in Japan? Who would benefit from high tariffs? Who might be hurt?

5. Should the United States try to expand its trade with communist countries, such as China and the U.S.S.R.? What would be some of the results?

Developing Your Attitudes, Values, and Skills

1. Take a survey of your home to find out whether you and the members of your family usually choose to purchase foreign or domestic goods. Make a list of the items, the names of the manufacturers, and the countries where the goods were made. Look at cars, kitchen appliances, home computers, electronic equipment, cameras, clothes, shoes, and furnishings. When you have completed the list, find out which country appears most often. Is it the United States, West Germany, Japan, Taiwan, or some other country? Now pick three or four items, such as a car, TV, stereo, or microwave, and interview the family members who purchased each of those items. Ask them why they chose each item. Were they influenced by price, quality, service, or other factors? Do the members of your family usually buy products they think offer the best value regardless of country of origin, or do they make a conscious effort to "buy American" even if a better foreign model is available? Prepare a report incorporating your list of items and interview results.

2. Pick a foreign country that trades heavily with the United States or that attracts large numbers of American tourists, such as Great Britain, France, Israel, West Germany, Mexico, Japan, Italy, Greece, or Canada. Find out what its unit of currency is. Then find out how many units of its currency equal $1. Next find out how this country's currency compared with the dollar five years ago, two years ago, and one year ago. You can find much of this information from travel agents, banks that have foreign currency tellers, stockbrokers, and almanacs and newspapers. The *Wall Street Journal* and *New York Times,* for example, list in U.S. dollars the current values of the Japanese yen, British pound, West German mark, Swiss franc, and Canadian dollar. By consulting back issues, you can determine how these currencies changed for each time period. You and your classmates can then make a chart showing the changes for each currency. What do you think these changes mean for U.S. exports, U.S. tourists, and for the citizens of each foreign country?

3. Throughout the early 1980s foreign competitors took larger shares of the U.S. market for goods such as cars, steel, electronic equipment, and textiles. The loss of American profits and jobs led to "buy American" campaigns and to demands for tariffs and import quotas. Research the arguments for and against

tariffs and import quotas by looking up magazine and newspaper articles on the subject, or by writing your members of Congress to ask for their comments on the subject. You can also ask your parents, local newspaper editors, or other adults what they think about the subject of tariffs and why. Be prepared during class discussion to offer and justify at least one argument for or against tariffs.

4. Although the United States produces a large amount of the gasoline and oil it uses, it also needs to import oil from other nations. The price and availability of imported gasoline and oil is affected by the countries that belong to OPEC (Organization of Petroleum Exporting Countries). You see and hear OPEC mentioned frequently in the news. Research either the history or the current operations of OPEC to find out which nations belong and how they affect oil prices. In your research on the history of OPEC, try to answer as many of the following additional questions as you can:

When was OPEC formed? Are there any large oil producing nations that do not belong to it? How does it function? What was the 1973 Yom Kippur War, and what did it cause OPEC to do? What effect did OPEC's actions have on the world supply of oil in the mid-1970s?

If you choose to research the current operations of OPEC, try to answer these additional questions: How much oil did OPEC export to the United States last year? How much oil did the United States produce itself, and how much did it import from non-OPEC nations? What was the average price per barrel? What was the average price per barrel five years ago? Ten years ago? Did the price go up or down during those periods? When did the OPEC nations last meet to make decisions about oil exports, and what decisions did they make? In what ways do the United States and other western industrialized nations influence the OPEC nations' decisions? Write a report summarizing your research.

FOCUS YOUR READING

How are personal and economic freedoms limited in the U.S.S.R.?

What special opportunities do some workers have in Yugoslavia?

Why do many Japanese workers stay with a single firm for their entire working lives?

CHAPTER 15

ECONOMIC SYSTEMS OF OTHER NATIONS

PREVIEW

In Chapter 1 you learned that free enterprise systems rely on decentralized decision making. That is, individuals are able to own property and are free to make their own choices about earning and spending activities. Similarly, managers of businesses are allowed to decide what they will produce and how much they will charge.

Chapter 1 also discussed command systems. In a command economy, the right to make decisions is centralized in a small group of people who control the government. Individ-

ual citizens may be able to own certain types of private property, but they usually have little to say about important economic choices.

There are no true free enterprise systems. Nor are there any true command systems. All the economies in the world today are mixed systems. In a mixed system, most choices are left to individual citizens, but some are made by government. However, there are great differences among these mixed economic systems.

In this chapter you will learn about economic systems of nations other than the United States. When you have completed the reading material and learning activities, you should be able to:

★ Compare how free enterprise and command economies answer the questions *what to produce, how to produce,* and *for whom to produce.*

★ Explain what is meant by central planning.

★ Discuss why Karl Marx thought that capitalism must fail and the kind of economic system he predicted would replace it.

★ Compare the management of businesses in Yugoslavia with the management of businesses in the United States and the U.S.S.R.

★ Discuss the special relationship that exists in Japan between workers and their employers.

FREE ENTERPRISE VS COMMAND SYSTEMS

As you have learned, there are no true free enterprise or command systems in the world today. However, some economies are primarily free enterprise systems, while others are much closer to being command systems. Figure 15-1 indicates where the economic systems of various countries fit along a free enterprise-command economy spectrum. Countries such as the United States, West Germany, and Japan rely heavily on principles of free enterprise. The U.S.S.R. and East Germany are examples of economic systems controlled primarily by government. Yugoslavia, Sweden, and France occupy middle positions, using many principles from both command and free enterprise systems.

FIGURE 15-1
There are no true free enterprise or command systems. Countries can be placed along a free enterprise-command spectrum.

PURE COMMAND SYSTEMS	MIXED ECONOMIES		PURE FREE ENTERPRISE SYSTEMS
None	U.S.S.R. East Germany	Yugoslavia Sweden France	U.S.A. West Germany Japan
			None

The questions *what to produce, how to produce,* and *for whom to produce* must be answered in every economic system. But the methods used to answer these questions in a free enterprise system are much different from those used in a command economy. In the pages that follow, you will learn how these two types of systems differ on each of these questions.

What to Produce

In a free enterprise system, the answer to the question *what to produce* is determined by the dollar votes of consumers. Businesses base their production decisions on consumer demand. If consumers vote for a product by buying it, more of that product will be produced. If a product is difficult to sell because consumers are not interested, firms will switch to producing other goods and services.

In a command economy, people in government decide what goods to produce. This method of decision making is called **central planning.** The planners may try to determine what consumers want, but this task is a difficult one because the planners do not have enough information. Often they pay little attention to consumer choice. Instead, they do what they believe is good for the country. For example, suppose they decide that most of the nation's resources should be used to make machinery. They reason that by increasing the country's supply of capital goods, more goods and services can be produced in the future. However, today's consumers will be deprived of food, clothing, and other products that they might have had.

How to Produce

Competition determines the answer to the question *how to produce* in a free enterprise system. Efficient firms are able to produce goods at lower cost than inefficient firms. Thus, inefficient firms must either change their methods of production or be forced out of the market.

In a command economy, the government decides what goods and services to make and how to make them.

Togliatti/Sygma

There is no competition in a true command economy. The government tells its factory managers what goods to produce and what quantity of each good to produce. The managers of each factory are provided with the resources to manufacture the assigned products, and they are responsible for meeting the government's production goals. Managers who fail to meet their production quotas may be replaced, demoted, or paid lower wages.

Sometimes this procedure of assigning production goals causes resources to be used inefficiently. For example, the output goal of glass-making firms in the U.S.S.R. used to be given in terms of the total weight of glass to be produced. Because the goal was easier to meet if thick glass was made, the firms turned out glass so thick that it was of little use. To correct this problem, the planners gave assignments in terms of total square meters of glass to be produced. This time it was easier to meet the goal by making very thin glass. Unfortunately, this glass was equally useless because it broke so easily. Consumers did not benefit in either case.

On other occasions, Soviet firms have been known to produce large quantities of shoes of the same size or thousands of identical dresses because mass production of one style or size was the easiest way to meet the goal set by the planners. Sometimes factory workers produce goods of very low quality. To avoid these problems, central planners must give firms detailed instructions about the products they are to produce. But it is a difficult task to give instructions to tens of thousands of factories concerning hundreds of thousands of products.

For Whom to Produce

In a free enterprise system, the question *for whom to produce* is answered by the distribution of income. People who have money and are willing to spend it receive the goods and services produced. Those with limited incomes buy less.

Individuals in a command economy usually are allowed to spend their incomes as they choose. However, the amount of income that they have may be determined largely by the government. By setting wages, assigning workers to specific jobs, and using the power to tax, government can control the distribution of income. Also, in a command economy many goods and services are provided directly by the government. For example, medical care and education are often free, and housing may be available at low cost. By controlling incomes and providing certain goods and services, the government in a command system plays an important role in deciding who will receive goods and services.

INSTANT REPLAY

The economic systems of the United States, Japan, and West Germany rely heavily on free enterprise principles. Those of the U.S.S.R. and East Germany are more like command economies.

Central planners in a command economy make decisions about *what to produce.* Decisions concerning *how to produce* are primarily the responsibility of plant managers.

In command systems, government affects the decision *for whom to produce* by controlling incomes and providing certain goods and services at little or no cost.

CAPITALISM AND SOCIALISM

In countries such as the United States, West Germany, and Japan, most of the large businesses are owned by individuals. These businesses use large quantities of capital goods to produce goods and services. The owners sometimes are called **capitalists,** and the systems are referred to as **capitalist economies.**

In contrast, large businesses in the U.S.S.R. and East Germany are owned by the government. For example, automobile manufacturing, steel production, oil drilling, and radio and television stations are all owned and controlled by the government in those countries. Systems in which the government owns most of the means of production are called **socialist economies.** Obviously, socialist economies are more like command systems than they are like free enterprise systems, because important economic decisions are made by those in government.

Perhaps the most important socialist thinker of all time was Karl Marx. Marx never held a position in government and he was not well known during his life, but his ideas have had an important influence on the world. Today hundreds of millions of people live in countries whose governments attempt to apply many of the principles advanced by Marx. In the next few pages you will read more about Marx's socialist philosophy and about his predictions concerning the failure of capitalism.

Marx As a Philosopher

Karl Marx believed that a society's economic system largely determines what that society is like. He claimed that government, culture, and even religion depend on how a society organizes to meet the economic needs and wants of its people. During his life, the economic systems that he observed were capitalist systems. As a result, much of his writing deals with the problems of capitalism.

Marx argued that the value of a good depends on the amount of labor that goes into producing it. For example, if it takes twice as many working hours to produce a pair of shoes as it does to make a pair of pants, the price of the shoes should be twice that of the pants. He recognized that capital goods are necessary to produce goods, but viewed the capital goods as the product of past labor. That is, it is human labor that originally created the capital goods.

Karl Marx's ideas on socialism and communism have had an important influence in the world.

The Bettmann Archive

Although he believed that the value of a good is determined by the amount of labor that went into it, Marx noticed that the capitalists kept most of this value and paid the workers low wages. He wrote that capitalists were "robbers who steal the fruits of the worker's toil." He saw a future in which the owners of capital would get richer and richer while workers get poorer and poorer.

Karl Marx believed that there would be constant conflict between workers and capitalists. He thought that government would be of no help because it always favored the interests of the capitalists. Finally, his study led him to the conclusion that there would be a revolution in which the workers would seize control of the economic system. A socialist society would emerge in which the means of production would be owned by a government controlled by workers.

But socialism was not the final goal in the eyes of Marx. He saw it as just a temporary step. In time, he believed, the socialist system would be replaced by a **communist society.** The communism written about by Marx is much different from the communism practiced in countries such as the U.S.S.R. In those nations, the government has power to control the lives of its citizens. In contrast, Marx's communist society had no government and no conflicts among different groups. Marx did not write very much about what this society would be like, but he did suggest that it would be a place where all people would earn their living by working. In Marx's utopia, no one would own the means of production; therefore, no one could exploit his or her co-workers.

One of his most famous phrases was that citizens would live and work "from each according to his abilities, to each according to his needs." In other words, all workers would contribute as much of their skills and labor to society as possible, and each would receive goods and services to fit his or her individual needs.

Marx As a Prophet

Marx predicted that capitalist societies would experience high rates of unemployment and bankruptcy. He saw a future in which many small business owners would lose their businesses to a few large firms, causing wealth to become concentrated in the hands of a few powerful capitalists. He believed that these capitalists would make life increasingly hard for workers until their lives became so miserable that they would be forced to revolt.

A few of Marx's predictions have occurred. For example, unemployment has been a problem in capitalist societies, and large corporations are much more prevalent and important now than they were in Marx's time. Also, in a number of important nations such as the U.S.S.R. and

China, revolutions did lead to the establishment of socialist economic systems.

But Marx's most dire predictions about the downfall of capitalism have not occurred. In many capitalist nations, such as the United States, there has been no revolution. One reason is that workers are much better off than they were in the past. Working conditions have improved and wages have increased, allowing workers to buy houses, automobiles, and other goods and services. Government regulations that did not exist in Marx's time have helped eliminate many of the negative aspects of capitalism, such as child labor and unsafe working conditions. Also, many workers are stockholders in large corporations. As a result, there are fewer conflicts between capitalists and workers today than there were during Marx's life.

Lenin and Imperialism

The failure of workers to rebel was unsettling to Marx's followers. They needed an explanation for the continuing success of capitalist systems. The reason was provided in the early 1900s by V. I. Lenin, a Russian revolutionary. Lenin argued that revolution by the workers had not occurred because capitalists were taking unfair advantage of poorer countries rather than of their own workers. For example, a multinational firm could take minerals from a poor country to satisfy human needs at home without making fair payment to the citizens of that country. Lenin called this practice **imperialism.** He predicted that wars and other problems would occur as capitalist nations competed for resources around the world. This prediction has not proved accurate. Although this century has had more than its share of wars, most were not the result of conflicts between capitalist nations.

INSTANT REPLAY

Economies in which the means of production are owned by individuals or corporations are called capitalist systems. In socialist systems the means of production are owned by government.

Karl Marx predicted that workers would rebel against capitalists and create a communist society with no classes and no government. Most of Marx's predictions did not occur.

Lenin believed that capitalists were able to postpone the revolution by practicing imperialism.

SOCIALIST ECONOMIC SYSTEMS: THE U.S.S.R.

The U.S.S.R. has a socialist economic system. The operation of that system can best be described by considering the four freedoms that exist in a free enterprise system. As discussed in Chapter 1, people living in a free enterprise system have the right to own private property, to buy what they can, to choose the kind of work they want to do, and to produce and sell goods and services. What about those four freedoms in the U.S.S.R.?

Freedom to Own Property

Soviet citizens are allowed to own certain types of private property. They can have goods such as cars, televisions, and tools. However, they are not allowed to own capital goods, houses, land, or other natural resources. All of these are owned by the government.

Freedom to Buy

Workers are paid wages and can use this income much as they choose. But the supply of goods available is often very limited. Consumers spend much of their free time standing in long lines to buy goods only to find that the stores have sold out of the items they want. Sometimes they will buy goods they do not want so that they can sell them or trade them with neighbors for other articles that they do want.

Frequently, the reason that goods are in short supply is that the U.S.S.R.'s central planners have decided to use the country's resources to produce other goods instead that the planners consider more important. In addition, the Soviet government sometimes deliberately seeks to reduce consumer demand for some products by raising prices or imposing heavy taxes on those goods. For example, in 1986 Russia tried to curb the nation's excessive alcoholism rate by raising prices and reducing the availability of vodka.

Freedom to Work

Soviet workers have considerable freedom to choose where they will work. Job openings are advertised, and a worker can move from one position to another. However, there are limitations. For example, college

Russian shoppers often have to stand in long lines to make purchases because goods are in such short supply.

Marlow/Magnum Photos, Inc.

graduates are assigned to their first jobs. And only a certain number of people are allowed to live in certain large cities. Also, those people who challenge the government may be prevented from having good jobs.

In a free enterprise system, wages are determined by supply and demand. In the U.S.S.R., government officials set wages. They use this power to encourage workers to take jobs in certain industries or locations. Wages may be high for unpleasant jobs or jobs in cold parts of the country. Automobiles or larger apartments also are used as rewards for productive workers.

Freedom to Produce and Sell

You have learned that in a command system the government owns all the large industries and imposes production goals or quotas on factories and businesses. In the U.S.S.R., central planners set up five-year plans for the entire economy. The planners then establish yearly output or production goals for each industry, and they allocate resources to each industry in order of importance. Thus, the most important industries, such as electricity, steel, and heavy machinery, receive the natural resources and capital goods they need to operate before industries that produce such consumer items as clothes, shoes, and home appliances.

Not all businesses are owned by the government in the U.S.S.R. Skilled workers such as tailors and barbers are allowed to operate their own businesses, but they cannot hire people to help them. It is a law in the U.S.S.R. that no person can work for another.

An Evaluation of the Soviet Economic System

In some ways, the economic performance of the U.S.S.R. has been impressive. In a fairly short period of time, that country has been transformed into one of the most powerful nations on earth. Over the past 40 years, gross national product in the U.S.S.R. has grown more rapidly than in some capitalist countries. At the same time, its unemployment and inflation rates have been much lower.

However, statistics do not tell the whole story. The rapid growth in the U.S.S.R. is the result of using many resources to produce capital goods. Thus, fewer goods were available for consumers to buy. Similarly, the low unemployment rate does not necessarily indicate that the Soviet system is superior to a system based on free enterprise principles. Finding a job in Russia is easy, because there is a shortage of workers. In fact, there are about 20 million jobs in the U.S.S.R. that cannot be filled because there are not enough workers.

Free Enterprise in the Soviet Union

Suppose that you live in a small town in Oregon and have two bushels of large apples grown on a tree in your backyard. One morning you catch a train to Portland and set up a street corner stand with apples for sale at $1 each. By evening you have sold all your apples and are on the train headed back home.

Such an experience is unlikely to occur in the United States but often happens in the U.S.S.R. Fruits and vegetables are usually in short supply in cities such as Moscow. As a result, peasants can make a handsome profit by bringing their produce to large cities. When they arrive, they go to a building or open area where other merchants are selling goods. As in a free enterprise system, prices are set by the forces of supply and demand. Although some sellers have to travel as much as a thousand miles, the prices they receive for their products are usually high enough to make the trip worthwhile.

Some of the fruits and vegetables sold in these markets are grown in backyards, but most come from small plots of ground on state-owned farms or collectives. In the U.S.S.R., farmers are allowed to have one acre of ground for their own use. Food grown on this land can be used by the family or sold to others.

Why do Soviet leaders permit this free enterprise in a socialist country? The answer is that the government-owned agricultural system has difficulty producing enough food for its citizens. However, farmers work much harder on their own plots than they do when working for the government. The result is that the 3 percent of the land farmed by individuals produces almost 25 percent of all the food grown in Russia. Although the government probably would like to do away with these private plots, it cannot because they are necessary.

It is also misleading to point to Russia's low inflation rate as a measure of success. Because the government controls prices, there can be no inflation unless government planners allow prices to increase. However, if prices are set too low, demand will exceed supply. When this occurs, Russian consumers often find themselves waiting in long lines to purchase the few goods that are available in government stores.

Finally, even if the economic performance of the U.S.S.R. is satisfactory, there are still the problems of personal and political freedom. A government that controls the economic system can exercise great control over its citizens. This economic power leads to political power. People living in the U.S.S.R. do not have the right to express their views, select their leaders, travel out of the country, or own their own houses. These are rights that are taken for granted in nations such as the United States.

INSTANT REPLAY

All large industries in the U.S.S.R. are owned by the government. Some workers are allowed to choose their own jobs, but wages and prices are set by planners.

Soviet leaders have favored production of capital goods at the expense of goods for consumers.

GNP in the U.S.S.R. has grown quite rapidly, but Soviet citizens have fewer personal and political freedoms than citizens of the United States.

WORKER-MANAGED BUSINESSES: YUGOSLAVIA

Before World War II, Yugoslavia had a capitalist economy, but when the war ended, the nation's new leader, Josip Broz Tito, set up a socialist economic system. In the beginning, Yugoslavia's economy was modeled after the Russian system, but over time it evolved into a mixed socialist and free enterprise economy called **market socialism.** Under market socialism, the government still owns most of the means of production, but the market forces of supply and demand also help determine what, how, and for whom to produce.

In Yugoslavia, individuals are allowed to own and operate some small businesses. For example, hotels, restaurants, and craft shops are run by private entrepreneurs. Unlike owners of businesses in the U.S.S.R., Yugoslavs can hire as many as five other persons to work for them. However, 80 to 90 percent of all goods and services in Yugoslavia are produced by **worker-managed firms.** The land and capital used by these businesses are owned by the government, and the business pays a fee to use them. But the firm itself is managed by its workers.

In each firm, a group of workers called the **worker's council** selects the managers and assists them in making decisions about what

In Yugoslavia's market socialist system, worker-managed firms are common.

© James Mason/Black Star

to produce. The objective of the business is like that of a firm in private enterprise—to make as much profit as possible. To accomplish this goal, the council decides to produce items it thinks will sell; then it borrows capital from the government to start up production. After paying production costs, salaries, and taxes, the workers can use their profits as they see fit. Usually they reinvest part of the profits to improve the business and share the rest among themselves.

In some ways, the workers in these Yugoslav firms are like stockholders in a corporation. The more profit that a business earns, the more money the worker–shareholders receive. Unlike stockholders in a free enterprise system, these shareholders actually work in the firm; therefore, they can do more to make the business profitable than stockholders can. One of the best features of worker-managed firms is that they provide an incentive for workers to produce more. In addition, because the workers are also the managers, there is usually less conflict between management and employees than in a company owned by capitalists.

Market socialism in Yugoslavia has worked fairly well. The economy has grown, and the system seems to do a better job of responding to consumer tastes than other socialist economies. However, inflation and unemployment have been serious problems.

A CAPITALIST SUCCESS STORY: JAPAN

At the end of World War II, Japan was a nation in ruins. Almost half of its cities had been destroyed, and its unemployment rate topped 50 percent. Even without wartime devastation, Japan lacked the land and natural resources to match the economic development of industrialized western nations. Thus, few would have predicted that this small island nation would transform itself into the industrial giant it has become.

Today, Japan challenges the United States as the world's leading economic power. More automobiles are produced in Japan than in any other country. Japan's steel industry is as large as that of the United States. Japan is also a leader in producing cameras, televisions, electronic equipment, ships, and many other goods.

In some ways, the destruction caused by World War II helped Japan develop economically. With most of its prewar industry gone, Japan was able to start over with modern plants and the latest management ideas. Japan also received a great deal of financial and professional aid from the United States to rebuild its economy. However, these were not the only reasons for the rapid growth of Japan's economy. Here are some other important factors in Japan's remarkable success story.

Spirit of Cooperation

Japan has a huge population living in a very small area. Most people live in small apartments in the nation's severely overcrowded cities. Thus, the Japanese have had to learn to live in harmony with one another. They have learned to work together for the good of the organization, because they believe that individual prosperity depends on group success. This communal spirit contrasts sharply with the United States, a land-rich nation where cooperation is less necessary and individuality is more highly prized.

This spirit of cooperation helps Japanese businesses. For example, unions and management have far fewer conflicts in Japan than they do in the United States. Strikes are rare. It is not uncommon for union members to accept reductions of wages if things are not going well for the business.

Lifetime Employment

In Japan, it is not unusual for workers to stay with a single company for their entire working lives. The lives of Japanese workers center on their jobs, and most workers are extremely loyal to their firms. They view their own welfare as dependent on the success of the business. In return, large Japanese firms take good care of their workers. They seldom lay off

Japanese workers bring a strong sense of cooperation to their jobs.

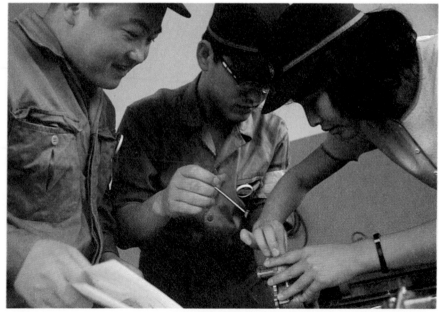

Hiroshi Hamaya/Magnum Photos, Inc.

employees and typically provide important fringe benefits. For example, a Japanese business may provide its workers with low-cost housing, meals, and medical care. In addition, when workers retire (55 is the usual age in Japan), they are given the equivalent of five or six years' wages.

Government Tax Policies

Tax policies of the Japanese government are designed to help the economy grow. Figure 15-2 shows taxes as a percentage of gross national product in various nations. The chart indicates that taxes in Japan are lower than in the United States and much lower than in countries such as West Germany, France, and Sweden. One reason taxes are so low is that Japanese businesses do many of the things that are done by government in other nations. For example, the money provided by firms to workers when they retire frees the government from the need to spend money on a social security program.

FIGURE 15-2
Taxes as a percentage of gross national product are lower in Japan than in most other nations.

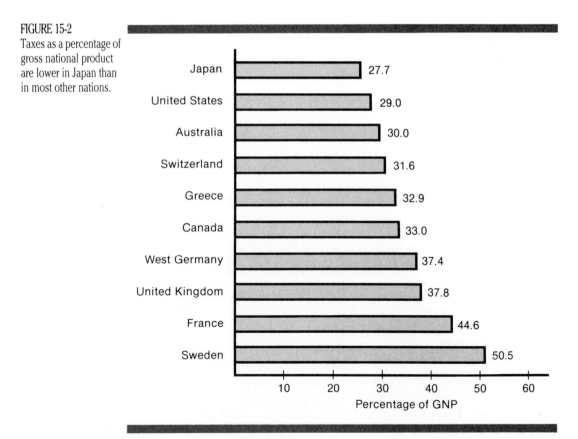

Source: United States Bureau of the Census, *Statistical Abstract of the United States: 1986*, 106th edition (Washington, D.C., 1986), p. 846.

Because Japanese citizens pay lower taxes, they have more money left to buy goods and services. Individuals and businesses also have more money to produce capital goods, and as you have learned, capital goods are a key ingredient in economic growth.

Japan in the Future

The Japanese economy has grown more rapidly than that of most other nations. At the same time, unemployment has remained low. Although Japan has enjoyed great success in the past, it could have some problems in the future. First, the country lacks natural resources. Thus, wars or other political problems could result in the loss of important supplies. Second, with such a large economy and so little land, pollution and crowding are major problems. Finally, there are some signs that the spirit of cooperation that has served Japan so well is being weakened by the very economic progress that this spirit helped create.

INSTANT REPLAY

Most large businesses in Yugoslavia are managed by workers.

Japan's remarkable economic progress is partly the result of the spirit of cooperation that exists in that country.

Other factors explaining Japan's success are loyalty between the firm and its employees and favorable government tax policies.

SUMMARY

In a command economy, the *what to produce* decision is made by central planners. The *how to produce* decision is left to plant managers who are given an assignment to produce a certain amount of goods. Government determines the *for whom to produce* decision by controlling incomes and by providing some goods and services at little or no cost.

In capitalist economies, most of the means of production are owned by individuals. In a socialist economy, government owns and operates the important industries. Karl Marx wrote about the problems of capitalism. He believed that capitalists treated workers unfairly. He predicted that there would be a revolution and that workers would establish a socialist system. Eventually this system would be transformed into a communist system in which there would be no government.

Marx's predicted revolution in capitalist countries has not occurred. According to Lenin, the reason is that capitalists have taken unfair advantage of poor countries rather than their own workers. This practice is called imperialism.

The U.S.S.R. has a socialist economy. By devoting resources to production of capital goods, the Soviet economy has grown rapidly. However, relatively few goods have been available for purchase by consumers. Much of the success of the U.S.S.R. has been achieved at the expense of personal and political freedom.

The economic system in Yugoslavia is based on market socialism. Most large businesses are owned by the government but managed by workers. Because the workers receive the profits earned by the firm, they have an incentive to work harder.

In recent years the Japanese economy has grown more rapidly than that of most other nations. Reasons include a spirit of cooperation among the Japanese people, loyalty between firms and workers, and government tax policies that favor economic growth.

☆ LEARNING ACTIVITIES ☆

Building Your Vocabulary

On a separate sheet of paper, write the numbers 1 through 9. Next to each number, write the term that correctly completes the sentence.

capitalists
worker's council
imperialism
capitalist economy
socialist economy
worker-managed firm
communist society
market socialism
central planning

1. In a command economy, the *what to produce* decision is made through _____ .

2. The owners of large businesses in a free enterprise economy are sometimes called _____ .

3. A _____ is an economic system in which the government owns the means of production.

4. A _____ is an economic system in which individuals are allowed to own capital goods.

5. A type of business ownership found in Yugoslavia is the _____ .

6. An economic system in which the government owns the means of production and which relies on markets to make *what, how,* and *for whom to produce* decisions is _____ .

7. Lenin called the practice of taking unfair advantage of poor nations _____ .

8. Marx believed that a _____ would not require any government.

9. Most businesses in Yugoslavia are governed by a _____ .

Reviewing the Facts

1. Give an example of a mixed economy that relies heavily on free enterprise principles.
2. Why did Karl Marx dislike capitalism?
3. How did Lenin explain the failure of Marx's revolution to occur in capitalist nations?
4. Discuss some ways in which capitalism has changed since Marx's time.
5. How does the Soviet government get workers to take jobs in certain industries?
6. How is the freedom to produce and sell in the United States different from that in the U.S.S.R.?
7. Who would be most likely to work harder, workers in the U.S.S.R. or those in Yugoslavia? Why?
8. Why are most Japanese workers so loyal to their firms?

Expressing Your Opinion

1. Why does the government of the U.S.S.R. limit the personal and political freedoms of its citizens.?
2. Could Marx's idea of "from each according to his abilities, to each according to his needs" really work? Explain.
3. Would Marx approve of communism as practiced in the U.S.S.R.? Why or why not?
4. In some economic systems, some goods and services, such as low-cost housing and free education, are provided by the government. Is this practice a good idea? Why or why not?
5. Do you think the Japanese system of giving retirees five or six years' wages is a better system than our social security system? Why or why not?

Developing Your Attitudes, Values, and Skills

1. Using periodical guides and reference books, research Japan's economy. Focus your attention on what the Japanese think about their own economy, what they see as its disadvantages and advantages, what their factories and stores are like, and how they view our economic system. Report your findings to the class.
2. Almost everybody has a few complaints about economic systems as they exist today. Describe in detail what you think would be the ideal economic system. Think about how your system would answer the four basic economic questions and how you would deal with the problem of scarcity. What would you retain from present economic systems? What would you change? Would free enterprise play any part? What role would government play? Compare your results with those of other classmates.
3. Germany's economy, like Japan's, was devastated by World War II. After the war, Germany was divided into two parts: Democratic West Germany, called the Federal Republic of Germany, has a mixed economy based on free enterprise, and Communist East Germany, called the German Democratic Republic, has a socialist economy. Using various almanacs and reference books,

explore how these two economies have recovered economically since the war. What is their current GNP, and what has the growth rate of their GNPs been for the last 10 years? What are their major imports and exports? How do they compare in size, population, natural resources, capital goods, unemployment, and inflation? How do their governments differ? How are production decisions made in each country? Which country has more consumer goods? Which country has more agricultural products? Which economy has recovered faster and grown more efficiently since the war? Which country fulfills its consumers' wants and needs more efficiently? In which country do citizens enjoy more political freedoms? What conclusions can you draw from your research? Which country would you prefer to live in?

UNIT 6

★ **Earning a Living**

★ **Borrowing, Saving, and Investing**

★ **Consumer Rights and Responsibilities**

★ **Consumer Economics**

In this unit you will examine the role of the individual in the economic system. You will learn about different types of jobs and about making wise borrowing, saving, and investment decisions. You will also learn how to be a more effective consumer.

FOCUS YOUR READING

Why are some athletes and entertainers paid more than $1 million each year?

How do education and training affect your chance of getting a good job?

Where can you obtain information about available jobs?

CHAPTER 16

EARNING A LIVING

PREVIEW

According to an old proverb, "The laborer is worthy of his hire." Does this mean that professional basketball players who earn an average of $250,000 a year or doctors who earn about $100,000 a year are worth that much? In general, the answer is yes, because salaries are determined by the same laws of supply and demand that determine the prices of goods and services. The owners of a basketball team are willing to pay a player $250,000 a year, because that player will add at least that much to the team's revenue from ticket sales and television contracts. Because there are relatively few people who have the skills required for professional basketball, the salaries are high.

In this chapter you will learn about earning a living. When you have finished the reading material and learning activities, you should be able to:

★ Explain the opportunity cost of going to work.

★ List six sources of income.

★ Describe what is meant by the distribution of income.

★ Explain why wage rates differ among jobs.

★ Discuss how education influences the range of job opportunities available to a person

★ List four ways of looking for a job.

THE OPPORTUNITY COST OF EARNING A LIVING

Soon you will be making choices that will determine the kind of work that you will be doing. In fact, you have already made some of these choices. For example, you have decided to stay in school rather than drop out, while some of your friends may have left school and are working.

Of course, there are opportunity costs almost every time you are faced with a choice. If you stay in school you forgo the money that you could be earning by working. But if you leave high school without graduating, you may be giving up the chance for a really good job in the future. By not quitting school to go to work, you give up some current income in order to have a greater lifetime income. Also, there probably are activities at your school that are fun. If you quit school to go to work, you give up those activities.

Going to school is like making an investment in your future, because education and training increase your skills and make you more valuable to an employer. Recall the concept of investment from Chapter 6. When you make an investment, you give up current consumption to have greater consumption in the future. Similarly, when you stay in school, you give up immediate earnings for greater earnings after graduation.

Going to school is an investment in your future.

Someone who has finished school has to choose how much time to spend working and how much time to devote to leisure. Think of a day as consisting of three eight-hour periods. One of those periods is devoted to sleep. The other two can be devoted to work, leisure, or a combination of the two.

No matter how people decide to divide their time between work and leisure, they have to consider the opportunity cost of their decisions. If you choose to do more work, you have less time to spend at leisure. If you choose more leisure time, you have less money to spend on goods and services.

SOURCES OF INCOME

Wages and salaries are usually thought of as the reward of work or the price of labor. As you learned in Chapter 7, a wage is typically paid per hour of work, whereas a salary is paid for a particular time period, such as a week or month, regardless of the number of hours worked. More than two thirds of all income in the United States comes from salaries and wages.

Another important source of income is transfer payments. A **transfer payment** is made when money is taken from one person and given to another. Usually the government takes the payments from workers in the form of taxes and pays it to recipients as part of social programs, such as social security, welfare, and unemployment compensation. In a sense, the money is simply taken from one pocket and put in another.

The government runs most transfer programs. However, many churches and private charitable organizations also have transfer programs. For example, members of a church may contribute money that is used to assist needy people. Most programs designed to help needy people are based on transfer payments.

Other sources of income are interest, profits, and dividends. As you learned in Chapter 11, interest is paid for the temporary use of money. If you have a savings account, you receive income in the form of interest. Business owners receive their income from profits, or the money they have left after they have paid all their expenses. As you learned in Chapter 7, if a corporation makes a profit, it shares the profit with its stockholders by paying them a dividend for each unit of stock they own.

Some people earn income by renting resources that they own to others. **Rent** is the money received for the use of land or a building. For example, if you live in an apartment, your parent makes a payment to the owner of the apartment each month. This rental fee is the payment that the owner receives in exchange for allowing you to use the apartment.

Sometimes people rent their land to oil or mining companies, which are then allowed to extract oil or minerals from the land. In some cities, rental rates are set and controlled by the government, but usually supply and demand determine the amount of rent to be paid for the use of a building or piece of land. For example, an acre of land in the middle of a desert may have no rental value, but an acre of prime farmland in Texas may earn an annual rent of $100. And an acre of land in midtown New York City may earn more than $1 million a year in rental fees.

Table 16-1 shows the importance of each source of income in the United States:

TABLE 16-1

SOURCES OF INCOME IN THE UNITED STATES	
Sources of Income	Percentage of All Income
Wages and Salaries	63.6%
Interest	13.8
Transfer Payments	13.2
Profits	4.9
Dividends	2.5
Rents	2.0

Source: U.S Department of Commerce, *Statistical Abstract of the United States*, 1986.

INSTANT REPLAY

Earning a living involves opportunity costs. Specifically, going to work means to have less time to spend in leisure activities.

Wages and salaries are the most important source of income. Other sources include transfer payments, interest, profits, dividends, and rents.

INCOME DISTRIBUTION

Some people in the United States earn more than others, because they enter different occupations, have different levels of training and skill, and own different resources. Generally, the more training and skill an occupation requires, the smaller the supply of workers and the higher the income people in that occupation will earn. Likewise, the more resources one person owns, the more income those resources will generate. Because of all these differences, there is a wide disparity between the highest and lowest income levels in the United States.

The way that income is divided among individuals and families in the population is called **income distribution.** The family income distribution for the United States is shown in Table 16-2. The table shows the number of families in each income category. For example, at the top of the income ladder, there are almost 10 million families that have an annual income of more than $50,000. At the other end of the distribution, there are about 9 million families whose income is less than $10,000 each year.

Clearly, income is not distributed equally. For example, the poorest 20 percent of the population receives only about 5 percent of all income. In contrast, the richest 20 percent of the population receives about 43 percent of all income

TABLE 16-2

FAMILY INCOME DISTRIBUTION IN THE UNITED STATES, 1984

Income Class	Number of Families (millions)	Percentage of Families
Less than $10,000	9.0	14.4%
$10,000 - $19,999	13.5	21.6
$20,000 - $34,999	18.6	29.7
$35,000 - $49,999	11.5	18.4
$50,000 and over	9.9	15.8

Source: U.S. Department of Commerce, *Statistical Abstract of the United States,* 1986.

A number of people in the United States live in **poverty.** This term means that they receive so little income that they cannot afford to buy an adequate amount of food, clothing, medical care, or housing. The poverty income level is set by the federal government and adjusted each year to reflect changes in the prices of goods and services. Any family whose income is below that figure is said to live in poverty. In 1984, a family of four with an income of less than $10,609 was living in poverty.

About 14.4 percent of the U.S. population, or about one out of every seven Americans, lives in poverty. The percentage of people living in poverty is far greater in some parts of the country than in others. For example, more than 18 percent of the families in Mississippi live in poverty compared with only 6 percent in Connecticut. Some poor people live in city slums, some are homeless, and some live in rundown shacks in rural areas. Some are elderly men and women who have no income except social security payments.

Government programs attack the causes of poverty by providing job training and low-cost housing.

HUD Photo

Many efforts have been made to help the poor and the homeless. Federal, state, and local government programs provide social security, Medicaid and Medicare, public housing, welfare, unemployment compensation, and free or low-cost school lunch programs. Private organizations, such as churches and charities, also operate programs for people living in poverty.

Considerable progress has been made in reducing the number of people living in poverty. The current level of about 14 percent compares with more than 22 percent of the population living in poverty in 1960.

INSTANT REPLAY

An income distribution shows how income is divided among individuals or families in a specific population.

People who cannot afford an adequate standard of living are said to be living in poverty. In the United States about one out of every seven people is living in poverty.

WHY SOME JOBS PAY MORE THAN OTHERS

Supply and demand explain why wage rates are higher in some occupations than in others. As more people want jobs in a particular field, the wage rate declines. But if businesses required more workers of a particular type, they must offer higher wages. Computer programmers and farm workers are good examples of occupations affected by supply and demand. Computers have become more and more important in our society. Demand for people who can write computer programs and operate computers has been increasing rapidly. However, colleges and technical schools are having difficulty training enough students to fill all the computer-related jobs offered. Because the demand has been growing faster than the supply, the wage rate for computer programmers has increased.

On the other hand, the demand for farm laborers has been declining as machines become increasingly important in farm operations. The supply of farm workers also has been decreasing, but not as rapidly as the decline in demand. As a result, the wage rate for farm workers has not increased as much as it has for computer programmers.

Supply and demand also explain the high salaries that are paid to star professional athletes. Baseball pitchers who attract fans to fill stadiums each time they pitch are worth a lot of money to the team owners. Because there are only a few people who are great pitchers, such players receive very high wage rates. In a few cases, these players receive more than a million dollars each season.

Table 16-3 shows average wage rates for several occupations for 1977 and 1985 in Dallas, Texas. Notice that not only do some jobs pay higher wage rates than others, but also the rate of increase has been much higher for some occupations.

You have learned that there are different wage rates or salaries for different jobs. Why do these differences exist? A few of the reasons are discussed here.

TABLE 16-3

OCCUPATIONAL WAGE RATES IN DALLAS, TEXAS, 1977 AND 1985

Occupation	Weekly Wage Rate 1977	1985	Percentage Change 1977–1985
Drafter	$258	424	64.3
Electronic Technician	256	490	91.4
Payroll Clerk	185	334	80.5
Secretary	215	381	77.2
Stenographer	199	408	105.0
Switchboard Operator/ Receptionist	150	264	76.0%

Source: U.S. Department of Labor, *Occupational Earnings and Wage Trends in Metropolitan Areas*, 1986.

The High Price of a Good Left-Hander

In his first season with the Los Angeles Dodgers, Fernando Valenzuela led the league in both shutouts and strikeouts. As a result, he won the Cy Young Memorial Award as the best pitcher in the National League. His salary for that season was $42,000. Before the next season began, he had an argument with the owners of the Dodgers about his salary. He finally accepted $350,000 but did not sign a contract. After that season Valenzuela again had a dispute about what he was to be paid. He wanted $1 million a season; but the Dodgers' highest offer was $750,000. An arbitrator was brought in to help the two parties reach an agreement. The arbitrator agreed that the pitcher was indeed worth $1 million a year. One of the determining factors in the arbitrator's decision was that attendance at

Dodger home games increased by about 5,000 people every time Valenzuela pitched. The average price of a ticket for a game was about $7, so the owners received an extra $35,000 every time Valenzuela pitched a home game. If he pitched in 18 to 19 home games during the season, the owners would receive an additional $630,000 to $665,000.

In addition, Valenzuela's pitching could help the team improve from being an average team to a championship team. If the team won a lot of games, more fans would come to all the games, not just to those in which Valenzuela was pitching. Also, if the team went to the league playoffs and the World Series, the owners would make even more profits. These factors made Fernando Valenzuela worth $1 million dollars a season.

Job Training, Experience, and Skill Requirements

Some jobs require more training or experience than others. Workers will not spend the time and money necessary for such training unless there is the promise of higher wages. Employers know that a highly trained or experienced worker can produce more than one who is untrained or inexperienced. As a result, the employer is willing to pay more to the trained or experienced worker. Note that in Table 16-3 the wage rates for the highly skilled jobs, such as a drafter, are much higher than those for the less skilled jobs, such as a switchboard operator.

Usually an experienced worker will produce more output and, therefore, will be paid more than an inexperienced worker. For example, the starting salary for a computer operator is about $15,200 a year; an experienced operator is paid about $18,800; and a senior operator earns an annual salary of more than $22,600.

Special Job Characteristics

Because some jobs are dangerous or undesirable, extra pay must be offered to attract people to work at them. For example, collecting garbage is not a highly skilled occupation, but wages are higher than in some jobs of greater skill because the collection of garbage, especially on a hot summer day, can be unpleasant work. In the military, people who perform dangerous jobs, such as submarine duty in the Navy, receive extra pay. Police and firefighters perform dangerous jobs and, therefore, they are often paid more than city employees with the same seniority who work in offices. You may have heard someone refer to this kind of additional payment as "combat pay" or "hazardous duty pay."

Location

Some jobs are located in remote, undesirable, or lonely places. For example, working in a lighthouse could be very lonely. Workers are often offered a higher pay rate to leave their families for a long period of time to take an assignment in a foreign country. If you look through the help-wanted advertisements in your local newspaper, you may find announcements of jobs available in far-off places. Usually the advertisement will mention an unusually high rate of pay and other incentives like free meals and housing. Figure 16-1 is an example of such an advertisement.

Some jobs pay more because they are dangerous.

AMERICAN IRON AND STEEL INSTITUTE

Even within the United States, the wage rate for a particular occupation can vary substantially. For example, in 1985 the United States Department of Labor conducted a survey of the wage rate for beginning computer programmers in 23 of the largest cities in the United States. The average wage rate was about $385 per week, but it ranged from $327 in Detroit, Michigan, to $442 in the Los Angeles area.

EDUCATION AND JOB OPPORTUNITIES

A high school diploma or its equivalent will probably be the minimum qualification for most jobs in the next 20 years. Of course, there are jobs for those who have not finished high school, but they usually are low paying and unfulfilling. Most of the high-paying skilled jobs such as those for electricians, nurses, plumbers, and secretaries, require training after high school. Vocational and technical schools offer many one- and two-year programs to provide this training.

Construction workers learn the skills of their trade in apprenticeship programs. In an **apprenticeship,** a young, unskilled worker works with a skilled craftsperson, such as a carpenter or bricklayer, to learn an

Construction workers learn skilled trades in apprenticeship programs.

occupation. Often the apprenticeship program also includes formal classroom training at night or on Saturdays. After a period of training that may last from one to three years, the apprenticeship is finished. The rate of pay for a fully trained craftsperson is increased at this time to reflect this higher level of skill.

A college education is required for many jobs. The proportion of jobs filled by college graduates has increased steadily over the past 30 years. In 1950 only about 10 percent of jobs were filled by college graduates. Now, college graduates account for more than 20 percent of all workers.

More college graduates are looking for work now than ever before. Some of them will not be able to obtain work in their chosen fields, and some will be hired for jobs that do not require a college education. In the

How Much Is a College Education Worth?

Usually the more education and training a person has, the more money she or he can earn. You have probably heard about people who have only a limited amount of education and who have become wealthy. But, generally, more years of school or training mean more dollars in the paycheck.

The United States Bureau of the Census recently published a study that estimated the amount a person would earn in a lifetime for different levels of education. The lifetime earnings for men and women are shown here:

Education Level	Lifetime Earnings	
	Men	Women
Five Years of College	$1,552,000	$833,900
Four Years of College	1,424,400	622,400
High School Graduate	1,027,800	455,700
High School Dropout	718,500	251,700

For men, the difference between having four years of college and being a high school graduate is almost $400,000 in lifetime income. The male high school graduate can expect to earn $300,000 more than a male who does not complete high school.

The data for women also show large increases in lifetime earnings as education increases. However, the average woman will earn considerably less than the average man for two reasons. First, in many cases, women earn less than men in the same type of job. This pay difference has been getting smaller but still exists. At the same time, the average woman spends less time in paid employment than the average man. For example, many women spend a large portion of their adult lives as homemakers. The services they provide in the home are valuable, but homemakers are not paid a wage or salary, so they do not have earnings. Studies have shown that the typical homemaker with children works about 55 hours a week. If she were paid for this household work, her lifetime earnings would be substantial.

next ten years, about 15 million people will graduate from college, but there will be only about 12 to 13 million job openings that will require a college education. Thus, some graduates will experience periods of unemployment, or they will have to take lower paying jobs.

In general, however, college graduates will have an advantage in the job market. The advantage is that many employers prefer to hire a well-educated candidate for a job even if it does not require a college education. The job will pay less and carry fewer responsibilities than jobs that college graduates normally expect to obtain. Nevertheless, the graduates who take these lower level jobs may gain useful experience that will help them compete later for more challenging and rewarding jobs.

INSTANT REPLAY

A high school education will be a minimum requirement for most jobs in the next 20 years. A growing percentage of jobs are being filled by those with college educations.

Generally, the more education and training a person has, the more income that person will earn.

Women have lower lifetime earnings than men, because they are usually paid less for the same type of job and they usually spend less time in paid employment.

FINDING A JOB

Suppose you have chosen a career and have completed the necessary training. How do you go about finding a job? There are a variety of ways to look for a job. A few are discussed here.

Direct Job Search

Once you have identified the types of business that are likely to employ people with your skills, you should identify specific firms to approach. You can go directly to each one and fill out an application for employment. In some cases, you may be referred to a company by a relative or friend. If you have graduated from a vocational or trade school, your school may be able to refer you to potential employers. The personnel offices of many companies keep applications on file and invite applicants to job interviews. If you are invited to an interview, always try to make the best possible impression on the person who interviews you. Keep in mind that even if the company does not hire you now, it may want to hire you later or it may be able to refer you to other firms. In addition, the people who interview you can be a valuable source of information about jobs in the field you choose.

Classified Advertising

An excellent source of job information is the classified section of the newspaper. Most major papers have hundreds of help-wanted advertisements each day. Figure 16-2 shows a few typical help-wanted advertisements. Most ads contain only a limited amount of information about the job, but usually it is enough to let you determine if you are qualified for the job and if you are interested in applying. If you need more information, you can telephone the company's personnel office. Or if you apply for the job, you can ask questions during the job interview.

Unfortunately, not all employers are completely honest in their help-wanted listings. Sometimes the potential salary listed for the job is much higher than what can actually be earned. In other cases, promises of travel or the possibility of working with movie stars or famous athletes is mentioned. Most of the time, such statements are exaggerated or not true. Be careful of advertisements that sound too good to be true.

Once you obtain the education and skills you need, the next step is to look for a suitable job.

FIGURE 16-2
These classified advertisements describe jobs that are available.

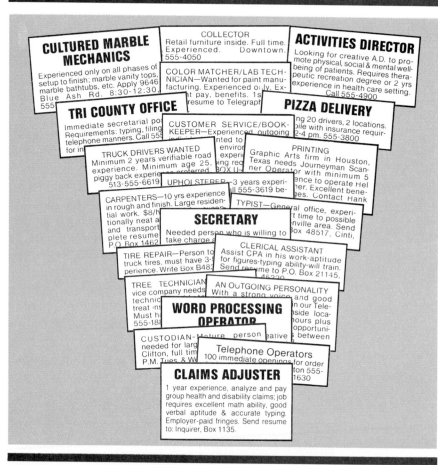

Employment Agencies

An employment agency provides the service of bringing buyers and sellers of labor together. Every state has a department of employment that serves as an employment agency. Usually this department is called the State Employment Office or Job Service.

State employment offices can be a good source of information about different occupations. They maintain files of available jobs and available workers. There are about 2,500 state employment offices in the United States. If you check your local telephone directory, you will probably find an office not far from where you live. There is no charge to either the employer or the worker for using the facilities of the state employment office, because federal and state tax monies pay for the service.

Privately owned businesses also provide services similar to those offered by state governments, but there is a charge to either the employer, the employee, or both. Ordinarily no fee is charged unless the applicant actually finds a job that has been listed with the agency. However, before using the agency's services, you should be sure that you understand exactly what charges are involved.

Career Counseling and Placement Offices

Career counseling and placement offices at most college campuses and in some high schools can be excellent sources of information about job openings. Usually their services are available only to current and former students of the school. At most colleges, company representatives come to the school's placement office to interview candidates for jobs. College placement centers also maintain listings of part-time and summer jobs. Check to see if your school has such an office or a person who provides these services.

High school and college placement offices can help you find a job.

Placement centers provide training for job hunting, writing résumés, and preparing for job interviews. A **résumé** is a summary of a person's education, training, and work experience. It is designed to give a prospective employer a quick look at the person's qualifications for a particular job. Figure 16-3 is an example of a résumé for a high school senior. This résumé will give you an idea of the kind of information to include and a useful way to organize it.

FIGURE 16-3
This résumé, for a high school senior, shows what kind of information should be included on a résumé and how it might be organized.

```
                                    RÉSUMÉ


        NAME:       Juli A. Parker
        ADDRESS:    302 North Ninth Street
                    Hamilton, Ohio  45013-9622
        TELEPHONE:  (513) 555-4497


        EDUCATION:  Senior at Hamilton High School, to graduate in June.
                    Majoring in business subjects.
        SUBJECTS STUDIED:

           Typing:  4 semesters        Free Enterprise:  1 semester
           Shorthand:  4 semesters     Business Math:  1 semester
           Secretarial                 Accounting:  2 semesters
           Procedures:  2 semesters    Business English:  2 semesters
           Business Law:  2 semesters


        STUDENT ACTIVITIES:  Secretary, Senior Class
                             Vice-President, Future Business Leaders of America
                             Member of Senior Prom Committee
        SPECIAL SKILLS:  Write shorthand at approximately 110 words per minute.
                         Type at approximately 65 words per minute.  Trained
                         in the operation of adding machine, calculator, and
                         copy machine.


        WORK EXPERIENCE:

           June 12, 19-- to September 2, 19--:  Butler County Park and
           Recreation Department, 132 Main Street, Hamilton, Ohio  45013-9624
           Duties:  Full-time general clerical work; operated adding machine,
                    answered telephone, greeted visitors.


        REFERENCES:

           Mrs. Juanita Cox, Shorthand and Typing Instructor, Hamilton High
           School, 1165 Eaton Avenue, Hamilton, Ohio  45013-9624
           Telephone:  (513) 555-3240

           Ms. Barbara Puccinelli, Assistant Director, Butler County Park and
           Recreation Department, 132 Main Street, Hamilton, Ohio  45013-9624
           Telephone:  (513) 555-1116
```

INSTANT REPLAY

Job-search techniques include direct search for a job, reviewing classified advertisements in newspapers, and using employment services and counseling centers.

A résumé showing one's experience and training is very useful when applying for a job.

S U M M A R Y

All choices involve opportunity costs. The decision to stay in school means that you forgo current income. However, the additional education will help you to earn more money in the future. After you finish school, your opportunity cost of going to work is the leisure time that you must give up.

Sources of income include wages and salaries, transfer payments, interest, profits, dividends, and rents. Wages are the most important source, accounting for 64 percent of all income. The government makes transfer payments when it takes money from one group of people and gives it to another group.

The income distribution shows the number of families in each income class. Those below an income level specified by the federal government are said to be below the poverty line. The proportion of families living in poverty in the United States has fallen since 1960.

A high school education is a minimum requirement for most jobs. Additional vocational or college training is usually required for the more skilled occupations. More than 20 percent of all workers are college graduates. The more training and education workers have, the more income they will usually earn.

Once someone has chosen an occupation and completed the necessary training and education, the search for a job begins. Classified advertisements in the newspapers, private and government employment services, and placement offices offer individuals help in finding a job.

☆ LEARNING ACTIVITIES ☆

Building Your Vocabulary

On a separate sheet of paper, write the numbers 1 through 6. Next to each number, write the term that correctly completes the sentence.

rent
transfer payment
income distribution
poverty
apprenticeship
résumé

1. _____ is a condition in which an individual cannot afford an adequate standard of living.

2. A _____ involves taking money from one group of people and giving it to another group.

3. _____ is a payment for the temporary use of land or a building.

4. _____ shows the way in which income is divided among individuals and families in a given population.

5. An _____ is a training program in which a worker learns a job skill.

6. A _____ is a summary of a person's education, training, and work experience.

Reviewing the Facts

1. List six sources of income.
2. What are the two largest sources of income in the United States?
3. What are two types of organizations that use transfer payments?
4. In what income category do most families in the United States fall?
5. What percentage of Americans lived in poverty in 1984?
6. List three reasons that some jobs pay more than others.
7. How many people will graduate from college in the next ten years?
8. Why do women have lower lifetime earnings than men?
9. What are three ways of looking for a job?

Expressing Your Opinion

1. Do you think it is fair for dangerous or unpleasant jobs to pay more even if the jobs require less training or education than jobs that are safer or more enjoyable? Why or why not?
2. Do you think that federal, state, and local governments provide too much, too little, or just enough help to the poor? Explain your answer.
3. Is it a good idea for employers to pay their workers to take job-related courses or technical training? Why or why not?
4. Should employers be allowed to reject job applicants for any reasons they choose? Why or why not?
5. Should newspapers and magazines be required to make sure that the help-wanted ads they carry are true? Explain your answer.

Developing Your Attitudes, Values, and Skills

1. People are paid for their work in different ways. Some work for salaries and some for hourly wages. Salespeople often receive a salary plus commission for every sale they make. Some people, such as waiters, work for a combination

of wages and tips, and others, called piece workers, are paid a rate for every unit of work they complete. A glove-maker, for example, may be paid for each glove produced. Locate and inter-view two or three people who are paid in these ways. Ask them whether they like or dislike the way in which they are paid and what they feel the advantages and disadvantages are. If they do not like the way in which they are paid, ask them how they would prefer to be paid. Com-pare and summarize your results, and be prepared to discuss them in class.

2. Many state and federal laws prohibit job discrimination, but it remains a major problem in the United States. Employers sometimes refuse to hire or promote people because of their age, sex, reli-gion, race, or handicap. To find out how to protect yourself from job discrimina-tion, choose one of the areas listed above, such as racial or sexual dis-crimination, and research a federal or state law enacted to prohibit that kind of discrimination. Find out what the law specifically prohibits, what agency is charged with enforcing it, what the penalties are for violating the law, and how a victim of discrimination can go about reporting it. Write a brief report summarizing your findings.

   To help you in your research, you can write or call the federal or state agency that is charged with enforcing it. The U.S. Labor Department and the U.S. Equal Employment Opportunity Com-mission both enforce anti-discrimination laws. In addition, most states have labor departments or human relations com-missions charged with enforcing state laws barring job discrimination. These agencies usually have information packets that they will mail to you.

3. Using an almanac, *Statistical Abstract of the United States,* or *Current Population Reports,* find tables that show charac-teristics of income distribution in the United States. These tables contain in-formation arranged by year, age, race, sex, size of family, geographic location, and poverty level. Choose one table, and make a graph to illustrate the in-formation that the table lists about income distribution in the population shown. Explain what your graph shows. How is the information arranged on the axes of the graph? What categories are used to divide the population? Have there been any changes in income dis-tribution in the time period covered by your graph? Describe these changes. What might have caused these changes?

4. "To get a good job today, a person almost always needs some specialized training, a certificate of achievement in a specific field from a recognized school, or a college degree." Test to see how correct this statement is by studying the help-wanted ads in your local news-paper. Select 15 ads at random, and for each one, write down the job being advertised and what skills are required. What does the ad say about diplomas or other credentials? Does it say you must have experience? If so, how much? Does it ask for both a diploma and experi-ence? Compare the ads, noting which jobs demand the highest requirements and which the lowest. Summarize your findings, and report to the class on the relationship between credentials and employment in today's job market.

FOCUS YOUR READING

How does the use of credit cards benefit both the buyer and the seller of a product or service?

How does a person buy and sell stocks and bonds?

What does it mean when someone in the investment business says, "IBM was up a point and one-half at the close today"?

CHAPTER 17

BORROWING, SAVING, AND INVESTING

PREVIEW

Borrowing and saving are two sides of the same coin. Borrowers pay for using other people's money, and savers are paid for providing it. Most people save money at some time in their lives and borrow money at others, but most people strive to be savers rather than borrowers. Each year the average American household spends about 95 percent of its income on goods and services and saves or invests the remaining 5 percent.

Most families go through a predictable cycle of borrowing and saving. Young people just starting out may have to borrow money to buy a house and car, because they do not yet earn a high salary. As their income increases, they can repay the loans and begin saving money. Thus, young families tend to borrow, and middle-aged families tend to save. Retired people usually spend more than they earn, because they are spending money they saved earlier.

In this chapter you will learn about some of the ways that money is borrowed, saved, and invested. When you have completed the reading material and learning activities, you should be able to:

★ Describe the different ways that individuals can borrow money.

★ Explain why people save money.

★ Discuss why credit and saving are important in a free enterprise system.

320

★ Describe how shares of stock are bought and sold.

★ Explain why stock prices continually change.

CREDIT AND BORROWING

Whenever you borrow money, you are using credit. **Credit** is an arrangement to pay in the future for goods, services, or money you are receiving now. Every day millions of consumers make credit transactions. Sometimes credit is primarily a convenience, such as when a family on vacation uses a credit card to pay for a motel room. In this case, using the credit card frees the family from the need to carry a large amount of money on the trip. On other occasions, credit may be used to make the purchase of expensive items possible. For example, an individual who does not have enough money to pay the total price of a new automobile may borrow the needed amount from a bank or other financial intermediary and repay the money over a number of months or years.

All credit transactions are based on trust. When the bank lends money to a person to help buy a car, the bank trusts that the loan will be repaid. The widespread use of credit in the United States means that, with few exceptions, users of credit can be depended on to make the payments required on their credit purchases.

Credit transactions benefit both parties involved in the exchange. Clearly, those making purchases on credit are better off, because the credit transaction is more convenient or because they are able to obtain goods and services that they otherwise might not be able to buy. But the banks and other financial intermediaries who make credit available also benefit, because they receive interest payments on the money they lend. Some of this interest goes to savers who provided the money, some is used to pay the costs of making credit available, and the remainder represents profit earned by the owners of the bank.

In a modern economic system, credit can be obtained in many ways and can be put to a variety of uses. Some of the most important methods of using credit are discussed here.

Credit Cards

Millions of people carry **credit cards.** These cards can be used in place of cash to pay for goods and services. When people use credit cards, they are promising to pay for their purchases later. Some credit cards can be used at only one store. Others, such as VISA or MasterCard, can be used at thousands of stores, hotels, service stations, and other retail establishments. Using a credit card to buy something at a store is a way of borrowing money. Suppose that a shopper has picked out a new dress. She takes the dress to the clerk and hands the clerk a credit card. The clerk makes an imprint of the cardholder's name and account number on a receipt, writes a description of the item purchased and its price, and has the purchaser sign the receipt. There are several copies of this receipt. The buyer keeps one copy for her records; the store keeps one for its records; and one is sent to the bank that manages the credit card account.

When the bank receives its copy of the receipt, it pays the store. However, the bank may pay the store only 96 percent of the amount on the bill. Thus, if the dress is $100, the bank will send the store only $96. A few weeks later the bank will bill the credit cardholder for $100. In effect, the bank has lent her $100 for a few weeks. The bank did not give the money directly to her, but allowed her to buy the dress without paying for it in cash.

Usually, the credit card holder will not be charged interest if the bill from the bank is paid within a few weeks. Then how can the bank afford to issue credit cards to customers? Remember that the bank has charged the credit card holder $100 and has paid the store $96. Thus, the bank keeps $4, or 4 percent. Some of this money will go toward paying the bank's expenses, and the rest will be profit. If the bank handles many

Using a credit card to buy merchandise at a store is one way to borrow money.

Photo reprinted from First Interstate Bancorp

thousands of credit card purchases each year, it can earn a substantial profit by acting as the intermediary in these credit card transactions.

Most people use credit cards because of the convenience, not because they need to borrow money. Having the credit card is much safer than carrying large amounts of cash. Also, the monthly statement provides a useful list of all the transactions that have been made.

Mortgage Loans

A **mortgage loan** is a loan secured by some kind of valuable property, such as land, buildings, or stocks and bonds. Mortgage loans are usually repaid in monthly payments for a period of 10 to 30 years.

Consider the purchase of a home. Suppose a family has found a house to buy. The price of the house is $75,000, and the family has saved $20,000 toward this purchase. They need another $55,000 to buy the house. A bank agrees to lend them this amount at 12 percent interest in return for a written promise to make a payment of $566 each month for the next 360 months (30 years). In addition, the family agrees to give the bank a mortgage against the property. A **mortgage** is a legal contract or deed in which the family agrees to put up the house as security against the loan. The bank will have a claim against the house for the amount of the loan until the loan is repaid. If the family fails to make its monthly loan payments, the bank may take the property and sell it to someone else to get its money back.

Installment Loans

People sometimes need to borrow money to pay the full amount of a major purchase. They may need to buy furniture, make a home improvement, buy a car, or pay for college tuition. Then they pay the money back in small monthly installments over a period of months or years until they have fully repaid the loan. This kind of borrowing is called an **installment loan.** Usually when the money is being used to purchase a large item, such as a car, the purchased item itself is used as collateral for the loan. **Collateral** is something of value that the borrower pledges to give to the lender if the borrower cannot repay the loan. The borrower keeps and uses the property, but if the borrower fails to repay the loan, the lender can take possession of the collateral and sell it to recover the amount of the loan. You may have heard of someone's car being **repossessed.** In that case, the borrower has failed to repay the loan, and the lender claims the car to satisfy the debt.

Sometimes banks and other lending agencies ask borrowers to furnish other types of collateral for a loan. Borrowers may pledge some kind of property, often bonds or stocks, as assurance that the loan will be repaid. The collateral that the borrower is able to offer the lender may have an effect on the interest rate. The greater the value of the collateral, the lower the risk to the lender and the lower the interest rate that will be charged. Sometimes borrowers cannot obtain a loan, because they have nothing to offer as collateral.

INSTANT REPLAY

Credit is a promise to pay in the future for goods, services, or money that people receive immediately.

Money is lent in a variety of ways. Three of these are credit cards, mortgage loans, and installment loans.

If someone fails to make the required payments on a loan, the lender may repossess the collateral used for the loan.

SAVING MONEY

As their incomes rise, people find that they do not have to spend all their money on goods and services. They can save some of it. In the Preview to this chapter, you learned that the average family saves about 5 percent of its income each year. Some families save more than 5 percent, and some save less. Once a family is able to put money aside, it must decide where to keep its savings.

As you learned in Chapter 6, during the Great Depression, many people lost their life savings in bank failures. The bank failures caused some people to mistrust banks and keep their savings at home. This practice is no longer a wise way to save money. Money kept at home is not safe from fire and theft, and it does not earn any interest or dividends. Today, banks are generally well managed, and the Federal Deposit Insurance Corporation insures depositors against losses. As a result, savers have lost very little money in banks in the last 50 years.

Why People Save

People save money for at least three reasons. First, saving can provide the money necessary to pay unexpected expenses. Although a well-designed budget may allow a person to pay the normal expenses of living, a large medical bill or extensive automobile repairs may far exceed the person's income during any one month. Without adequate savings, the individual may be forced to borrow money at high interest rates or to greatly reduce his or her standard of living until the bill is paid. Similarly, saving offers protection against illness or unemployment, which may reduce income for long periods of time.

A second reason that families save is to accumulate enough money to make a large purchase in the future. A family may want to buy a boat or a recreation vehicle. By forgoing smaller purchases today and putting the money into an interest-bearing account, the family saves enough money to make a larger purchase or to purchase more goods and services in the future. For example, if the interest rate is 10 percent, $100 dollars saved today will grow to $200 in about seven years. By waiting, the consumer could have twice as many goods and services. Of course, inflation might have increased prices, but usually a saver will be able to buy more at the end of the time period than at the beginning.

Finally, people save for their retirement. Most retired persons spend more than they earn. Typically, retired people do not use borrowed money; instead, they use money they saved while they were working. To provide for this period without wages or earnings, most people have some sort of retirement savings program. They save each year while working and then use these savings to support themselves when they retire.

One reason people save is to accumulate money to make a big purchase in the future.

Pace Arrow motorhouse produced by Fleetwood Enterprises, Inc.

People save for their retirement years, when they will no longer be earning income.

Indiana Department of Commerce

Ways to Save Money

Many kinds of savings accounts are offered by banks, insurance companies, and other financial intermediaries. Some of the key differences among these accounts have to do with how much interest is paid, whether or not the account is insured, and how easily the money can be withdrawn.

Banks and savings and loan associations offer checking accounts, passbook savings accounts, certificates of deposit, and money market accounts. You learned about checking accounts in Chapter 3. Until recently, most checking accounts did not pay interest. However, because of changes in banking laws and increased competition among banks and other financial institutions, most banks now offer checking accounts that pay interest.

For many years, the **passbook savings account** was the primary means of saving, and today it is still a major method of saving for many people. The saver brings or mails a deposit to the bank, and it is recorded in a small booklet called a passbook. Every three months, the bank adds interest to the account. When the saver wants to make a withdrawal, he or she brings the booklet to the bank and requests payment. The bank then records the withdrawal as a subtraction from the balance in the savings book.

A **certificate of deposit (CD)** is a form of savings account in which a minimum amount, perhaps $1,000, is deposited for a specified period of time ranging from three months to seven years at a guaranteed rate of interest. Financial institutions offer a variety of these certificates. Usually the interest rate on CDs is higher for longer time periods. For example, a two-year CD might pay 8 percent interest, while a five-year CD might pay 9 percent.

A **money market account** is another way of saving money. It offers the advantage of a checking account, while it pays a higher rate of interest. Often, the interest rate increases if the account balance is higher than $10,000. The interest rate is determined by supply and demand; therefore, the rate can vary daily. With money market accounts, the saver can write only a limited number of checks on the account each month.

INSTANT REPLAY

Individuals save money to provide security in the event of unexpected expenses or reductions in income due to illness or unemployment, to purchase more goods and services in the future, and to provide for income during retirement.

Checking accounts, passbook saving accounts, certificates of deposit, and money market accounts are ways to save money.

THE ROLE OF CREDIT AND SAVINGS IN THE ECONOMY

Perhaps the best way to understand the role of credit in a free enterprise system is to imagine an economic system in which credit does not exist. Every day, people would have to carry enough cash with them to take care of all necessary transactions. They would have to carry money for such unforeseen events as car repairs and medical emergencies. Most families would have difficulty purchasing a home or a car. It would take them many years to save enough money to buy these things. In fact, for a family with children it might take so long that by the time enough was saved, the children would be grown and there would be no need for the new house.

Without credit, business transactions would be much more difficult to make. Today, many business orders are made over the telephone, delivery is made within a few days, and the bill is paid at the end of the month. Without credit, the purchaser would have to go to the seller with the money, make payment, and pick up the materials. This method of doing business would be much more difficult and costly for both the buyer and the seller.

By using credit, businesses are able to produce more goods and services and generate more jobs. Although there may be problems associated with the use of credit, especially when some people are unable to meet the payments due on their credit obligations, credit offers advantages to the day-to-day operation of the economic system.

There are at least five specific ways that the use of credit benefits the economic system:

1. Credit makes it more convenient and less costly for consumers and businesses to make a large number of transactions. Consumers can use credit cards instead of cash, and businesses can place orders over the telephone. Then the consumers and businesses can pay for their purchases and orders later.

2. The availability of credit helps new businesses and young families get started. A new business may not have enough money to purchase inventory and rent a building. By borrowing the money and using credit to buy inventory, an entrepreneur can start up a new business. The business will then start generating income to enable the entrepreneur to repay the loans. Similarly, young people do not usually have enough money to purchase a car or home. Credit allows them to obtain these things and pay for them gradually.

3. Credit also benefits the economic system by helping to offset declines in economic activity. When people are temporarily laid off from work, their incomes are reduced. By using credit to buy goods and services, they can provide for their families until they are rehired. These purchases increase the demand for goods and services, and the increase in demand helps offset the decline in economic activity.

4. A well-developed credit system increases gross national product. When businesses borrow money to increase production, not only does GNP increase, but more jobs are created. The banks that lend these funds earn additional profits. The profits are then used to expand the bank's operations; in turn, the expansion increases output and employment.

5. Credit results in an increase in the standard of living. Using credit, individuals or families can buy cars, homes, or education that they could not otherwise afford. For the entire economy, credit results in an increase in GNP, and this increase means a higher standard of living for the average individual or family.

Saving is as essential as credit to economic growth; without saving, there could be no borrowing. Obviously, before a bank can lend money to borrowers, it must have the money to lend. This money comes from the savers who deposit their savings in the bank to earn interest. Similarly, corporations depend on savers to buy stock and thus provide the corporation money in exchange for shares of ownership.

In Chapter 6 you learned that savings is the part of the economy's total income that becomes available for investment in capital goods. These capital goods are used to increase production in the future. It follows that GNP will be higher in the future if part of today's income is saved and invested. Thus, the principle of giving up some consumption now for greater consumption in the future operates not only for individual savers but also for the entire economy.

INSTANT REPLAY

Credit makes economic transactions easier and less expensive.

There can be no credit unless savers make money available for borrowing.

The use of credit results in a greater production of goods and services and an increased number of jobs.

Saving promotes economic growth by making money available to purchase capital goods.

INVESTING IN STOCK

Although we usually think of saving money in a bank account, another way to save is to invest money in stock. In Chapter 7 you learned that corporations such as General Motors and American Telephone & Telegraph are owned by thousands of people whose ownership is represented by shares of stock. Of course, people buy these stocks to make money. A stockholder is usually paid a dividend on a regular basis—typically every three months. In addition to dividends, stockholders often make money when the price of stock they own increases. Indeed, fortunes have been made and lost in the stock market.

Thus, investing in stock is another way of earning a return on money that has been saved. But such investments are riskier than depositing money in bank accounts. Bank accounts do not fluctuate in value. In contrast, the value of stock may rise or fall dramatically.

Stock Prices

The prices of stock shares change continually. On a recent day on the New York Stock Exchange, 89 million shares of stock in 1,952 companies were traded. Of these, 914 increased in price and 695 decreased. The prices of the remaining stocks were unchanged. Of all stocks traded that day, the average price per share increased by 18 cents.

Sometimes, the prices of most stocks increase or decrease steadily for a period of time. When most stock prices are increasing, it is said to be a **bull market.** When most stock prices are decreasing, it is said to be a **bear market.** You may hear investors asking, "Are you bullish or bearish on the market?" In other words, do you expect stock prices generally to increase (bullish) or to decrease (bearish)?

The **Dow Jones Industrial Average** is the best-known indicator of changes in the overall price of common stocks. This average is a measure of the stock prices of 30 leading corporations in the United

Investing in stock is another way of earning a return on money that has been saved.

States. Included in this group are IBM; Sears, Roebuck and Co.; General Electric; and General Motors. Because of the way it is calculated, the Dow Jones Industrial Average does not tell you anything about the actual prices of any one of these stocks. Only the overall level of stock prices is measured.

Newspapers and radio and television newscasts regularly report changes in the Dow Jones average, sometimes on an hourly basis. Changes in the Dow Jones average are measured in points. For example, if the Dow Jones average has been about 1,800 and you hear that it has increased by 18 points, this means that stock prices have increased, on average, by about 1 percent (18 ÷ 1800 = 0.01).

Figure 17-1 shows the Dow Jones average since 1929. Note the many ups and downs. Some of these were caused by changes in economic or industrial conditions or by political developments. Other fluctuations, however, are simply the result of changes in the attitudes of investors.

FIGURE 17-1
This chart shows the Dow Jones Industrial Average since 1929.

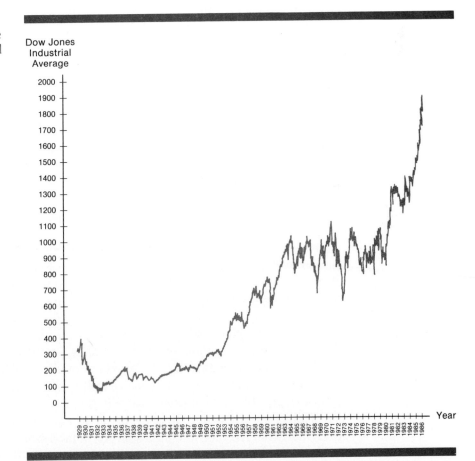

There are four basic reasons that stock prices change: company profitability, industry conditions, general economic conditions, and international developments.

Company Profitability. At any time, some companies are achieving large increases in profits, while others are recording profit decreases and possibly even losses. Investors prefer to own stock in those companies that are earning high profits and avoid those that are not. These preferences will be reflected in the price of the stock. The value of stock in successful companies will increase, while the value of stock in unsuccessful companies will decrease.

Consider an example. A few years ago, the state of New Jersey passed a law that made gambling legal in Atlantic City. Resorts International, Inc., was the first business to be granted a license to open a casino. In fact, for some time that company had the only legal gambling casino in the area. The casino was a huge success. The year before it received this license, the company's profit had been only $2.5 million. The next year, largely because of the new casino, the company made profits of $51 million; the year after that, profits increased to $86.5 million. As a result, its stock increased in value. Before the casino opened, a share of common stock sold for $8. A year after the casino opened, the price of a share was almost $70.

Industry Conditions. The ability of a company to earn a profit depends on conditions within the industry of which it is a part. For example, in the 1980s the computer industry was growing rapidly and profits were increasing. Because of this situation, investors were attracted to the industry. As a result, there was a strong demand for the stock of computer companies. Thus, the stock prices of many of these computer companies increased significantly.

Industries experiencing slower growth in sales and profits are less popular with investors. Some companies in an industry may be successful; but if the industry as a whole has a poor profit record, the price of stock for successful companies within the industry may still be low.

General Economic Conditions. Because economic conditions affect the sales and profits of companies, they also affect stock prices. In an economy in which GNP is growing, the profits of business will also increase. As a result, stock prices will increase as well. Conversely, during a recession or depression, stock prices usually decline. Refer again to Figure 17-1. Note that when the Great Depression started in 1929, the Dow Jones Industrial Average declined sharply. In fact, stock values declined by about 80 percent. It was not until 1956 that the Dow Jones stock average returned to the level achieved in 1929 before the depression. In contrast, between 1982 and 1986 stock prices increased rapidly. During this period, the Dow Jones Industrial Average rose more than 130 percent. This means that on average a $10,000 investment in 1982 increased in value to $23,000 in just four years.

Political and International Developments. Changes in our government such as the election of a president or senator often have an effect on stock prices, because some politicians are perceived as being more favorable toward business than others. When these people are elected, stock prices tend to go up. For example, when Ronald Reagan was running for the presidency in 1980 and 1984, he promised greater government spending for national defense. Upon his election, the stock prices increased for many companies producing goods and services for defense.

On other occasions, individuals who favor higher taxes and more government control of business have been elected. Sometimes, the promise of higher taxes and more control of business has resulted in falling stock prices.

National emergencies also can affect stock prices. When President John F. Kennedy was assassinated in 1963, the Dow Jones average declined about 30 points, or 3 percent in one day. When a national emergency occurs, investors often are not sure how the emergency will affect the economy. As a result, more investors try to sell stocks than try to buy stocks, and prices decline.

Problems and crises on the international front also can have an effect on the stock market. During the last 20 years there have been several wars in the Middle East. At the time it seemed possible that these small wars could develop into major wars involving the United States and other countries. Stock prices tended to decrease during these periods.

How to Buy and Sell Stock

If you wanted to buy stock, you would go to a brokerage company, such as Merrill Lynch or E. F. Hutton. These firms, like most big brokerage companies, have offices all over the United States and in many foreign countries. In each office, salespeople called **stockbrokers** assist investors in buying and selling stock.

Shares of stock in large corporations are bought and sold in organized **stock exchanges.** For example, the New York Stock Exchange is a central place where stock of more than 2,000 corporations is traded. Other U. S. stock exchanges include the American Stock Exchange and several regional exchanges such as those in Denver, Philadelphia, and Chicago. Many other nations also have stock exchanges. Two of the largest are in London and Tokyo.

Within an exchange, there are places for the various stocks traded. Representatives of brokerage companies go to a certain place if they have orders from customers to buy or sell a particular stock. An exchange employee at each place keeps track of all orders to buy or sell particular stocks.

Suppose that you want to buy 100 shares of General Motors and that Merrill Lynch is your brokerage company. Your stockbroker communicates your order to a Merrill Lynch employee at the New York Stock Exchange, who takes the order to the General Motors station. Other stockbrokers are arriving with orders to sell. Your order to buy is matched with another's order to sell. The result is that you have purchased 100 shares, perhaps from someone hundreds of miles away. You will never know who sold the stock to you. On a typical day, 80 to 120 million shares of stock are traded on the New York Stock Exchange alone.

Stockbrokers trade millions of shares of stock at the New York Stock Exchange every day.

Dana Duke Photography

The cost of buying or selling stock can vary considerably depending on the price of the stock, the number of shares purchased, and the particular brokerage company you use. For example, one company may charge a commission of 2 percent of the total value of the transaction. Thus, if you bought 200 shares of stock at $25 per share, the total value would be $5,000. The brokerage commission would then be about $100 ($0.02 \times \$5,000$). The same fee is charged when you sell the 100 shares.

Stock for thousands of smaller companies is traded in the **over-the-counter market.** There is no central place where this trading occurs. Rather, hundreds of brokerage offices are linked together by telephone lines and computer terminals. Each of these offices buys and sells the stock of many companies. These firms make money by charging one price if you want to sell and a slightly higher price if you want to buy. For example, a brokerage company that buys and sells a particular stock may offer to buy at $30 per share (the bid price) and sell at $30.50 per share (the asking price). Thus, on every 100 shares bought or sold, the company will make 50 cents per share, or $50. Hence, the investor who wants to buy would pay $30.50 per share plus the usual commission. A seller would receive $30 per share and also would pay a commission.

INSTANT REPLAY

Investing in stock is one way of saving money. Stock prices are constantly changing because of company and industry conditions, general economic conditions, and political developments.

Individuals buy and sell stock by working with a stockbroker in a brokerage company.

Stocks are bought and sold in central stock exchanges and in the over-the-counter market.

Reading the Financial Page

Reports on stock prices are found in most major newspapers each business day. The information looks complicated, but it is not difficult to learn what it means. Part of a typical report from the New York Stock Exchange is shown on page 336. Stocks are listed alphabetically so that it is easy to find a particular company.

Stock	Dividend	Sales	High	Low	Close	Net Change
General Mills	2.32	1,856	81½	75¼	80½	+4½
General Motors	5.00	5,348	79⅛	78	78½	—
Georgia Pacific	0.80	3,031	33⅜	33¼	33¼	+ ⅛

What does all this information mean? Consider the first row, which reports on activity of the stock of General Mills. This corporation pays a dividend of $2.32 per share. Thus, a stockholder would receive $2.32 each year for each share owned. The sales figure refers to the number of shares sold in hundreds. So, 1,856 means 185,600 shares. *High* and *low* refer to the high and low prices that the stock sold for during the day. The high price of 81½ translates into $81.50 per share, because the decimal equivalent of ½ is 0.50.

Close refers to the last price before the market closed for the day. *Net change* means the change in price from the close of the previous day. General Mills' *net change* +4½ means that the closing price was $4.50 per share above the closing price of the previous day. If you owned 100 shares, your stock would now be worth $450 more than it was the previous day. This is a rather large increase for one day, but stock prices can go up and down dramatically.

SUMMARY

Credit allows individuals to borrow money to buy goods and services and pay for it later, using future income. There are many ways to use credit. These include the use of credit cards, mortgage loans, and installment loans. Many people use credit cards as a convenient way to make purchases now and pay for them later.

People save to provide for unexpected expenses, to have greater consumption in the future, and to have income for their retirement. Ways to save include passbook savings, certificates of deposit, and money market accounts. When people save part of their current income, money becomes available for investment in capital goods, which are important in economic growth. Also, saving provides money that individuals can borrow to purchase goods and services.

When people save and use the credit available in an economy, more goods and services are produced and more jobs are available. Credit benefits the free enterprise system by making it easy for consumers and business managers to make transactions; by helping young families and new businesses get started; by offsetting declines in economic activity; by increasing GNP and employment; and by increasing living standards.

Another way to save is to invest in stock. Every day millions of shares of stock are bought and sold in organized stock exchanges and in the over-the-counter market. Individuals buy and sell stock by working with a stockbroker at a brokerage company. The prices of these shares change constantly; prices depend on the company's financial success, the industry, the performance of the economy, and international and political developments. The Dow Jones Industrial Average is the best-known indicator of the overall level and change in stock prices.

☆ LEARNING ACTIVITIES ☆

Building Your Vocabulary

On a separate sheet of paper, write the numbers 1 through 10. Next to each number, write the term that correctly completes the sentence.

credit card
mortgage loan
installment loan
collateral
repossess
passbook savings
    account
certificate of deposit
money market
    account
bull market
stock exchange

1. To _____ property is to take someone's property for nonpayment of a loan.

2. A _____ is secured by a house, land or a business building.

3. A _____ gives a consumer the privilege of buying goods and services today and paying for them later.

4. A central place where stocks are bought and sold is a _____.

5. When stock prices generally are rising, a _____ is said to exist.

6. A _____ is a type of savings account that pays a stated rate of interest for a specified time period.

7. A _____ is like a checking account but pays a higher rate of interest.

8. With a _____, deposits, withdrawals, and interest payments are recorded in a small book.

9. An _____ is generally used to borrow money to make large purchases such as an automobile or a boat.

10. Property pledged as security for a loan is known as _____.

Reviewing the Facts

1. List three kinds of loans.
2. Why do young families tend to borrow money?
3. How does the bank make money on credit card purchases?
4. Identify three reasons for saving money.
5. Describe three ways in which a person can save money.
6. Discuss the ways that credit benefits the economy.

7. Give four reasons that stock prices fluctuate.
8. What does it mean if someone says, "General Motors was up a half at the close today"?
9. Explain how a brokerage company in the over-the-counter market makes a profit when buying or selling stock.

Expressing Your Opinion

1. What are the dangers of using credit cards?
2. If you were given $2,000 to save for your college education, should you put it in a passbook account, certificates of deposit, or a money market account? Why?
3. Some savings institutions are not insured. Why would anyone deposit money in one of these organizations?
4. If you use your credit card to buy an item that sells for $100, the store will receive only $96 from the bank. What would the store manager say if you offered to pay $97 in cash instead of using your credit card?
5. What is happening to the purchasing power of your savings if the interest rate is 5 percent but the inflation rate is 10 percent? In this situation, would there be any reason to save?

Developing Your Attitudes, Values, and Skills

1. Different banks offer different rates of interest and other incentives to attract savers. Suppose that you have inherited $3,000 and are looking for a bank to open an account. Visit at least three banks, and determine the rates of interest they offer on passbook savings accounts, money market accounts, and certificates of deposit. Find out what the interest rates and terms are for each kind of savings account. What other incentives is the bank offering? Some banks give away appliances or other items to new depositors. Banks offer certificates of deposit for various lengths of time from a few months to several years. Find out the rates for each time period. In addition, money market accounts usually require that you maintain a minimum average monthly deposit to earn the money market rate. Find out what the required minimum deposit is at each bank. When you have finished gathering your data, prepare a chart showing how each bank compares on rates and terms for each kind of account. Using your research, decide which bank you would use and which kind of savings account you would open. Write a brief report explaining your choice.

2. Assume that you decide to invest your $3,000 in the stock market instead of in a savings account. For one week, read a newspaper that carries stock market listings. Then choose five stocks, and follow their performance for a month. (See page 336 for an explanation of how to read stock market listings.) Make a chart showing each stock's daily performance. Also include a listing on your chart showing the daily performance of the Dow Jones Average. Your newspaper will report changes in this average

somewhere on the stock pages. At the end of the month, you will have to decide which stock to purchase with your $3,000. Consider these factors: Which stock increased in value the most? Did any decline in value? How did each stock perform in comparison with the Dow Jones Average? How many shares of each stock could you purchase with your $3,000? When you have examined all these factors, write a report stating which stock you would purchase. Explain why.

3. Think of an item you would like to have, such as a television or bicycle. Find out the cost of the item by comparison shopping. Plan how long it would take you to save the money needed to buy the item. To help you plan, develop a budget based on your sources of income (allowances, gifts, earnings, etc.), your typical weekly expenses, and your savings. Devise credit terms for a plan that would allow you to "buy now and pay later." Plan a credit agreement based on what you can afford to pay each month. Assume that the interest rate is 10 percent each month. How easy or difficult would it be to meet the monthly payments? Do you think that having the item would be worth the commitment to meet regular payments? How would the monthly payments limit your ability to make other purchases?

4. Interview a member of your family or a friend who has recently financed a car. Find out the cost of the automobile, the down payment, the monthly payment, and the number of months the payments must be made. Do you think the terms of the loan were fair? Explain why or why not. What do you think is the most important factor to the car buyer—the interest rate, the absolute amount of interest in dollars, the down payment, or the monthly payment? In your opinion, which should be of most concern?

CHAPTER 18

CONSUMER RIGHTS AND RESPONSIBILITIES

PREVIEW

"I've been poor and I've been rich.... and believe me, rich is better."
Actress Sophie Tucker

"The very rich are different from you and me.... They have more money."
Writer Ernest Hemingway

Most people would agree with Sophie Tucker that being rich is better than being poor. Almost everyone dreams of a life in which decisions such as which car to buy, where to go on vacation, and how much to spend on clothes can be made without first looking to see if there is enough money in the checking account.

Unfortunately, few people acquire enough wealth to allow them to stop worrying about how their income is spent and how much things cost. Ernest Hemingway was correct when he observed that "the very rich are different from you and me." Unlike the very wealthy, most people must be constantly concerned about consumer decisions. The difficulties faced by the average person are summarized by this short saying:

If your outgo is greater than your income, then your upkeep will be your downfall.

The main purpose of economic activity is to meet the needs and wants of consumers. This chapter will help you understand your rights and responsibilities as a consumer. It will also help you improve the decisions that you make as a consumer. When you have completed the reading material and learning activities, you should be able to:

★ List and explain four rights of consumers.

★ Discuss the responsibilities of consumers.

★ Explain how the economic principles of opportunity cost, marginal cost, and sunk cost can be used to improve consumer decision making.

CONSUMER RIGHTS

In many ways the choices that today's consumers face are much more complicated than those of people living in earlier times. Consider farm families during the nineteenth century. Usually these families had only enough resources to provide for their basic needs—food, shelter, and clothing. Their choices were simple and few in number. About the only way they could get a new home was for the family members to build it. Most of the food they consumed was grown on their own farms, and they either made their own clothing at home or purchased it from the limited selection at a local store.

In contrast, today's consumers normally purchase all the goods they need to satisfy their basic needs, and many have extra income to purchase a wide variety of goods and services to satisfy their tastes in entertainment and recreation as well. Although you are still a student, you are already one of these modern consumers. You choose your own clothes, purchase restaurant meals, buy records and tapes, and go to concerts and movies.

As a consumer, you usually have to make choices in order to make a wise purchase. Suppose, for example, that you decide to buy a new car. First, you need to decide what make and model you should buy. Should it be a Chevrolet, a Chrysler, or a Toyota? Should it be a sports car, a four-door sedan, or a station wagon? What color would you prefer? What optional equipment do you want? Do you want air conditioning, a stereo system, or power windows? You also have to decide where to purchase your new car by determining which dealer offers the best price and service. Then you have to decide how to pay for the car. Will you pay cash, or will you borrow the money? If you borrow the money, should you go to a bank or finance it through the dealer?

Consumers often find themselves at a disadvantage when they make these kinds of decisions, because the sellers of goods and services have considerable information about the things they sell. As such, they are well aware of the strengths and weaknesses of the products they sell. But an individual consumer may buy a car only once every five years. During that time, prices, models, and features would have changed a great deal. What the consumer learned about cars five years ago will be little help in selecting a new car today.

In addition to the complexity of choosing goods and services, today's consumers are occasionally victimized by fraudulent advertising, shoddily made goods, and dangerous or tainted products. In recognition of these problems, in 1962 President John F. Kennedy set forth four basic rights of consumers:

★ The right to accurate information

★ The right to safe products

★ The right to adequate variety

★ The right to be heard

In a free enterprise system, these rights are protected to some extent by competition. In those cases in which the marketplace does not regulate itself adequately, government or private groups have stepped in to protect and promote consumer rights. In the next few pages, you will see how each of these forces—competition, government, and private organizations—work to secure the four basic rights of consumers.

The Right to Accurate Information

To make good decisions, consumers must have accurate information about available goods and services. A diabetic may need to know whether a product contains sugar, a traveling salesperson may want to buy a car that gets good gas mileage, or a person who is allergic to wool may need to know what fabric a coat is made of. When producers provide accurate information, it helps consumers make purchasing decisions and thus helps producers sell their goods and services.

Much of the information that consumers receive comes to them through advertising. But advertising information may be biased in favor of the product that is being advertised. Sometimes an advertiser's claims are exaggerated or false. When a product is inexpensive (such as a bar of soap), consumers can find out for themselves whether the product performs as advertised. But for many products, consumers cannot afford to buy and test several brands. To make their purchasing decisions, they must rely on the information that the producers and advertisers have provided.

Competition can work in different ways to provide consumers with accurate information. Many businesses depend on repeat customers, and others depend on their good reputations to bring them new customers. In either case, these companies know they must deal fairly and honestly with every customer. If they do not provide exactly what they claim they are providing, their customers will go elsewhere. If a company does make exaggerated or false claims about a product, its competitors may advertise to inform consumers about the product's flaws. Of course, the competitor's ads may be biased, but consumers can still take them into consideration, along with other product information, when making a purchasing decision.

The labels and tags that producers put on their goods also help inform consumers. Labeling is an area in which government has taken steps to help consumers. Congress passed laws that require processors of food to list all the ingredients on the can or package. Thus, a diabetic who needs to avoid sugar or a consumer with high blood pressure who needs to avoid salt can read the labels on each food product to check the ingredients in the product. The number of calories and the nutritional content of the food may also be shown.

Similarly, manufacturers of clothing must indicate on the label what materials have been used to make the garment, and gasoline stations must post the octane ratings of the fuel they sell. The intent of rules like these is to strengthen consumers' rights to have accurate information about goods and services they purchase.

Labels help inform consumers about products.

The Right to Safe Products

Consumers have a right to assume that the goods and services they purchase are safe. Competition can work to promote product safety. Firms that sell an unsafe product will soon lose business. When consumers become aware of the product's safety problems, they will buy from a company that provides a safer product. In many cases, however, a product is so widely distributed that it is not possible for all its potential buyers to learn about its defects. A consumer in Maine, for example, has no way of knowing that the product that he or she is thinking of purchasing has killed or injured users in Texas and Oregon. Consequently, there is a need for government to be involved in product safety.

Some of the activities of government in this area were discussed in Chapter 10: The *Consumer Product Safety Commission* has power to remove an unsafe product from the market; the *National Highway Traffic Safety Commission* can require that automobiles have certain types of

The government establishes safety standards for new products.

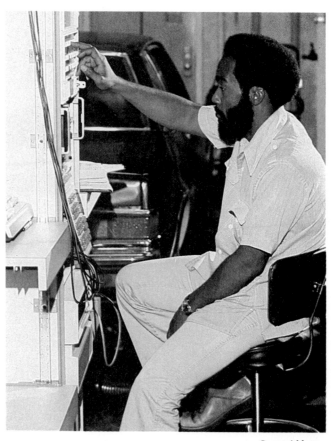

General Motors

safety equipment; and the *Food and Drug Administration* requires that extensive tests be conducted on drugs before they are approved for human use.

The court system is also used to promote the consumer's right to safety. An individual who has been injured while using a product can sue the manufacturer. If the court decides that the injury occurred because the product was unsafe, the seller may be forced to pay the customer's medical bills and replace any income that was lost as a result of the injury. In some cases, the manufacturer may also be required to pay additional money as a penalty. This system helps consumers who have been injured and also gives firms an incentive to make safer products.

The Right to Adequate Variety

Consumer wants vary from person to person. Some consumers may demand high-quality products and are willing to pay high prices for them. Others, because they have little money or different tastes, may be willing to settle for a lower-quality product that is less expensive. For example, one buyer may choose a big-screen television complete with remote tuner and four-year warranty. Another may select a 13-inch black-and-white set. A single person with a high income may buy a Mercedes Benz sports car, while a married couple with three children may select a Ford station wagon.

The free enterprise system meets the various preferences of these consumers. As long as demand is adequate to allow entrepreneurs to earn a profit, competition will assure that a wide variety of goods and services are available to the consumer. In some cases, however, consumers may have little choice among products or prices. A monopoly may offer only one product or a few similar products, or the firms in an oligopoly may band together and fix the prices of their products. As you learned in Chapter 10, the government can use antitrust laws to increase competition in these cases either by breaking up monopolies or by prosecuting companies that engage in price fixing.

The Right to Be Heard

Consumers have a right to complain if they are not satisfied. Even when a business tries to be fair with its customers, there will be times when the buyer is not happy with the product. If a product is unsatisfactory, most reputable stores will refund the customer's money or replace the product. Some large retail stores have departments where products are tested for safety, durability, and effectiveness. If products are not acceptable, the store will not sell them. Thus, customers of these stores can have confidence in the items they buy.

Competition helps ensure consumer satisfaction by providing alternatives to unhappy buyers. For instance, if a consumer buys a defective radio, it is usually in the seller's best interest to replace the radio or give the customer a refund. Otherwise, the consumer may decide never to buy that brand of product or shop in that store again. The consumer may also tell friends and relatives not to shop there either. But this consumer power works only if there are many other radio manufacturers and stores to patronize. If there are few competitive sellers and a limited number of models, shoppers will not have this power because they will have few alternatives.

If a consumer cannot achieve satisfaction by dealing directly with the seller, there are other ways to resolve the problem. Many newspapers and radio and television stations have consumer advocates who assist people in their disputes. If these advocates believe that a consumer has been unfairly treated, they may write about the issue in the newspaper or discuss it on the radio or television. Often, the unfavorable publicity will cause the business to be more responsive to consumers.

Better Business Bureaus are another source of help for consumers. These bureaus are formed by businesses that join together to encourage good business practices in a community. Individuals can go to the local Better Business Bureau to obtain information about specific

Consumers have the right to be heard when they purchase defective products.

businesses. If other consumers have been dissatisfied with the business's performance and have complained to the bureau, the bureau will provide this information. In this way the consumer can avoid dealing with dishonest businesses. The bureau may also be able to help consumers who have been treated unfairly by a local business. In some areas, the state or local government also has employees assigned to help individuals resolve disputes with sellers of goods and services. These employees inform consumers of their rights and may also contact businesses directly.

If none of the ways discussed above is successful, consumers can take their disputes to court. If the amount of money involved is small, a small claims court would be the place to go. If a large sum of money is involved, the person can hire a lawyer and take the matter to the regular court system. The courts have the power to force the business to live up to its obligations or return the consumer's money.

INSTANT REPLAY

Companies help consumers obtain accurate information by reporting the shortcomings of their competitors' products.

Competition lowers the demand for unsafe products. Manufacturers are required by law to list the contents of canned or packaged goods. Government agencies can require that unsafe products be improved or removed from the market.

Competition ensures a wide variety of goods and services to consumers. Government promotes competition by breaking up monopolies and prosecuting price fixers.

Competition promotes customer satisfaction, because unhappy customers can go elsewhere. Government agencies, Better Business Bureaus, consumer advocates, and the court system all help consumers resolve complaints.

CONSUMER RESPONSIBILITIES

The rights that consumers have also carry with them certain basic responsibilities. If businesses must provide information, satisfaction, safety, and variety to their customers, consumers must also carry out certain obligations to the businesses they patronize. These rights and responsibilities are inseparable. Businesses provide information about their goods and services, but it is up to the consumer to collect the information, examine it, evaluate it, and make a decision. Similarly, businesses provide safe products and satisfy customer grievances, and consumers, in turn, are expected to deal honestly with business.

The Responsibility to Be Informed

In Chapter 3 you learned that the dollar votes of consumers guide businesses in their decisions about what to produce. That is, businesses provide the goods and services, and consumers vote on which things they prefer by either buying or not buying. Thus, consumers are the real decision makers in a market economy.

But to make good decisions, consumers must have information about the goods and services available, their important features, and their prices. How do consumers get this information? How can consumers keep up to date on new products and on any changes in price? Some of the best ways are discussed here.

Informal Information Gathering. Good consumers are alert to developments, such as a new product on the market, a sale at a local department store, or the opening of a new business in the community. Sources of information for these events include advertisements in newspapers and magazines and commercials on radio and television. Word-of-mouth reports from friends and neighbors are also important.

Advertisements can provide consumers with a great deal of information. They tell what products are available; they announce sales and price reductions; and they provide important details about sizes, colors, styles, brands, and so on. Consumers can evaluate the information contained in the ads to decide whether or not to visit a store or purchase an item. Suppose a consumer has decided to buy a Panasonic VCR. The consumer may see an ad announcing that this brand is on sale at a certain store. If the consumer buys the VCR at that store, she or he may save a lot of money. Ads can also save consumers time as well as money. For instance, a couple who is shopping for a house in a certain price range will not spend time looking at houses that have been advertised for sale at higher prices.

Friends and neighbors are an excellent source of information. For example, reports on the food and service at a new restaurant can be valuable. You may be planning to go out for dinner. Your friend's recent

Consumers have the responsibility to be informed.

experience at a particular restaurant can help you decide whether to go there or to another place. However, you should remember that people have different preferences. Your friend may not recommend the restaurant because it specializes in Chinese food, which she does not like. In that case, her views may not be useful. Good consumers always make a careful evaluation of the source of the information.

Acquiring consumer information is a continual process. This information must be developed over a long period of time. As you become familiar with certain kinds of products, brand names, and stores, you will be better able to decide which manufacturers and stores provide the goods and services that you want. You will also learn which manufacturers and stores to avoid.

Information from Business and Government. Most businesses provide brochures or other written material about the goods and services they sell. These are valuable sources of information, especially for expensive, complicated goods for which detailed information is needed. Automobile dealers are a good example. They often have color brochures that show the cars they sell and describe many features of the cars.

State and federal government agencies also publish reports to help consumers make wise purchasing decisions. Booklets on amounts of energy used by different products, automobile performance and safety, and methods for avoiding dishonest businesses are typical of the information available from government. Most of these booklets are either free or very low priced.

Consumer Information Services. Several private organizations provide information about goods and services. Two of the better known are Consumers' Research, Inc., and Consumers' Union of the United States. Both are nonprofit corporations that evaluate and test products for effectiveness and safety. The results of these tests are reported in monthly magazines published by the organizations. Features on new consumer protection laws, ratings of movies, and reports on questionable business practices are also included.

Consumer Reports, the Consumers' Union magazine, is the best-known magazine of its kind. A recent issue contained reports on video cassette recorders, small cars, oven cleaners, and travel in the Hawaiian Islands. Typically, these reports compare products of different sellers and recommend good quality products.

Consumer Reports does not accept advertising. Thus, the magazine does not have to worry about offending advertisers. In contrast, some consumer-oriented publications do accept advertising. These magazines may have a problem when a business that is a major advertiser introduces a poor-quality product. An unfavorable report on the product may cause the company to cancel its advertising. As a result, some magazines rarely publish a negative report on a product. Consumers should be cautious about recommendations of products found in such publications. Only when a magazine does not accept advertising can it be totally objective in evaluating goods and services.

The Responsibility to Be Honest

Consumers expect stores to be honest in their business dealings. But businesses also have the right to expect consumers to be honest. Unfortunately, some people choose not to play by the rules. One of the most serious problems faced by businesses today is shoplifting. In a recent year, over $35 billion in merchandise was stolen from stores—more than 100 times the amount taken each year by bank robbers. Some shoplifters justify their theft by claiming that businesses charge high prices to earn large profits. But in Chapter 5 you learned that the average business earns only 5 cents in profit for every dollar of sales. Thus, for every dollar of merchandise that is stolen, a store must sell $20 of goods to make up for the loss.

Shoplifting not only hurts businesses, it also punishes honest consumers. To compensate for the cost of goods stolen by a few dishonest

Stores must guard against shoplifting, which costs businesses and consumers billions each year.

people, businesses must charge all consumers higher prices. Also, to protect against shoplifting, stores often change their methods of displaying merchandise. For example, tape stores often keep audio tapes in cases that can be opened only by a salesperson. This practice makes shoplifting more difficult, but it also prevents customers from reading the labels on the tapes. Thus, it is harder for consumers to obtain information about the product.

Shoplifting is not the only way that consumers can behave dishonestly. A person might buy a dress from a clothing store, wear it for a special occasion, and then return it to the store for a refund. Some people switch the price labels on merchandise so that at the checkout counter the good appears to cost less than the original price. Others buy goods on sale and then try to get the full price when they return them. Some credit purchasers do not pay their bills promptly, and others do not pay at all. Thieves often steal credit cards or obtain credit card numbers illegally and use the cards or numbers to purchase goods and services. Then either the credit card owner is billed for those purchases, or the businesses that sold the goods are forced to absorb the losses.

Not all businesses earn large profits. For some, the losses suffered because of dishonest consumer behavior cause the business to fail. Even if a business does not fail, it can be forced to charge its customers higher prices. For a market economy to operate successfully, consumers need to recognize their responsibility to be honest.

INSTANT REPLAY

Consumer rights and responsibilities are inseparable. They must be exercised together.

Consumers have the responsibility to gather and evaluate information from other consumers, advertisements, government publications and private agencies.

Consumers have the responsibility to be honest. Shoplifting and other dishonest practices force all consumers to pay higher prices.

CONSUMER DECISIONS AND PRINCIPLES OF ECONOMICS

In Chapter 4 you learned that consumers make buying decisions based on opportunity costs. Opportunity costs are the alternatives that a consumer gives up when making a choice. If you have $10, for example, you may have to choose between taking a date to the movies, buying a new record, or filling the gas tank of your car. Opportunity cost is an important economic principle that affects consumer decisions. Two others are marginal costs and sunk costs. By learning about these principles, you will be able to make better consumer decisions.

Opportunity Costs and Consumer Decisions

When you make a purchasing decision, you should calculate the opportunity costs in both money and time. If you have only $10, you cannot choose to spend $25 for concert tickets. However, you may have the $25 you need to buy the tickets, but you may decide that it is not worth your time to stand in line for several hours waiting to purchase the tickets. You could be spending that time watching television or going to a ball game. Thus, the opportunity cost is too high not in terms of money but in terms of time. Still, for some goods and services, it often pays to take the time to shop around for the best price or quality.

Goods purchased by consumers can be classified as either consumer durables or consumer nondurables. As the name suggests, a **consumer durable** refers to a product that can be used repeatedly and that will last a number of years. Some examples are automobiles, washing machines, refrigerators, and television sets. **Consumer nondurables** are goods that are purchased and then consumed, or goods that are quickly worn out and discarded. Food, paper products, medicine, and gasoline are examples of nondurables. A camera is a consumer durable. Film for the camera is a consumer nondurable.

There is an important difference in the way a consumer shops for these two kinds of goods. Usually when buying a nondurable, a consumer goes to a favorite store and buys one or more of the items. Most people do not take time to get information about the different products. Because each item is relatively inexpensive, the consumer can try it out. If it is not satisfactory, the person can try another brand the next time. Consumers find those brands that they like best by a trial-and-error process.

On a typical shopping trip for nondurables, a consumer might go into one store and buy three rolls of film, two tubes of toothpaste, and a dozen rolls of toilet paper. Although the person might quickly compare the prices of the different brands of each product in the store, he or she probably would not go to several stores to shop for the lowest price. The opportunity cost of spending that much time would be much greater than any cost savings.

Shopping for consumer durable goods is quite different. Many of these goods cost hundreds or thousands of dollars. An intelligent consumer would not simply walk into a store and buy the first product model available. This approach would almost guarantee buying the wrong brand or paying too much.

A better approach would be to read ads and consumer magazines to obtain information on the different models and brands, and then go to a number of stores to compare prices for those goods. This shopping approach might take several weeks or even months in the case of a very expensive product. Finally, after choosing a brand and model, the consumer would purchase it at a store that offered the best price. Because of the amount of shopping that is often required, consumer durables are sometimes referred to as **shopping goods.**

The prices of consumer durables can vary considerably. Because a consumer can save a lot of money by buying at one store rather than another, it is worthwhile to invest some time in shopping. A recent issue of a consumer magazine reported on the prices of refrigerator-freezers. It found that the price of the same model of refrigerator ranged from $410 to $620 in different stores. To most consumers a savings of $100 to $200 on the purchase of a refrigerator is well worth the time spent shopping.

Marginal Costs and Consumer Spending Decisions

Recall that marginal cost refers to the additional cost of producing or buying one more unit of a product. This concept is important for wise consumer spending. An example will help explain why.

Suppose a family has a large station wagon. It is a good car except that it gets only 15 miles per gallon of gas. It has a market value of $4,000. The family is considering trading in this car on a small economy model, because the small car would get 35 miles per gallon of gas. The new car would cost $9,000, so they would have to pay $5,000 in addition to trading in their station wagon.

Does this proposal make good economic sense? Consider the amount saved by buying less gas. Suppose the car is driven 10,000 miles each year and that gasoline costs about $1 per gallon. If the station wagon is kept, it will use 667 gallons of gas each year, costing $667. If the new compact car is purchased, it will use only 286 gallons at a cost of $286 per year. Thus, the family will save $381 each year on gas.

It pays to comparison shop for expensive consumer durables like these motorcycles.

The decision to trade the car should be based on the *marginal cost* of the two alternatives. Think about the costs over the next four years. If the station wagon is kept, the cost of the gasoline used will be $2,668. If the compact car is purchased, the family will spend $1,144 on gasoline plus $5,000 to buy the compact car, a cost of $6,144.

If the decision is to be based on cost alone, buying the compact car cannot be justified. The marginal cost of buying the compact car is almost $3,500 more than keeping the station wagon. The money saved by purchasing less gas will not make up for the additional cost of the new car.

The point here is that consumers must consider the entire marginal cost of a consumption decision. If you consider only part of the cost, you may make a poor choice. In the 1970s the price of gasoline increased dramatically. Some people were selling large cars at relatively low prices and buying small cars at relatively high prices simply because they were going to save a few hundred dollars each year on gasoline. This approach was not sound, because it did not account for all the marginal costs.

Sunk Costs and Consumer Decisions

Sunk costs are expenditures that have already been made and cannot be recovered. For example, $75 paid last week for repairs on a motorcycle would be a sunk cost. Sunk costs are not important to consumer decisions. The only costs that are important are the future costs over which a person has some control. For example, the motorcycle that was just repaired may soon need an engine overhaul that will cost $150. If the motorcycle is an older model, it is questionable whether it is worth spending that much for repairs. One may be tempted to think that because $75 was spent on repairs last week, further repairs should be made to protect last week's expenditure. Actually the money spent last week is totally irrelevant. It cannot be recovered and should have no bearing on what is done this week.

What should be done about the engine overhaul? If the owner wants to keep the motorcycle, he or she should go ahead and make the repairs. But what if the owner decides to sell the bike? Suppose that without the engine overhaul its market value is $400 and with a rebuilt engine the market value is $500. The cost of the repair is $150; the additional market value is $100 (the difference between $500 and $400). Because the cost exceeds the increased value, the owner should not rebuild the engine, but should sell the bike as is. No matter what is decided, the sunk costs should not be considered.

INSTANT REPLAY

There is an opportunity cost associated with making any purchase.

Consumer durables are goods that can be used repeatedly and will last a number of years. Consumer nondurables are goods that are used up quickly.

Marginal costs are important to many consumer purchases.

Sunk costs are irrelevant to consumer decisions.

SUMMARY

Competitors can help consumers obtain information about another firm's product. Another source of information is labels. Manufacturers are required by law to list the contents of canned or packaged goods.

Competition assures that a wide variety of goods and services will be available. Competition also protects consumers against unsafe products, because firms that sell such products will quickly lose business. Consumers are also protected by government agencies and the courts. Those who are injured by unsafe products have the right to sue the manufacturers.

Consumer advocates assist unsatisfied consumers by publicizing unfair business practices. Better Business Bureaus and government agencies also help consumers. Consumers can also take their disputes to court.

Consumers can obtain useful information from other consumers and from advertisements. Businesses provide brochures that provide details about their products. Government agencies also provide product information. Private information services evaluate different products in magazines such as *Consumer Reports*.

Over $35 billion of merchandise is taken by shoplifters each year. Businesses make up for this loss by charging higher prices to consumers. Shoplifting also causes business to display some products in ways that are less convenient for consumers who wish to inspect the merchandise.

When consumers select goods, they should consider the opportunity cost of the time they spend shopping. Consumer durables are goods that can be used repeatedly and will last a number of years. Consumer nondurables are goods that are used up quickly. Marginal costs are important to decision making, while sunk costs are irrelevant.

☆ LEARNING ACTIVITIES ☆

Building Your Vocabulary

On a separate sheet of paper, write the numbers 1 through 6. Next to each number, write the term that correctly completes the sentence.

Better Business
   Bureau
Consumer Reports
consumer durables
consumer
   nondurables
shopping goods
sunk costs

1. _____ are used repeatedly and last for a long time.

2. _____ is a magazine that compares different products and makes recommendations to consumers.

3. Food, paper products, and other goods that are quickly used up or worn out are called _____.

4. Consumer durables are also called _____.

5. A _____ provides information to consumers about dishonest businesses.

6. _____ are expenditures that have already been made and cannot be recovered.

Reviewing the Facts

1. List and describe the four rights of consumers.
2. How does competition help ensure the consumer's right to choose?
3. How does the government help secure the consumer's right to safe products?
4. What are three ways that consumers can exercise their right to be heard?
5. Describe at least three ways that consumers can gather information about goods and services.
6. How does opportunity cost, calculated in terms of time, affect consumer decisions?
7. How does the principle of marginal cost help consumers make purchasing decisions?
8. Why are sunk costs irrelevant in making consumer decisions?

Expressing Your Opinion

1. Do you think it is fair to pass shoplifting losses on to honest consumers in the form of higher prices? Why or why not?
2. Would you wait in line all night to buy concert tickets? Which performers would you be willing to spend this much time to see? Why?
3. Would a store be obligated to refund your money if you failed to supply a sales slip with the purchase you are returning? Why or why not?
4. In your opinion what is the most important right of consumers? What is the most important responsibility?

Developing Your Attitudes, Values, and Skills

1. Choose a name brand consumer durable, such as a television set, VCR, camera, microwave oven, or stereo center. Visit three or four stores to compare their prices for the same brand and model. If possible, try to shop in different kinds of stores—department stores, discount stores, catalog stores, appliance stores, and so on. What was the highest price you found for the item? What was the lowest price? How much would you have saved if you had purchased the item for the lowest price? How much time did you spend comparison shopping? Do you feel that the savings justified the time you had to spend? Summarize and compare your results with those of your classmates.

2. Choose ten advertisements from magazines and newspapers, and analyze them to determine what kinds of information they provide. List each ad on a sheet of paper. Leave enough room under each to note whether it tells you what the item does, how much it costs, where it can be bought, what its advantages are, and any other information (such as model, color, or size) that might help you decide whether to buy it. Rate each ad, on a scale of 1 to 4, on each of these qualities: informativeness, persuasiveness, and accuracy. How do the majority of the ads you selected compare on each quality? Write a report on your findings, and state your own conclusions about whether advertising helps secure the consumer's right to be informed.

3. Write a letter to a store, Better Business Bureau, or consumer agency, describing an imaginary consumer problem. You could pretend that a store is refusing to replace a defective product, that the workers you hired to fix your roof did a poor job, that you found pieces of glass in a jar of applesauce, or that you returned a credit card purchase but the seller has failed to credit your charge account. Use your own imagination to think of an appropriate problem. When you have finished your letter, exchange it with a classmate and write an answer to your classmate's letter. When you have finished the exercise, your teacher will ask some of you to read your letters and answers to the class. As you listen to the letters being read, think about whether you think they are effective in explaining the problem and asking for help, whether they are polite in tone, and whether the imaginary consumers and businesses fulfilled their responsibilities toward one another.

4. Most expensive consumer durables carry a warranty, which is a promise by the manufacturer to repair or replace any defective products or parts of a product for a specified period of time. Find three of four warranties that someone in your family has kept. Examine each one to find out what product the warranty covers, what the manufacturer specifically promises to do, what responsibilities the buyer is expected to fulfill, and how long the warranty will last. Some manufacturers require that the buyer ship the product back to the factory for repairs. Some exclude labor costs, and others use very specific language to exclude from the warranty

damage due to normal wear and tear. Ask family members if they have ever had a product repaired while it was under warranty. If so, find out whether they had to pay to ship the product to the factory or whether they had to pay any part of the repair costs. Were they satisfied with the warranty? If not, why not? Write a brief report summarizing your findings and comparing the terms of the warranties.

FOCUS YOUR READING

How can a budget help a family manage its income?

What are the disadvantages of owning your own home?

When a person borrows money to buy a car, are lower monthly payments always better?

CHAPTER 19

CONSUMER ECONOMICS

PREVIEW

Since you are still in school, you probably live with an adult who provides the basic necessities you require. In a few years' time, however, you will have to provide for your own needs. Thus, you will be responsible for major consumer decisions. You will need to find a place to live; you will need to furnish and decorate your home; and you may need to buy a car. At first, you will probably be concerned only about your own needs and wants, but eventually, you may marry and have children. Then you will need to provide food, shelter, and transportation for your family as well, or you will need to share in providing those essentials. And once you have a family, you may want to purchase life insurance so that your family will be financially secure.

In this chapter you will learn about budgeting and making decisions about housing, automobiles, and life insurance. You also will learn about some of the ways that dishonest people try to take advantage of consumers. When you have completed the reading material and learning activities, you should be able to:

★ Prepare a budget for yourself or your family.

★ List the advantages and disadvantages of owning versus renting housing.

★ Describe how automobile loans are arranged.

★ Discuss the two basic types of life insurance.

★ List some ways that unscrupulous firms take advantage of consumers.

BUDGETING SCARCE RESOURCES

Economics is defined as the study of how scarce resources are allocated among people's unlimited wants and needs. For the family or individual, needs and wants almost always are much greater than income. Therefore, consumers need to apply sound principles of economics when managing their money. An important part of good money management involves developing and using a budget. A **budget** is a plan to organize and match income and expenses.

Preparing an individual or family budget involves six steps:

1. Determine the time period to be covered by the budget. Usually this period will correspond to the frequency that income is received. For example, if salary is received once a month, a monthly budget is appropriate.

2. Determine income available for spending and saving by subtracting taxes from total income. This amount is referred to as **disposable income.**

3. Identify all **fixed expenses.** These are costs that are essentially the same each month. Fixed expenses typically include the rent or mortgage payment, utility bills, and payment on an automobile loan.

4. Determine a saving goal. That is, determine how much money should be set aside each month for saving in a bank account or investing in stock.

5. Estimate other expenses such as those for food, clothing, gasoline, and entertainment. By reviewing spending for previous months, you can estimate these items.

6. Compare income and expenses; then adjust spending so that spending and income are in balance.

Table 19-1 shows the budget for a family of four people. Consider the first column of numbers. If total income is $1,800 per month and taxes are $400 per month, disposable income is $1,400. That is, $1,400 is available each month for spending and saving. Assume the family's goal is to save 10 percent of total income, or $180 per month. Spending in each category was estimated by reviewing actual expenses for the past three months. These amounts are also shown in the first column of Table 19-1. Note that this column is labeled "preliminary."

TABLE 19-1

PRELIMINARY AND FINAL FAMILY BUDGETS			
	Preliminary	Change	Final
Total Income	$1,800		$1,800
Less: Taxes	400		400
DISPOSABLE INCOME	$1,400		$1,400
SAVINGS	180	-30	150
EXPENSES			
Fixed: Rent	350		350
Auto Insurance	30		30
Utilities	80		80
Car Payment	225		225
Other: Food	360	-25	335
Clothing	70		70
Entertainment	90	-50	40
Medical Care	60		60
Gas & Auto Repair	80	-20	60
TOTAL SAVINGS & EXPENSES	$1,525		$1,400

In the preliminary budget, spending and saving totaled $1,525, which is $125 more than disposable income. Therefore, some changes had to be made. Some families would simply reduce the amount of saving to balance the budget. However, as you learned in Chapter 17, saving is important, so family members should make an effort to reduce their spending on goods and services before they change the amount to be saved each month. For example, they can reduce entertainment expenses by switching from movies and concerts to biking, hiking, and other low-cost activities. This change could reduce entertainment expenses by $50, but it still leaves an additional $75 to be cut somewhere.

After giving it some thought, the family members decided they could reduce food expenses by $25 and automobile expenses by $20 each month. They still had to cut $30 from their budget, but no other reductions in expenses seemed possible. In this case, the family had to reduce its saving goal. Specifically, it decided to reduce its saving by $30, to $150 per month. The last column of Table 19-1 shows the spending and saving changes. It is referred to as the "final" budget. Note that the saving and spending amounts total $1,400, which is the same as disposable income.

Preparing a budget is an excellent way for individuals or families to monitor how they are spending their money. It allows them to set and meet realistic goals for spending and saving. Unless you are one of the few people who have more money than you can spend, you should have a budget.

I N S T A N T   R E P L A Y

Budgeting is a method of matching spending and saving plans with the amount of income available.

Disposable income is the amount of money available for spending and saving.

IMPORTANT CONSUMER DECISIONS

Consumers make many important decisions when they purchase goods and services. Three areas of particular importance are choosing housing, borrowing to finance an automobile purchase, and buying life insurance.

Housing

The average American family spends about 25 percent of its income on housing. In this section you will learn about the relative merits of living in apartments versus single-family homes and about the advantages and disadvantages of renting versus owning your home.

Apartments vs Single-Family Homes. An apartment is one of a number of separate dwellings within a building; a single-family home is a building occupied by one family. People rent or buy both apartments and single-family homes. As you may recall from Chapter 16, rent is a fee that is paid to use a building or land. The primary advantage of living in an apartment rather than a house is that apartments generally cost less to rent or buy. When several housing units are combined in one building, the costs of buying the land and constructing the building are lower than they would be for an equal number of single-family homes.

Another advantage of apartments is that, in addition to living space, some apartment buildings offer swimming pools, tennis courts, and other recreational facilities. Because a number of residents share these facilities, the cost per person is low. Apartment buildings that rent to only young singles often offer a range of organized social activities to attract renters, while apartments that rent to families may provide parks and playgrounds for children. Another advantage of apartment living over home ownership is that chores such as mowing the lawn, painting,

Some apartment buildings offer swimming pools and other recreational facilities.

© Burt Glinn/Magnum Photos, Inc.

and making repairs are done by others. Residents share the cost of these services either as part of the rent they pay or as a monthly maintenance fee.

The disadvantages of apartment living are that people are crowded together and there is less privacy than in single-family dwellings. Apartment dwellers sometimes have to put up with considerable noise from the people living above, below, and on both sides of them. Also, many apartments do not provide much storage and parking space.

Single-family homes usually offer more living space and privacy than apartments. For example, a house typically has an attic or basement for storage, a garage to house the family car, and a yard for children and pets to play in. One disadvantage of a single-family house is that the homeowner must either do all the yardwork and maintenance chores or pay someone else to do them.

As with all choices, decisions about where to live involve opportunity costs. You may choose to spend more to live in a single-family house because the added space, yard, and garage are worth the additional cost to you. Or you may choose to live in a small midtown apartment, despite the lack of space and privacy, because it is cheaper and closer to your work. The right choice for you depends on your income, your needs, and your preferences.

Renting vs Owning. Housing can be rented or owned. People who rent houses or apartments are called **tenants,** and the people who own those dwellings are **landlords.** When a dwelling is rented, the tenant and landlord sign a **lease.** This is a contract that specifies the rights and obligations of both parties. Usually the lease specifies that the tenant has a right to live in the dwelling for a certain period of time, typically one year. It sets the monthly rental fee for the period of the lease, and it spells out any other necessary terms and conditions. For example, it may state that the tenant is required to pay for electricity, while the landlord must supply heat and water.

One advantage of renting is that renters can easily predict their housing expenses. Because landlords normally cannot raise the rental fee during the period of a lease, tenants know exactly how much rent they will pay each month for that time period. They do not have to worry about paying for unexpected maintenance and repair costs, because it is the landlord's responsibility to pay for those. A disadvantage of home-owning is that homeowners must pay all expenses, including those that

Choosing housing is the most expensive consumer decision the average family ever makes.

they cannot anticipate. If the roof leaks or the furnace breaks down, the homeowner must pay to fix them.

Renting also offers greater flexibility than owning a home. Renters can move whenever they want. When the lease period ends, they may choose to stay in the apartment and negotiate another lease with the landlord, or they may choose to move elsewhere. If they choose to move before the lease is up, they can usually pay the rental fee for the remaining months of the lease or pay some smaller amount to compensate the landlord for having to find new tenants. People who are transferred frequently, such as members of the military, usually rent.

Homeowners can also move whenever they wish, but selling one house and buying another is an expensive and complicated transaction that can take months to complete. Buyers and sellers incur thousands of dollars in expenses every time a house is sold. They have to pay real estate agents, buy title and homeowner's insurance, pay extra fees to get a new mortgage loan, and so on. Sometimes, a family has to buy a new house before it can sell the last. Then the family has to make payments on two mortgage loans until the first house is sold. Clearly, the average person cannot afford to buy and sell a home every year or two.

Despite the drawbacks of unexpected expenses and the lack of flexibility, homeowning has important economic advantages over renting. First, when a family pays off its mortgage loan, it owns the home. In addition, the owners can use the home for collateral on loans. The owners will receive all the proceeds when the home is sold and will probably make a profit on the home when they sell it, because property values have been rising for many years.

Another advantage of home ownership is that interest payments on a home mortgage and property taxes are deductible from total income when computing income taxes. These deductions can result in a sizable tax reduction. For example, if interest and property taxes totaled $4,000 for the year and the marginal tax rate was 28 percent, the tax saving would be $1,120 (i.e., $4,000 \times 0.28$). In contrast, renters get no tax advantages on the money they spend on rental fees.

Perhaps the greatest advantage of owning housing is that it provides almost total control over the use of the property. In general, as long as you do not violate the law, you can do anything you want to on your own property. A homeowner can have pets, paint the living room pink, or grow tomatoes in the backyard. A renter may not be able to do any of these things. In fact, many leases specifically prohibit pets and do not allow tenants to do their own painting. Further, renting involves an ongoing relationship with the landlord. Some landlords are hard to deal with. For example, a landlord may fail to make needed repairs, violate lease obligations, or prohibit tenants from having houseguests.

INSTANT REPLAY

Apartment living offers the advantages of lower cost, special recreation facilities, and freedom from home and yard maintenance.

Single-family homes are generally more expensive than apartments but usually offer greater privacy and more space.

Renters know what their housing costs are going to be, and they have more flexibility to move whenever they want.

Owning a home or apartment offers tax advantages, the possibility of increased value, and almost complete control of the use of the property.

Financing Automobile Purchases

Buying a car is one of the largest expenditures a person can make. Usually only buying a home and paying for a college education are more expensive. Most people purchase automobiles on credit. Typically the buyer must make an initial payment, called a down payment, of about 20 percent of the purchase price of the car. The buyer can then borrow the remaining 80 percent of the car's cost and repay it in monthly installments over the next three or four years.

Competition between lenders is common. You can see advertisements offering "low interest rates" and "low down payments" regularly

Because cars are expensive, buyers commonly purchase automobiles on credit.

in the newspaper. Sometimes when sales are slow, automobile manufacturers offer loans at very low interest rates in an attempt to sell more cars.

When a buyer goes to a bank to borrow money for a car, the bank consults a publication called the *National Automobile Dealers Association Blue Book* to determine how much to lend. The *Blue Book* is a monthly publication that lists the retail prices of all domestic and foreign cars for the past seven years. In addition to price, the book shows the average loan amount for each car. This loan amount, usually about 80 percent of the value of the car, is the maximum that the bank will lend.

Suppose you find a two-year-old Chevrolet that you want to buy. The seller's price of $9,000 is the same as the average retail price shown in the *Blue Book,* and the loan value listed in the book is $7,200. That is, you probably could borrow $7,200 to buy the car. The difference between the loan value and the selling price is $1,800. Thus, you will need to have $1,800 for the down payment plus some additional money for sales tax and the licensing fee. In most states, you must pay sales tax when you purchase a car. If the sales tax rate is 5 percent, the sales tax on the $9,000 car will be $450. Fees for registration and license plates typically are $10 to $50.

When you apply for the loan of $7,200, the bank will want to know where you work and how much you earn. This information is important to the bank, because you have to demonstrate that you have enough income to be able to make the monthly payments. If the interest rate charged by the bank is 12 percent per year, the monthly payment on a $7,200 loan would be $239.14 on a three-year loan and $189.60 on a four-year loan. Although the monthly payment is lower for a four-year loan, the total interest paid over the entire period would be considerably more because you would make 12 more payments before you paid off the loan. In this case, the interest on the three-year loan would be $1,409, while the total interest for the four-year loan would be $1,901—a difference of nearly $500. Clearly, the faster you can pay off a loan, the better. However, if you need a car and cannot afford to pay $239 a month, then a longer loan period with lower payments may be the only way you can buy it.

Until the loan is paid off, the bank will hold the title or ownership document for the car as collateral. Thus, you would not be able to sell the car without making arrangements with the bank to use the money received from the sale to pay off the loan. If the payments on the loan are not made, the bank can and probably will repossess the car. It will then be sold to pay the loan. In some states, if the car is sold for less than the remaining balance on the loan, the bank can require you to pay the difference.

I N S T A N T   R E P L A Y

Credit is commonly used to finance the purchase of automobiles.

Automobile loans are usually repaid in monthly payments over a period of three or four years.

If the payments are not made, the car can be repossessed and sold to pay off the loan.

Annual Percentage Rate (APR)

A number of different methods are used to determine the rate of interest on a loan. Each method means something different, and these differences can be confusing to a borrower. The best measure of an interest rate is the **annual percentage rate (APR).** The APR provides the best estimate of the cost of borrowing money, because it compares the interest paid each year to the average amount owed each year.

In the past, some advertisements contained misleading statements about the interest rate being charged. For example, some advertisements for new cars included statements like this: "We have 6 percent loans available. Borrow at only $6 per $100 per year."

These statements usually meant the following. If $1,000 was borrowed for 12 months, $60 of interest (that is, $6 for each $100 borrowed) was subtracted in advance and the borrower was given $940. This means that the interest was actually paid in advance. The borrower would then make a payment of approximately $83 per month, thus repaying the $1,000 in 12 months.

This advertising was misleading and is against the law today. The real annual percentage rate is the total interest paid during the year divided by the average amount of money that is borrowed. In the example above, the total interest is $60. To figure the average amount borrowed, remember that part of the money is being repaid each month. At the first of the year, $940 is owed, but each month part is repaid. By the twelfth month, only about $83 is owed. Actually, the average amount owed over the 12-month period is $940 ÷ 2 or $470. Therefore, the true or annual percentage interest rate would be:

$$\text{APR} = \left(\frac{\text{Total Interest}}{\text{Average Amount Owed}} \right) \times 100$$

$$\text{APR} = (\$60/\$470) \times 100 = 12.8\%$$

Thus, the true interest rate (i.e., the APR) is more than double the rate indicated in the advertisement.

Look in your local newspaper for advertisements for new cars or houses. Look closely at any information about interest rates. Sometimes the ad will say "9.8 percent financing available." The fine print below it will say "10.4 percent APR." If the advertisement does not state the APR, it is in violation of federal law.

When you are thinking about borrowing money, it is important to find out what the APR is. The rate of interest is an important part of any loan agreement.

Life Insurance

Anyone who provides financial support for another person probably should have **life insurance.** Under a life insurance contract an individual makes payments each year to an insurance company, which agrees to make a large cash payment to those who are specified as **beneficiaries** (e.g., usually a spouse or children) if the insured person dies. The primary purpose of life insurance is to protect against financial problems in the event of death. Clearly, a family can be in serious financial trouble if the breadwinner dies without adequate insurance. The funeral costs, payments for rent or a home mortgage, and day-to-day living expenses have to be paid. Life insurance provides an excellent way for meeting these expenses. As will be discussed later, a life insurance policy can also be used as a way of saving money.

How Much Insurance Is Enough? Many financial planners suggest that the family head have life insurance equal to six times annual income. Because most families also participate in the Social Security program, they also will receive monthly checks from this source in the event of death. The combination of both the interest on the life insurance pay-

Life insurance provides financial security for the insured's family in the event of his or her death.

COURTESY, AMERICAN BRANDS, INC.

ment received and the Social Security benefits should provide enough income to meet the family's expenses.

Using the "six-times income" rule, a family breadwinner earning $25,000 per year should have a $150,000 life insurance policy. If the person died, the remaining family members could invest the $150,000 life insurance benefit. If the money could be invested at a 9 percent interest rate, for example, this investment would provide annual interest income of $13,500. This amount each year, together with Social Security payments, should provide enough income to meet the family's basic expenses.

Types of Life Insurance. Although insurance companies offer a bewildering variety of policies, life insurance comes in two basic kinds—term and whole life. A **term insurance** policy is the simplest form of life insurance and provides a specified level of insurance for a fixed period of time. For example, a 5-year term policy may specify that $150,000 in protection is provided for the next five years as long as the annual premium (i.e., the yearly payment for the insurance protection) is paid. Usually, such a policy is renewable for additional five-year periods, although the annual premium will increase as the insured person gets older. The cost rises because as people get older, they are more likely to die.

Table 19-2 shows the annual premiums on a $150,000 policy offered by one company. Note that the premium is $203 per year at age 25 and $1,698 at age 60. Thus, if a 25-year-old person buys a policy by paying the annual premium of $203 and dies at any time during the next year, the person named as beneficiary will be paid $150,000 by the insurance company. Similarly, for an annual payment of $1,698, the beneficiary of a deceased 60-year-old person would receive $150,000.

TABLE 19-2

TYPICAL ANNUAL INSURANCE PREMIUMS FOR $150,000 TERM LIFE INSURANCE POLICY

Age	Annual Premium
25	$ 203
30	209
35	254
40	356
45	530
50	821
55	1,388
60	1,698

As people get older, their need for insurance usually declines. One reason is that their children may have reached adulthood and may no longer be dependent on their parents. Also, the parents may have accumulated some wealth in the form of stocks, bonds, and real estate that could be sold if additional money was needed. As a result of the reduced need for life insurance and the higher cost as one gets older, many people cancel their insurance later in life. This is a perfectly reasonable thing to do.

The other type of insurance, **whole life,** provides a combination of insurance protection and a savings program. That is, part of the premium each year goes toward providing insurance protection while the remainder goes into a type of savings account that is called the cash value of the policy. By canceling the policy, the owner can receive the cash value of the policy at that time.

Unlike term insurance, the annual premium on a whole life policy remains constant over the life of the policy. Each year the amount of insurance is less but the cash value is greater. At any time, the combination of insurance and cash value is equal to the face amount of the policy.

One problem with whole life insurance is that it is much more expensive than term insurance. For example, at age 25 an annual premium of $203 will buy $150,000 in term insurance but only about $20,000 in whole life insurance. A young family may need $150,000 in insurance coverage but may be able to afford only $203 per year. Such a family probably should buy a term policy. A whole life policy for $150,000 would cost a 25-year-old man about $1,400 per year. This may be too expensive for most families. Many people have a life insurance policy with inadequate coverage because they bought a small whole life policy for the same premium that would have purchased a large term policy.

INSTANT REPLAY

Life insurance is an important way of protecting against financial problems.

The family breadwinner should have life insurance equal to about six times annual earnings.

A term policy provides basic insurance at low cost, whereas whole life combines insurance and saving, but at a much higher cost.

CONSUMER FRAUD

In Chapter 18 you learned that you, as a consumer, have a responsibility to deal honestly with businesses and that they have an obligation to treat you fairly. The majority of businesses are run by honest people who take this obligation seriously. These business owners strive to provide consumers with high-quality goods and services at reasonable prices. However, there are a few firms that take advantage of consumers. Usually these firms cannot operate this way for very long before losing customers. Sometimes, however, a business is able to make substantial profits in a short period of time by selling poor-quality goods and services, often at inflated prices. In extreme cases, these firms take consumers' money and give nothing in return. The following are examples of unfair or illegal practices that have been used to cheat consumers.

Door-to-Door Repair Services

The door-to-door home repair industry has had a number of dishonest firms. A common practice among these businesses is to go from house to house offering a free inspection of a furnace, water heater, or other appliance. During the inspection the furnace is dismantled and the unsuspecting consumer is informed that it is not working properly. The repairer then says that the furnace will not be put back together, because it is unsafe to use. A sales pitch for a new furnace is then made. In most cases, of course, there is nothing wrong with the furnace. The whole process is designed to frighten the consumer into buying a new furnace.

Door-to-Door Sales

Although there are many reputable firms that sell goods and services on a door-to-door basis, there are some that are not honest. One type of misrepresentation occurs when young children are sent to sell candy or similar items door-to-door at prices several times higher than in stores. The children offer a story of how they represent a charity or how they themselves are disadvantaged. Often they report that if they sell just another $5 worth of candy, they will win a trip to Hawaii or some other vacation spot. Many of these reports simply are not true.

Most door-to-door sales programs are sponsored by worthy organizations and managed by responsible people. However, because some are not, the consumer must be cautious. An important principle of being a good consumer is to be wary of salespeople you do not know representing organizations you are not familiar with.

Mail-Order Sales

Many quality products are sold through the mail by reputable business firms. Often these firms are able to sell at relatively low prices, because they do not need to maintain expensive retail stores or employ salespersons to display and demonstrate the various products. Instead, the merchandise is kept in cartons in a warehouse, and orders are taken by clerks over the telephone. These firms have low-cost operations and usually can set their prices below those of a full-service retail store.

Unfortunately, there are a number of dishonest people in the mail-order business. In some cases, consumers send in payment but receive no products. In other cases, the advertisement greatly overstates the quality or features of the product. Be wary of advertisements that offer products at prices that seem too good to be true—they probably are not true.

Big-Screen Television—Only $19.95

An advertisement in a newspaper promised a device that would turn your television set into a "super sharp projected TV picture that measures up to seven feet diagonally," and all this for $19.95. This device sounded like a bargain, because most big-screen television sets sell for $1,500 to $3,500.

Consumer Reports magazine responded to the advertisement and received two cardboard boxes—a big one and a little one—and a six-inch plastic lens. The lens was taped into the little box, which was then slid into the big box. Then the whole thing was fitted over a table-model television set. The picture was projected onto a screen or light-colored wall,

but was upside down! This problem could be corrected by turning the television set upside down, or by having a repairer rewire the circuits so the set could remain right side up.

As for the super sharp picture, the quality was poor. Although fairly clear in the center, the picture became increasingly blurred toward the edges. *Consumer Reports* concluded: "It would be nice to find a low-cost, uncomplicated way of turning out a large, sharp TV picture. Product X is not the answer."*

---

*See *Consumer Reports,* July 1980.

Some mail-order firms are dishonest, but most are reputable.

INSTANT REPLAY

Although most businesses make every effort to provide good quality goods and services at reasonable prices, a few firms attempt to cheat consumers.

Examples of consumer fraud may be found in all types of businesses but are more common in the door-to-door and mail-order sales industries.

S U M M A R Y

Preparing and using a budget is an excellent tool for allocating a family's limited income among its needs and wants. By planning and monitoring spending, a family or individual can keep expenses under control and achieve goals for saving.

Housing decisions are among the most important that a consumer will make. Apartment living offers lower cost, availability of recreation facilities, and freedom from home and yard maintenance. The cost of renting is fixed for the period of the lease, and renters do not have to worry about selling the housing unit if they decide to move. In contrast, single-family homes provide more space and greater privacy. Home ownership also offers tax advantages, the chance of increased value of the property, and greater control over the use of the property.

Credit is used to make many automobile purchases. A bank or other finan-cial institution will usually lend a buyer 80 percent of the car's value, which is then repaid in monthly installments over a three- or four-year period. Until the loan is paid, the bank will hold title to the car as collateral. If the loan is not paid, the bank will repossess the car, sell it, and use the money to pay the loan.

Anyone who provides financial support for another person should have life insurance. A rule of thumb is that the amount of insurance should be six times annual income. Term insurance provides insurance protection only, whereas whole life insurance provides a combination of insurance and saving.

Most businesses provide consumers with high-quality goods and services at reasonable prices, but there are some dis-honest people who take advantage of con-sumers. Consumer fraud can be found in all industries but is more common in door-to-door and mail-order sales.

☆ LEARNING ACTIVITIES ☆

Building Your Vocabulary

On a separate sheet of paper, write the numbers 1 through 8. Next to each number, write the term that correctly completes the sentence.

budget
disposable income
tenants
landlord
lease
annual percentage
  rate
life insurance
beneficiaries

1. _____ are the people who receive life insurance payments after the insured person dies.

2. People who rent houses or apartments to live in are called _____.

3. _____ is the interest rate on the average amount of money owed each month over a 12-month period.

4. A _____ is a plan to match income and expenses.

5. A contract to make a large cash payment in the event of a person's death is called _____.

6. A _____ is the owner of a house or apartment that is rented to a tenant.

7. The income that remains after taxes are deducted is _____.

8. A contract that spells out the rights and obligations of tenants and landlords is a _____.

Reviewing the Facts

1. What are the six steps that you must follow to prepare a budget?
2. What percentage of its income does the average family spend on housing?
3. Why are apartments generally less expensive than single-family homes?
4. Compare the advantages and disadvantages of living in an apartment and living in a single-family house.
5. Compare the advantages and disadvantages of renting versus owning a home.
6. Why do banks want to know your employer and income before they will provide you with a car loan?
7. What is the difference between whole life and term insurance?
8. Why can mail-order firms sell goods cheaper than retail stores can?

Expressing Your Opinion

1. If you lived in an apartment house, how could you deal with noisy neighbors?
2. Do you think it is fair for the owner of an apartment house to restrict occupancy to one particular group, such as young singles or senior citizens? Why or why not?
3. Homeowners can deduct mortgage interest and property tax payments from their federal taxes. Should renters receive similar tax advantages? Why or why not?
4. If you are a young, single adult, do you need life insurance? Explain your answer.

Developing Your Attitudes, Values, and Skills

1. When you own a car, you have to insure it each year against a variety of possible mishaps. You may damage another person's car or your own in an accident. You may injure or kill someone, your car may be stolen or vandalized, or you may be struck by an uninsured motorist. The typical auto insurance policy covers each of these possibilities separately, and you must pay for each kind of coverage. Each state usually requires that automobile owners purchase a minimum amount of insurance. Research the auto insurance costs and requirements in your state. Five or six members of the class can be appointed to telephone different auto insurance agents and interview the agents about the kinds and amounts of auto insurance the state requires and the cost of each kind of coverage. Find out what specific hazards each category covers. What other kinds of insurance coverage are available? For example, can you

purchase insurance to cover towing and car rental costs if your car is in an accident? When the students have finished gathering information from the insurance agents, they should present their findings to the class in the form of a chart that shows each kind and amount of coverage and the costs for each. Discuss your classmates' findings in class; make certain that you understand any special terms that were used to describe insurance coverage, such as collision, comprehensive, and liability.

2. The class needs to be divided into relatively equal groups for this exercise. Each group will explore one kind of housing cost in your area. Members of Group One should telephone or visit four or five apartment rental offices to find out the monthly rental fee for one-, two-, and three-bedroom apartments. Members in Group Two should visit two or three real estate agents to find out how much condominium and cooperative apartments are selling for in the area. Are prices based on square footage, number of bedrooms and baths, or location? Are there any maintenance fees required, and if so, how much are they? Members of the third group should also visit two or three real estate agents to examine prices for single-family homes. Prices will vary greatly depending on the house, location, and size. Choose one or two representative houses in each of the low, middle, and high price ranges; compare the differences in features and prices among them. Students who are researching the purchase prices for houses and apartments should ask the real estate agent to determine approximately how much the monthly mortgage payments would be at current interest rates if a buyer made a 20 percent down payment on each house. (The agents have charts that help them calculate these figures quickly.) If the average family spends 25 percent of its income on housing, how much would a family have to earn each month to rent an apartment or to purchase a medium-priced house or apartment? When the students have finished their research, each group should make a presentation to the class describing their results.

3. Many individuals have made significant contributions to consumer safety and protection. Among them are Ralph Nader, Rachel Carson, Upton Sinclair, Dr. Harvey W. Wiley, Charles Evans Hughes, Ida Tarbell, and Dr. Frances Kelsey. Choose one of these individuals, and prepare a brief biography explaining who the person was, or is, and what she or he did to help consumers. Did your subject's work result in any new laws or changes in business behavior? If so, what were they? What did your subject have to do to gather information? Was there some particular aspect of your subject's background, education, or upbringing that helped her or him achieve distinction? Be prepared to describe your subject's contributions to the class.

absolute advantage The ability of one country to produce a product at a lower cost than any other nation.

agent A person or firm who has been given the right to act for others.

allocate To divide or direct to specific uses.

American Federation of Labor–Congress of Industrial Organization (AFL–CIO) The national organization that represents organized labor in political lobbying and public relations.

annual percentage rate (APR) The annual interest on a loan divided by the average amount owed during the year.

antitrust law A law designed to increase competition between firms.

apprenticeship A program in which a person is taught a skill or a trade.

assembly line A device that moves a product from one worker to the next as it is being manufactured.

assessed value The tax base of the property tax.

automation The replacement of human labor by machines.

balance of payments The total of all money received from other countries minus the amount spent in other nations.

balance of trade The difference between money received from exports and money spent for imports.

bankruptcy A legal procedure used when a person or business is not able to repay the money that is owed.

barter The exchange of goods and services without the use of money.

bear market A period when stock prices generally are falling.

beneficiary A person named in an insurance policy to receive the insurance benefits upon the death of the insured.

Better Business Bureau An organization that provides background information on local businesses and encourages good business practices.

Board of Directors A group of three or more individuals who act as the governing body for a business.

Board of Governors A group that consists of seven members with overall responsibility for administering the Federal Reserve System.

bond A printed promise to repay a certain amount of money, at a certain interest rate, at a certain time.

bondholder A person or organization that owns a bond.

budget A plan to organize and match income and expenses.

bull market A period when stock prices generally are rising.

business cycle A period when GNP is increasing followed by a period when GNP is decreasing.

capital gain An increase in the value of shares of stock.

capital good Goods that are used to produce other goods.

capital loss A decrease in value of shares of stock.

capital resource One of the many kinds of equipment, tools, buildings, and machinery used to produce goods or services.

capitalist The owner of a business in a free enterprise economy.

capitalist economy An economic system in which individuals are allowed to own capital goods.

central bank An organization responsible for all banking in a country.

central planning A procedure whereby economic decisions are made by a small group of people in government.

centralized decision making A method whereby decisions for the entire system are made by a small group of people and individuals have little freedom of choice.

certificate of deposit A form of savings account in which money is deposited for a specified period of time at a guaranteed rate of interest.

channel of distribution The path that goods take as they move from the original producer to the final consumer.

charter A document that gives a business legal authority to operate.

circular flow of economic activity The continuous movement of income between product and resource markets.

closed shop A place of business that hires only union members.

coin Money made of metal.

collateral Property pledged as security for a loan.

collective bargaining Contract discussions between union leaders and their employers.

command system An economic system in which decisions are made by government or a small group of people.

commercial bank A bank owned by private citizens.

commodity money Money made of valuable metals.

communist society A form of socialist economy described by Karl Marx.

comparative advantage The ability of one country to produce a product relatively more efficiently than another nation.

competition Efforts by business to attract customers and factors of production.

construction industry Those businesses that build structures like roads, buildings, and bridges.

consumer Someone who buys goods and services.

consumer durable A product that lasts for a number of years.

consumer good A product that is useful to consumers.

consumer nondurable A product that is quickly used or worn out.

consumer price index (CPI) An index that measures the change in the overall cost of a market basket of goods and services purchased by the average family.

consumer sovereignty The concept that consumers determine what is produced through their purchases.

consumption The use of goods and services by consumers.

contract A legal agreement between two or more people or firms.

corporation A business owned by several persons, each of whom has limited liability.

cost-push inflation An increase in prices resulting from increases in the cost of production.

craft union A labor union consisting of workers who have particular skills.

credit An arrangement to pay in the future for goods, services, or money received.

credit card A form of identification that allows people to receive small loans in order to buy consumer goods and services.

credit union A financial institution owned by its depositors.

creditor Someone who is owed money.

currency Money made of paper.

cyclical unemployment Unemployment resulting from a decrease in economic activity.

debt financing Money that is borrowed to start or run a business.

decentralized decision making A method whereby decisions are made by each individual rather than by one person or a small group of people.

deduction An expense that can be subtracted from taxable income.

deficit The result of government expenditures exceeding revenues.

deflation A decrease in the overall price of a market basket of goods and services.

demand The relationship between the price of a good and the quantity of that good consumers want to purchase.

demand curve A graph showing the relationship between price and quantity demanded.

demand deposit Money held in a checking account that may be withdrawn at any time by writing a check.

demand-pull inflation An increase in prices resulting from too much money chasing too few goods.

demand schedule A table showing the amount demanded by consumers at different prices.

depression A period when GNP has fallen significantly and the number of people without jobs is very high.

devalue To lower the value of a nation's currency.

direct marketing A channel of distribution through which products are sold directly to the consumer.

discount rate The interest rate charged to commercial banks on money borrowed from the Federal Reserve System.

discouraged worker Someone who wants to work but who has given up trying to find a job.

discrimination The practice of paying some workers less than others for the same job.

disposable income Total income minus tax payments.

dividend A portion of a corporation's profits that management sets aside for payment to stockholders.

Dow Jones Industrial Average An indicator of changes in the price of stocks.

economic freedom The individual's right to make earning and spending decisions.

economic resource Human, natural, and capital resources that can be used to produce the goods and services that people consume.

economic system The organizations, laws, traditions, beliefs, and habits that affect decision making in the society.

economics A science that explains how societies allocate scarce resources.

economies of scale Lower costs resulting from larger-scale production.

economy The system used in a nation for making decisions on what, how, and for whom to produce.

efficiency A concept which involves using scarce resources to produce the maximum amount of goods and services.

employee A person who works for someone else.

entrepreneur An individual in a free enterprise system who organizes the factors of production and is willing to take risks in order to earn profits.

equilibrium price The price at which supply equals demand.

equity Fairness in the distribution of goods, services, and resources.

equity financing Money obtained from stockholders to start or run a business.

excess demand A situation in which more is demanded than supplied.

excess supply A situation in which more is supplied than demanded.

exchange rate The price of one currency in terms of another.

excise tax A tax on the purchase of a specific good or service.

exemption A situation that causes taxable income to be reduced.

expansion The period of economic growth during which GNP increases.

export A good that a nation sells to other countries.

extractive industry Those businesses that take natural resources from the earth.

factor of production Human, natural, and capital resources when used in production of goods and services.

Federal Deposit Insurance Corporation (FDIC) A government agency that insures bank deposits.

Federal Insurance Contribution Act (FICA). The law that established the social security system.

Federal Reserve System (Fed) The central banking system of the United States.

fiat money Money by government order or decree.

financial intermediary A person or business who brings buyers and sellers of money together.

financing Obtaining or providing the money to operate a business.

firm Another name for a business.

fiscal policy Changes in government spending or taxation designed to increase GNP or to reduce unemployment and inflation.

fixed exchange rate An exchange rate set by the government of a country.

fixed expenses Costs that are the same each month.

floating exchange rate An exchange rate that changes with market conditions.

foreign exchange market The market in which different currencies are traded.

fractional reserve banking The practice of lending out much of the money that has been deposited in a bank.

franchise The legal right to sell a good or service in a specific area.

free enterprise system An economic system in which households and the managers of firms are free to make their own choices about earning and spending activities.

frictional unemployment Unemployment resulting from workers changing jobs.

full employment An unemployment rate of about 5 percent.

good An object of value that can be measured or weighed.

grievance procedure A way of settling disagreements between employers and workers.

Gross National Product (GNP) The value of all final goods and services produced in the economy.

household A small group of people who make their earning and spending decisions together.

human resource The effort and skill that an individual can contribute to producing goods and services.

imperialism The practice of taking unfair advantage of poor nations.

import A good purchased from other countries.

income The total value of earnings that a household receives from the sales of its resources.

income distribution The way in which income is divided among individuals and families in a given population.

independent union A national labor union that is not part of the AFL-CIO.

indirect marketing A channel of distribution in which goods pass through various businesses on their way to consumers.

industrial good A product that is used by industries in producing goods and services.

Industrial Revolution The period when machines were first widely used to increase efficiency and cut costs in manufacturing.

industrial union A labor union that includes all the workers in an industry.

industry All of the firms that make a particular type of product.

inflation An increase in the price of a market basket of goods and services.

installment loan Money that is to be repaid in regular payments over a period of time.

interdependence The reliance of workers and businesses on one another.

interest A payment for the temporary use of another person's money.

intermediary A person or business whose job is to bring buyers and sellers together.

intermediate good A good that is used to produce other goods.

international finance The process of paying for goods and services in international trade.

international trade The exchange of goods and services among different countries.

investment Money used to purchase capital goods.

labor force People who have or are seeking employment.

landlord Someone who owns rental property.

law of demand A principle stating that people tend to buy more of something at lower prices than they do at higher prices.

law of supply A principle stating that firms will produce more of a good at higher prices than they will at lower prices.

lease A contract that specifies the rights and obligations of renters and landlords.

legal tender Money that must be accepted as payment for goods, services, and resources.

life insurance A financial plan in which an individual makes small payments each year to a company that agrees to make a large cash payment to specified people if the individual dies.

limited liability A situation where a business owner cannot lose more than he or she invested in the business.

limited partner A partner who cannot lose more than the amount of money originally invested in the business.

line of credit An arrangement that allows a business to borrow part or all of a specified amount from a bank as the need arises.

manufacturing industry Those businesses that convert unfinished goods into products that are useful to consumers or other industries.

marginal cost The extra cost of producing one more unit of output.

marginal tax rate The proportion of extra dollars of income that must be paid as taxes.

market An arrangement that allows buyers and sellers to come together to trade goods, services, and resources.

market basket A set of goods and services purchased by the typical family.

market economy An economic system that relies on markets to make economic decisions.

market power A situation in which a business has only a limited need to compete.

market socialism An economic system in which the means of production are owned by government, but which relies on markets in making decisions concerning what, how, and for whom to produce.

marketing All the activities involved in getting goods and services from the producer to the consumers.

mass production Producing goods and services in large quantities using specialized labor.

medium of exchange Something that is generally accepted in trade.

merger Two or more firms joining to form a new firm.

mill One tenth of 1 percent.

mixed system An economic system in which some economic decisions are left to individuals, and some decisions are made by government.

monetarist Someone who claims that changes in the rate of growth in the money supply can affect the level of GNP, the unemployment rate, and the rate of inflation.

monetary policy Changes in the supply of money designed to influence rates of economic growth, inflation, and unemployment.

money Anything that people are willing to accept as payment for things they sell or work they do.

money market account A form of savings account that offers the features of a checking account but pays a higher rate of interest.

monopoly A firm that is the single seller of a good or service.

mortgage A legal contract or deed that pledges the property as security against the loan.

mortgage loan Money borrowed in order to buy a house, building lot, or other type of property.

national bank A bank that receives its charter from the federal government.

national debt The total amount of money owed by the federal government.

National Labor Relations Act A law that gave unions a legal right to exist and requires employers to negotiate contracts with union representatives.

National Labor Relations Board A government agency responsible for labor-management relations.

natural resource A material that comes from the air, water, or earth.

need A good or service that people must have

to continue living.

officer An individual responsible for the day-to-day operations of a corporation.

oligopoly A market with few important sellers.

open market operation The buying and selling of government bonds by the Federal Reserve System.

opportunity cost The value of resources in their best alternative use.

over-the-counter market A market for stocks that consists of hundreds of brokerage offices linked by telephone.

partnership A business owned by two or more people.

passbook savings account A form of savings account in which withdrawals and deposits are recorded in a small book.

peak The high point of the business cycle.

personal income tax A tax on income earned by individuals.

picket line A group of workers marching in front of a business to call attention to their demands.

political freedom The individual's right to voice his or her opinions.

positive externality A benefit received by someone other than the person who buys a good or service.

poverty A condition of being unable to meet minimum standards with regard to food, clothing, housing, and medical care.

price fixing An agreement among managers of firms to charge the same price.

price system A method of putting monetary value on products.

principal The amount of money that is initially borrowed.

private enterprise system An economic system in which people make decisions as private individuals rather than as part of a public or government group.

private property Property owned by individuals.

product market A market in which goods and services are exchanged.

productivity increase An increase in the amount of goods and services produced from the same amounts of capital and labor.

profit The money left over after a business has paid all its expenses.

profit motive The desire to earn profits.

progressive tax A tax with an increasing marginal tax rate.

property tax A tax on land, buildings, and vehicles.

public good A good that everyone can consume whether they pay for it or not.

Public Service Commission (Public Utility Commission) A state agency that regulates the operations of public utilities.

public utility A business that provides an important good or service and for which economies of scale cause a single firm to be most efficient.

recession A period of economic slow-down during which GNP declines.

regressive tax A tax with a decreasing marginal tax rate.

rent Money received for the use of land or a building.

repossess To take property back because of nonpayment of a loan.

reserve Bank funds kept on hand for the immediate needs of depositors.

reserve ratio The portion of total deposits that cannot be lent out by a bank.

resource Something that is available for use.

resource market A market that exists to assist in exchanging human, natural, and capital resources.

résumé A summary of a person's education, training, and work experience.

retailer A business that buys goods and sells them to consumers.

revenue The income a government receives from all sources, including taxes, fees, and fines.

right-to-work law A state law that outlaws the union shop.

salary A regular income paid for work over a

set time period.

sales tax A tax on the goods and services that consumers purchase.

savings The part of income held back from consumption.

savings and loan association A financial intermediary that accepts deposits and makes loans, primarily for use in buying homes.

scarce A condition in which more goods or services are desired than are available.

seasonal unemployment Unemployment resulting from changing demand for labor at different times during the year.

sector A group of industries producing similar goods or services.

service Help received from other people.

service industry Those firms that provide services directly to consumers or other businesses.

share One unit of ownership in a corporation.

shopping good A consumer durable, or a product that will last for several years.

small claims court A place for resolving disagreements involving small amounts of money.

Social Security Tax A tax that employed persons pay during their working years to provide income for retired people and for those unable to care for themselves.

socialist economy An economic system in which the government owns the means of production.

society A group of individuals who have similar goals or interests.

sole proprietorship A business owned by only one person.

specialization of labor The assignment of workers to specific tasks.

state bank A bank that receives its charter from the state in which it operates.

stock certificate A document showing ownership in a corporation.

stock exchange A place or arrangement in which shares of stock are bought and sold.

stockbroker Someone who assists buyers and sellers of stocks.

stockholder Someone who owns a share of a corporation.

store of value Something that can be held to buy goods or services in the future.

strike An agreement by workers to stop working.

structural unemployment Unemployment caused by changes in technology or consumer tastes.

sunk cost Money that has been spent and cannot be recovered.

supply The quantity of a good or service that firms will provide at a given price.

supply curve A graph showing the amount of a good or service that firms will provide at different prices.

supply schedule A table showing the amount or quantity of a good or service that firms will provide at different prices.

supply-side economics The use of government policies that promote maximum production.

Taft-Hartley Act A law which limits the power of unions and allows the President of the United States to delay a strike.

tariff A tax on imported goods.

tax base The number of dollars to be taxed.

tax rate The proportion of each dollar in the tax base that must be paid as taxes.

tax withholding The practice of deducting income taxes from an employee's paycheck.

taxable income That portion of total income which is taxed.

tenant Someone who rents a house or an apartment.

term insurance A type of life insurance that provides a specified level of protection for a stated period of time.

trade The voluntary exchange of goods, services, and resources.

trade industry Those businesses that sell goods primarily to consumers and other businesses.

transaction cost An expense associated with a trade or a purchase.

transfer payment Money taken from one person and given to another by government.

trough The low point of the business cycle.

trustee Someone appointed by a court to protect the interests of both a business and its creditors during bankruptcy proceedings.

unemployed worker Someone who seeks, but does not have, a job.

unemployment rate The percentage of the labor force without jobs.

union shop A place of business in which new workers must join a union within a short time after starting work.

unit of account The means by which prices are expressed.

wage Compensation that depends on the amount of time worked.

want A good or service that people desire but could live without.

whole life insurance A type of life insurance that combines insurance protection and a savings program.

wholesaler A business that buys goods from producers and then sells them to retailers.

worker-managed firm A business in which the land and capital used by the firm are owned by the government, but the firm itself is managed by its workers.

worker's council The governing body in worker-managed firms.

INDEX

A

absolute advantage:
  defined, 259
  principle of, 259–261
account:
  money market, 327
  passbook savings, 326
  unit of, 47
accurate information, right to, 342–343
activities, government, financed by
    taxation, 221
adequate variety, right to, 345
advantage:
  absolute. *See* absolute advantage
  comparative. *See* comparative advantage
advertising, 150–153
  classified, and finding a job, 313
  cost of, 150–152
  false, 191–192
  good or bad?, 152–153
  and market power, 92
advertising competition, 87–88
AFL–CIO, 169–170
  defined, 165
age, and human resources, 19
agencies, employment, 314–315
agents, defined, 148
allocate, defined, 24
allocation, resource. *See* resource
    allocation
American Federation of Labor, 165. *See also*
    AFL–CIO
annual percentage rate (APR), defined, 369
antitrust, 187–188
  and conduct, 187–188
  and size, 187
antitrust laws, defined, 187
apartments, vs single-family homes, 363–365
apprenticeship, defined, 310
assembly line, defined, 142
assessed value, defined, 231–232

assistance, government, and market power, 92
automation:
  and capital goods, 144
  defined, 144
automobile purchases, financing, 367–369

B

balance of payments, defined, 270
balance of trade, defined, 270
banking, fractional reserve, 204–205
banking activities, supervised by Fed, 211
bankruptcy, 157–158
  defined, 157
banks:
  central, 208
  commercial, 205–206
  Fed as supplier of currency to, 209
  as financial intermediaries, 201–203,
    205–206
  member, loans made to by Fed, 211
  national, 205
  state, 205–206
bargaining, collective, 175
barter:
  defined, 44
  and need for money, 44–46
base, tax, 223
bear market, defined, 330
beneficiaries, defined, 370
benefits:
  of competition, 89–90
  of free enterprise system, 6–8
  fringe, and unions, 171
  of government regulation, 195–196
  of international trade, 259–262
Better Business Bureaus, defined, 346
board of directors, defined, 128
Board of Governors of the Federal Reserve,
    213–214
  defined, 214

bond, defined, 154
bondholder, defined, 154
borrowing:
   and credit, 321–324
   and inflation, 114
budget:
   defined, 361
   government, 245–249
budgeting scarce resources, 361–363
bull market, defined, 330
business, information from, 349–350
business cycles, 109–110
   defined, 109
businesses, worker-managed, 290–291
business ownership, forms of, 121–123
buy:
   freedom to, 7
   freedom to in U.S.S.R., 286

C

capital gain, defined, 156
capital goods, 21–22
   and automation, 144
   defined, 21
capitalism, 282–285
capitalist economy, defined, 282
capitalists, defined, 282
capital loss, defined, 156
capital resources, 21–22
   defined, 21
   increasing, 103–104
cards, credit, 321–323
career counseling, 315–316
central bank, defined, 208
centralized decisions, defined, 9
central planning, defined, 280
certificate, stock, 128–129
certificate of deposit (CD), defined, 327
channels of distribution, 147–149
   defined, 147
charter, defined, 129
checks, Fed as clearinghouse for, 209–210
circular flow of economic activity:
   defined, 38
   and markets, 37–39

classified advertising, and finding a job,
   313
clearinghouse for checks, Fed as, 209–210
closed shop, defined, 166
coins, defined, 49
collateral, defined, 323
collective bargaining, defined, 175
command systems, 9–10
   defined, 9
   and for whom to produce, 281
   vs free enterprise system, 279–281
   and how to produce, 281
   and what to produce, 280
commercial banks, 205–206
   defined, 205
commodity money:
   defined, 51
   vs fiat money, 51–53
communist society, defined, 284
company profitability, and stock prices, 332
comparative advantage:
   defined, 261
   principle of, 261–262
competition, 85–90, 92–93
   advertising, 87–88
   benefits of, 89–90
   defined, 86
   and government, 186–189
   methods of, 86–89
   price, 86–87
   quality, 88
   variety, 88–89
conduct, and antitrust, 187–188
Congress of Industrial Organizations (CIO),
   165. *See also* AFL–CIO
construction industries, defined, 134
consumer decisions:
   changed by taxation, 221–222
   important, 363–372
   and marginal costs, 354–355
   and opportunity costs, 352–354
   and principles of economics, 352–355
   and sunk costs, 355
consumer durable, defined, 353
consumer fraud, 373–374

consumer goods, defined, 134
consumer information services, 350
consumer nondurables, defined, 353
consumer price index (CPI), defined, 111
Consumer Product Safety Commission, 190, 344
consumer protection, and government, 189–191
consumer responsibilities, 347–352
consumer rights, 341–347
consumers, defined, 17
consumer sovereignty, defined, 40
consumption, defined, 17
contracts:
    defined, 184
    government as enforcer of, 184–185
control over resources, and market power, 91
cooperation, spirit of, in Japan, 292
corporations, 128–132
    advantages of, 130
    defined, 122
    disadvantages of, 130–131
    importance of, 131
    officers of, 128
cost:
    of advertising, 150–152
    of government regulation, 195–196
    marginal. See marginal cost
    opportunity. See opportunity cost
    sunk, 355
    transaction, 46
cost-push inflation, defined, 113
council, worker's, 290
counseling, career, 315–316
court, small claims, 185
craft union, defined, 165
credit:
    and borrowing, 321–324
    defined, 321
    line of, 154
    role of in economy, 327–329
credit cards, 321–323
    defined, 321
creditor, defined, 157
credit unions, defined, 206

currency, 49–50
    defined, 49
    supplied to banks by Fed, 209
curve:
    demand, 66–68
    supply, 68
cycle, business, 109–110
cyclical unemployment, defined, 107

D

debt, national, 249–252. See also national debt
debt financing:
    defined, 154
    difference from equity financing, 156–157
decentralized decision making, defined, 6
decision making, decentralized, 6
decisions:
    centralized, 9
    consumer. See consumer decisions
deductions, defined, 226
defense, national, and government, 243–244
deficit, defined, 249
deflation, 111–115
    defined, 111
demand, 64–68
    defined, 64
    excess, 71
    law of, 65
demand curve, 66–68
    defined, 67
demand deposits, 50–51
    defined, 50
demand-pull inflation, 112–113
    defined, 113
demand schedule, 65–66
    defined, 65
deposit:
    certificate of, 327
    demand, 50–51
depression, defined, 110
developments, political and international, and stock prices, 333
direct marketing, defined, 147
directors, board of, 128

direct search, for job, 312–313
disagreements, honest, government as resolver of, 185–186
discount rate, defined, 211
discouraged workers, defined, 105
discrimination, defined, 193
disposable income, defined, 361
distribution:
    channels of, 147–149
    income, 303–305
dividend, defined, 155
door-to-door repair services, 373
door-to-door sales, 373–374
Dow Jones Industrial Average, defined, 330
durable, consumer, 353

E

earning a living, opportunity cost of, 301–302
economic activity, circular flow of, and markets, 37–39
economic conditions, general, and stock prices, 332–333
economic freedom, defined, 9
economic growth, 100–104
    achieving, 102–104
    importance of, 101
economic incentive, profits as, 78–85
economic questions:
    three basic, 28–30
    three basic, and markets, 39–43
economic resources, defined, 19
economics:
    defined, 24
    principles of, and consumer decisions, 352–355
    supply-side, 240
economic systems:
    command, 9–10
    defined, 4
    free enterprise. *See* free enterprise system
    of society, 3–5
economies of scale:
    defined, 91
    and market power, 91–92

economy:
    capitalist, 282
    defined, 5
    managed by taxation, 222–223
    market, 40. *See also* market economy
    reasons for government involvement in, 242–243
    role of credit in, 327–329
    role of savings in, 327–329
    socialist, 282
education:
    and government, 244–245
    and human resources, 19
    and job opportunities, 310–312
efficiency:
    defined, 30
    vs equity, 30–31
employee, defined, 121
employment:
    full, 107
    lifetime, in Japan, 292–293
employment agencies, 314–315
entrepreneur, 78–80
    defined, 78
environmental protection, and government, 194–195
Environmental Protection Agency, 195
equilibrium price:
    defined, 72
    determining, 70–73
equity:
    defined, 30
    vs efficiency, 30–31
equity financing, 154–156
    defined, 154
    difference from debt financing, 156–157
excess demand, defined, 71
excess supply, defined, 72
exchange:
    medium of, 46
    voluntary, and markets, 35–37
exchange rates, 268–269
    defined, 268
    fixed, 269
    floating, 268

exchanges, stock, 333
excise tax, defined, 231
exemptions, defined, 226
expansion, defined, 109
expenditures, government, 247–249
expenses, fixed, 361
experience, and wages, 307
exports:
    defined, 263
    of the United States, 264–265
externality, positive, 244
extractive industries, defined, 133

F

factors of production, defined, 78
false advertising, 191–192
Fed. *See* Federal Reserve System
Federal Deposit Insurance Corporation
        (FDIC), defined, 206
Federal Insurance Contribution Act (FICA),
        defined, 229
Federal Reserve System, 207–215
    Board of Governors of, 213–214
    as clearinghouse for checks, 209–210
    defined, 208
    functions of, 208–212
    independence of, 214–215
    and loans to member banks, 211
    organization of, 213–215
    and regulation of money supply, 211–212
    reserves held by, 210–211
    as supervisor of banking activities, 211
    as supplier of currency to banks, 209
Federal Trade Commission, 191
fiat money:
    vs commodity money, 51–53
    defined, 51
finance, international, 268–270
financial intermediaries:
    banks as, 201–203, 205–206
    defined, 202
financing, 153–158
    automobile purchases, 367–369

    debt, 154
    defined, 154
    difference between equity and debt,
        156–157
    equity, 154–156
finding a job:
    and career counseling, 315–316
    and classified advertising, 313
    and direct search, 312–313
    and employment agencies, 314–315
    and placement offices, 315–316
firm:
    defined, 5
    multinational, 265–266
    worker-managed, 290–291
fiscal policy:
    defined, 237
    evaluation of, 238–239
fixed exchange rate, defined, 269
fixed expenses, defined, 361
fixed payments, and inflation, 114
fixing, price, 187
floating exchange rate, defined, 268
Food and Drug Administration, 191, 345
force, labor, 105
foreign exchange market, defined, 268
for whom to produce, 29–30
    in command system, 281
    in free enterprise system, 281
    in market economy, 43
fractional reserve banking, 204–205
    defined, 205
franchise, defined, 92
fraud, consumer, 373–374
freedom:
    economic, 9
    political, 9–10
freedom to buy, 7
    in U.S.S.R., 286
freedom to own property, 6–7
    in U.S.S.R., 286
freedom to produce and sell, 7
    in U.S.S.R., 287–288
freedom to work, 7–8
    in U.S.S.R., 286–287

free enterprise system:
　characteristics and benefits of, 6–8
　vs command systems, 279–281
　defined, 6
　and for whom to produce, 281
　and how to produce, 280
　market power in, 90–94
　and what to produce, 279–280
frictional unemployment, defined, 107
fringe benefits, and unions, 171
full employment, defined, 107

G

gain, capital, 156
general economic conditions, and stock
　　prices, 332–333
goals of unions, 170–174
goods:
　capital, 21–22
　capital, and automation, 144
　consumer, 134
　defined, 17
　industrial, 134
　intermediate, 101
　public, 243
　shopping, 353
goods and services, 17
　government as producer of, 241–245
　and resources, 19–23
　to satisfy human needs and wants, 16–18
government:
　and competition, 186–189
　and consumer protection, 189–191
　and education, 244–245
　as enforcer of contracts, 184–185
　and environmental protection, 194–195
　and inflation/unemployment, 237–240
　information from, 349–350
　involvement of in economy, reasons for,
　　242–243
　and national defense, 243–244
　as producer of goods and services, 241–245
　and protecting against theft and violence,
　　184
　as referee, 183–186

　and resolving honest disagreements,
　　185–186
　and worker protection, 192–193
government activities, financed by taxation,
　　221
government assistance, and market power, 92
government budgets, 245–249
government expenditures, 247–249
government regulation, benefits and costs
　　of, 195–196
government revenues, 245–247
　defined, 245
government tax policies, Japanese, 293–294
Governors, Board of, of the Federal Reserve,
　　213–214
"greenbacks," 52
grievance procedures, defined, 174
gross national product (GNP), defined, 100
growth, economic. See economic growth

H

health, and human resources, 19–20
history of organized labor, 164–165
honest, responsibility to be, 350–352
honest disagreements, government as resolver
　　of, 185–186
household, defined, 5
housing, 363–366
how to produce, 29
　in command system, 281
　in free enterprise system, 280
　in market economy, 41–42
human needs and wants, goods and services
　　satisfy, 16–18
human resources, 19–20
　and age, 19
　defined, 19
　and education, 19
　and health, 19–20

I

imperialism:
　defined, 285
　and V.I. Lenin, 285

imports:
    defined, 263
    of the United States, 265
improving resource allocation, 103
incentive, economic, profits as, 78–85
income:
    disposable, 361
    redistributed by taxation, 222
    redistribution of and national debt, 251
    sources of, 302–303
    taxable, 226
income distribution, 303–305
    defined, 304
income tax, personal, 223, 225–228
income tax rates, 225–226
increase, productivity, 102
increasing capital resources, 103–104
increasing labor resources, 103–104
independent unions, defined, 170
index, consumer price, 111
indirect marketing, defined, 147
industrial goods, defined, 134
Industrial Revolution, defined, 164
industrial union, defined, 165
industries:
    construction, 134
    extractive, 133
    manufacturing, 134
    service, 135
    trade, 135
    types of, 133–135
industry, defined, 5
industry condition, and stock prices, 332
inflation, 111–115
    and borrowing and lending, 114
    causes of, 112
    coping with, 113–115
    cost-push, 113
    defined, 111
    demand-pull, 112–113
    and fixed payments, 114
    and government, 237–240
    and planning, 115
information:
    accurate, right to, 342–343
    from business, 349–350
    from government, 349–350
information gathering, informal, 348–349
information services, consumer, 350
installment loan, 323–324
    defined, 323
insurance:
    life, 370–372. See also life insurance
    term, 371
    whole life, 372
interdependence, 144–145
    defined, 144
interest, defined, 201
interest rates, high, and national debt, 252
intermediaries, 147–148
    defined, 135
    financial, banks as, 201–203, 205–206
intermediate goods, defined, 101
international developments, and stock
        prices, 333
international finance, 268–270
    defined, 268
international trade:
    benefits of, 259–262
    defined, 259
    importance of, 263–266
    and multinational firms, 265–266
    problems created by, 272–273
    restrictions on, 271–273
investing in stock, 329–335
investment, defined, 103
"invisible hand," and Adam Smith, 43

J

Japan:
    as capitalist success story, 291–294
    in the future, 294
    and government tax policies, 293–294
    and lifetime employment, 292–293
    and spirit of cooperation, 292
job:
    and career counseling, 315–316
    and classified advertising, 313
    direct search for, 312–313
    and employment agencies, 314–315
    finding a, 312–316
    and placement offices, 315–316

job characteristics, special, and wages, 307–308
job opportunities:
    and education, 310–312
    and unions, 172–173
job training, and wages, 307

L

labor:
    organized. *See* organized labor
    specialization of, 141–142
labor force, defined, 105
labor resources, increasing, 103–104
landlords, defined, 365
law of demand, defined, 65
law of supply, defined, 70
laws:
    affecting organized labor, 165–167
    antitrust, 187
    right to work, 166
lease, defined, 365
legal tender, defined, 51
lending, and inflation, 114
Lenin, V.I., 285
    and imperialism, 285
liability, limited, 122
life insurance, 370–372
    defined, 370
    how much is enough, 370–371
    types of, 371–372
lifetime employment, in Japan, 292–293
limited liability, defined, 122
limited partners, defined, 127
limited resources, and scarcity, 23–25
line: assembly, 142
    picket, 175
line of credit, defined, 154
loans:
    installment, 323–324
    to member banks, made by Fed, 211
    mortgage, 323
local unions, 168
location:
    and retailers, 149
    and wages, 308–309
loss, capital, 156

M

mail-order sales, 374
management skill, and market power, 91
manufacturing industries, defined, 134
marginal costs:
    and consumer spending decisions, 354–355
    defined, 70
marginal tax rate, defined, 223
market:
    bear, 330
    bull, 330
    foreign exchange, 268
    over-the-counter, 335
market basket, defined, 111
market economy:
    defined, 49
    and for whom to produce, 43
    and how to produce, 41–42
    and three basic economic questions, 40–43
    and what to produce, 40–41
marketing, 146–149
    defined, 146
    direct, 147
    indirect, 147
market power:
    and advertising, 92
    causes of, 91–92
    and control over resources, 91
    defined, 90
    and economies of scale, 91–92
    in free enterprise system, 90–94
    and government assistance, 92
    and management skill, 91
    problems created by, 92–94
markets:
    and the circular flow of economic activity, 37–39
    defined, 35
    product and resource, 37
    and the three basic economic questions, 39–43
    and voluntary exchange, 35–37
    at work, 36–37
market socialism, defined, 290
Marx, Karl, 282–285
    as philosopher, 283–284

as prophet, 284–285

mass production, 142–143
  defined, 142

medium of exchange, defined, 46

member banks, loans made to by Fed, 211

merger, defined, 187

mill, defined, 232

misunderstandings about national debt,
  250–251

mixed systems, 10–11
  defined, 11

monetarists, defined, 239

monetary policy:
  defined, 237
  evaluation of, 238–239

money:
  commodity, 51–53
  defined, 45
  fiat, 51–53
  as medium of exchange, 46
  need for, and barter, 44–46
  saving. *See* saving money
  as store of value, 48
  three functions of, 46–48
  in the United States, 49–53
  as unit of account, 47

money market account, defined, 327

money supply, regulated by Fed, 211–212

monopoly, 93–94
  defined, 93

mortgage, defined, 323

mortgage loan, defined, 323

motive, profit, 80–81

multinational firms:
  defined, 265
  and international trade, 265–266

N

national banks, defined, 205

national debt, 249–252
  defined, 249
  and high interest rates, 252
  misunderstandings about, 250–251
  and redistribution of income, 251
  size of, 249–250
  valid concerns about, 251–252
  and waste, 251

national defense, and government, 243–244

National Highway Traffic Safety
  Administration, 190, 344

National Labor Relations Act, 165–166
  defined, 166

National Labor Relations Board (NLRB), 166,
  174–175
  defined, 166

national unions, 169

natural resources, 20–21
  defined, 20

need for money, and barter, 44–46

needs, defined, 16–17

needs and wants, 16–17
  human, and goods and services, 16–18

nondurables, consumer, 353

O

Occupational Safety and Health
  Administration, 192–193

officers of corporation, defined, 128

offices, placement, 315–316

oligopoly, 93–94
  defined, 93

open market operations, defined, 211

opportunities, job. *See* job opportunities

opportunity cost:
  and choices, 26–28
  and consumer decisions, 352–354
  defined, 27
  of earning a living, 301–302
  and prices, 59–60

organized labor:
  history of, 164–165
  laws affecting, 165–167
  in the United States, 168–170

over-the-counter market, defined, 335

ownership:
  business, forms of, 121–123
  form of, and retailers, 149

owning a home, vs renting, 365–366

P

partners, limited, 127

partnerships, 126–128

advantages of, 126–127
defined, 122
disadvantages of, 127–128
passbook savings account, defined, 326
payments:
  balance of, 270
  fixed, and inflation, 114
  transfer, 302
peak, defined, 109
personal income tax, 225–228
  defined, 223
  problems with, 227–228
picket line, defined, 175
placement offices, 315–316
planning:
  central, 280
  and inflation, 115
policy:
  fiscal, 237–239
  government tax, Japanese, 293–294
  monetary, 237–239
political developments, and stock prices, 333
political freedom, defined, 9–10
positive externality, defined, 244
poverty, defined, 304
price competition, 86–87
price fixing, defined, 187
price index, consumer, 111
prices:
  equilibrium, 70–73
  and opportunity costs, 59–60
  and resource allocation, 62–64
  and scarcity, 25
  as signals, 60–62
  stock. See stock prices
price system, defined, 59
principal, defined, 154
principle of absolute advantage, 259–261
principle of comparative advantage, 261–262
principles of economics, and consumer
    decisions, 352–355
private enterprise system, defined, 6
private property, defined, 7
produce:
  freedom to, 7
  freedom to in U.S.S.R., 287–288

producing, 141–146
product, gross national, 100
production:
  factors of, 78
  mass, 142–143
productivity increase, defined, 102
product markets, defined, 37
products:
  safe, right to, 344–345
  unsafe, 190–191
profitability, company, and stock prices, 332
profit motive, 80–81
  defined, 81
profits:
  defined, 78
  as economic incentive, 78–85
  as signals, 82–84
  uses of, 84–85
progressive taxes, 223–224
  defined, 224
property:
  freedom to own, 6–7
  freedom to own in U.S.S.R., 286
  private, 7
property tax, 231–232
  defined, 231
proprietorship, sole, 121. See also sole
    proprietorship
protecting against theft and violence, and
    government, 184
protection:
  consumer, and government, 189–191
  environmental, and government, 194–195
  worker, and government, 192–193
public goods, defined, 243
public service commission, defined, 189
public utility, defined, 189
public utility commission, defined, 189
purchases, financing automobile, 367–369

Q
quality competition, 88
questions, economic, three basic, 28–30,
    39–43

R

rate:
annual percentage, 369
discount, 211
exchange, 268–269
fixed exchange, 269
floating exchange, 268
income tax, 225–226
interest, high, and national debt, 352
marginal tax, 223
tax, 223
unemployment, 105
ratio, reserve, 210–211
rationing, 25
recession, defined, 109
referee, government as, 183–186
regressive taxes, 224–225
defined, 224
regulation, 188–189
government, benefits and costs of, 195–196
rent, defined, 302
renting a home, vs owning, 365–366
repair services, door-to-door, 373
repossessed, defined, 323
reserve ratio:
defined, 210
set by Fed, 210–211
reserves:
defined, 204
held by Fed, 210–211
resource allocation:
improving, 103
and prices, 62–64
resource markets, defined, 37
resources:
budgeting scarce, 361–363
capital, 21–22
control over, and market power, 91
defined, 19
economic, 19
and goods and services, 19–23
human, 19–20
labor and capital, increasing, 103–104
limited, and scarcity, 22–25
natural, 20–21

responsibilities, consumer, 347–352
responsibility to be honest, 350–352
responsibility to be informed, 348–350
restrictions on international trade, 271–273
résumé, defined, 316
retailers, 148–149
defined, 148
and form of ownership, 149
and location, 149
and types of stores, 149
revenue, government, 245–247
right to accurate information, 342–343
right to adequate variety, 345
right to be heard, 345–347
rights, consumer, 341–347
right to safe products, 344–345
right-to-work law, defined, 166

S

safe products, right to, 344–345
safety, worker, 192–193
salary, defined, 121
sales:
door-to-door, 373–374
mail-order, 374
sales tax, 230–231
defined, 230
saving money, 324–327
reasons for, 324–325
ways to, 326–327
savings:
defined, 103
role of in economy, 327–329
savings account, passbook, 326
savings and loan associations, defined, 206
scale, economies of, 91–92
scarce resources, budgeting, 361–363
scarcity:
defined, 24
and limited resources, 23–25
and prices, 25
and unlimited wants, 23–25
schedule:
demand, 65–66
supply, 68

search, direct, for job, 312–313
seasonal unemployment, defined, 107
sectors, defined, 133
sell:
    freedom to, 7
    freedom to in U.S.S.R., 287–288
service industries, defined, 135
services:
    consumer information, 350
    defined, 17
    repair, door-to-door, 373
share, defined, 129
shop:
    closed, 166
    union, 166
shopping goods, defined, 353
signals:
    prices as, 60–62
    profits as, 82–84
single-family homes, vs apartments, 363–365
size, and antitrust, 187
skill, management, and market power, 91
skill requirements, and wages, 307
small claims court, defined, 185
Smith, Adam, and "invisible hand," 43
socialism, 282–285
    market, 290
socialist economic systems, 286–289. See
    also U.S.S.R.
socialist economy, defined, 282
social security taxes, 229–230
    defined, 229
society:
    communist, 284
    defined, 3
    economic system of, 3–5
sole proprietorship, 124–126
    advantages of, 124–125
    defined, 121
    disadvantages of, 125–126
sovereignty, consumer, 40
specialization of labor, 141–142
    defined, 142
spirit of cooperation, in Japan, 292
state banks, defined, 205–206

stock:
    investing in, 329–335
    how to buy and sell, 333–335
stockbrokers, defined, 333
stock certificate, defined, 128–129
stock exchanges, defined, 333
stockholders, defined, 128
stock prices, 330–333
    and company profitability, 332
    and general economic conditions, 332–333
    and industry conditions, 332
    and political and international
        developments, 333
store of value, defined, 48
stores, type of, and retailers, 149
strike, defined, 175
structural unemployment, defined, 107
substitution, 25
sunk costs:
    and consumer decisions, 355
    defined, 355
supply, 68-70
    excess, 72
    defined, 68
    law of, 70
    money, regulated by Fed, 211–212
supply curve, defined, 68
supply and demand, and wages, 305–309
supply schedule, defined, 68
supply-side economics, defined, 240
systems:
    command, 9–10
    economic, 9–10
    free enterprise. See free enterprise
        system
    mixed, 10–11
    price, 59
    private enterprise, 6
    socialist economic, 286–289

T

Taft-Hartley Act, 166–167
    defined, 166
tariffs, defined, 273
taxable income, defined, 226

taxation:
    to change consumer decisions, 221–222
    to finance government activities, 221
    to manage the economy, 222–223
    purposes of, 221–223
    to redistribute income, 222
tax base, defined, 223
taxes:
    excise, 231
    other types of, 229–232
    personal income, 223, 225–228
    progressive, 223–224
    property, 231–232
    regressive, 224–225
    sales, 230–231
    social security, 229–230
tax policies, government, in Japan, 293–294
tax rate:
    defined, 223
    income, 225–226
    marginal, 223
tax withholding, defined, 227
tenants, defined, 365
tender, legal, 51
term insurance, defined, 371
theft, government protection against, 184
three basic economic questions, 28–30
    and markets, 39–43
trade:
    balance of, 270
    defined, 35
    international. *See* international trade
trade industries, defined, 135
training, job, and wages, 307
transaction cost, defined, 46
transfer payment, defined, 302
trough, defined, 109
trustee, defined, 157

U

unemployment, 105–108
    cyclical, 107
    defined, 105
    frictional, 107
    and government, 237–240
    and inflation, 237–240
    measuring, 105–107
    seasonal, 107
    solving problem of, 107–108
    structural, 107
    types of, 107
unemployment rate, defined, 105
unions:
    in action, 174–177
    craft, 165
    credit, 206
    and fringe benefits, 171
    goals of, 170–174
    and grievance procedures, 174
    independent, 170
    industrial, 165
    and job opportunities, 172–173
    local, 168
    national, 169
    in the United States, 168–170
    and wages, 170–171
    and work conditions, 172
    and work hours, 171–172
union shop, defined, 166
United States:
    exports of, 264–265
    imports of, 265
    money in, 49–53
    organized labor in, 168–170
    unions in, 168–170
unit of account, defined, 47
unlimited wants, 18
    and scarcity, 23–25
unsafe products, 190–191
U.S.S.R.:
    evaluation of economic system of, 288–289
    freedom to buy in, 286
    freedom to own property in, 286
    freedom to produce and sell in, 287–288
    freedom to work in, 286–287
utility, public, 189

V

value:
    assessed, 231–232
    store of, 48

variety, right to adequate, 345
variety competition, 88–89
violence, government protection against, 184
voluntary exchange, and markets, 35–37

W

wages:
  defined, 121
  and experience, 307
  and job training, 307
  and location, 308–309
  and skill requirements, 307
  and special job characteristics, 307–308
  and supply and demand, 305–309
  and unions, 170–171
Wagner Act, 166
wants:
  defined, 17
  unlimited, 18
  unlimited, and scarcity, 23–25
waste, and national debt, 251

what to produce, 29
  in command system, 280
  in free enterprise system, 279–280
  in market economy, 40–41
whole life insurance, defined, 372
wholesalers, defined, 148
withholding, tax, 227
work:
  freedom to, 7–8
  freedom to in U.S.S.R., 286–287
work conditions, and unions, 172
worker-managed businesses:
  defined, 290
  in Yugoslavia, 290–291
worker protection, and government, 192–193
workers, discouraged, 105
worker safety, 192–193
worker's council, defined, 290
work hours, and unions, 171–172

Y

Yugoslavia, and worker-managed businesses, 290–291

Gov oral — Monday
SP test — Fri
Math test — Fri
English oral Thu – Fri
Bio test Thu.

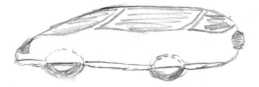